Christina Latham-Koenig
Clive Oxenden
Mike Boyle

ENGLISH FILE

Intermediate Plus Student's Book A

OXFORD
UNIVERSITY PRESS

Paul Seligson and Clive Oxenden are the original co-authors of
English File 1 and *English File 2*

OXFORD
UNIVERSITY PRESS

Great Clarendon Street, Oxford, OX2 6DP,
United Kingdom

Oxford University Press is a department of the
University of Oxford. It furthers the University's objective
of excellence in research, scholarship, and education by
publishing worldwide. Oxford is a registered trade mark
of Oxford University Press in the UK and in certain other
countries

ISBN: 978 0 19 450133 0   MULTIPACK A
ISBN: 978 0 19 450131 6   STUDENT'S BOOK /
                       WORKBOOK A
ISBN: 978 0 19 455837 2   iTUTOR
ISBN: 978 0 19 471993 3   OOSP ACCESS CARD
ISBN: 978 0 19 455838 9   OOSP CONTENT

Printed in China

This book is printed on paper from certified and
well-managed sources.

ACKNOWLEDGEMENTS

*The authors would like to thank all the teachers and students round
the world whose feedback has helped us to shape* English File.

The authors would also like to thank: all those at Oxford
University Press (both in Oxford and around the world) and
the design team who have contributed their skills and ideas
to producing this course.

A very special thanks from Clive to Maria Angeles, Lucia,
and Eric, and from Christina to Cristina, for all their support
and encouragement. Christina would also like to thank
her children Joaquin, Marco, and Krysia for their constant
inspiration.

Mike Boyle would like to thank his wife Christine for her
support, as well as Christina and Clive for their invaluable
assistance.

*The publisher and authors would also like to thank the following for
their invaluable feedback on the materials*: David Silles McLaney,
Alfredo Ramos Benedito, Juan J. Lago Leis, Enrique Pilar
Narros, Jonathan Grimes, Asunción Calderón González,
Ignacio Bermejo, Isabel Corral Prieto, Marta del Arco, Beatriz
Martin Garcia, Brian Brennan, Gill Hamilton, Jane Hudson,
Lucie Cotterill, Marcus Mattia, Sophie Rogers, Donna
Hutchinson, Rachel Buttery-Graciani, Lenka Slunečková,
Ivona Cindlerová.

*The Publisher and Authors are very grateful to the following who have
provided information, personal stories, and/or photographs*: Debbie
Kuan, (p.4), Wendy Woodward (p.9), Catherine Ball, Emi
Kinoshita, (p.19), Brian Voce (pp.28–29), Samantha Richter
(pp.31, 113), Krysia Cogollos (p.31), Steve and Joan Boyle
(pp.31, 48), Joe Kenyon (p.39), Wendy and Lizzie Molyneux
(pp.44–45), Tim Bentinck (p.51)

*We would also like to thank all the friends, colleagues and people in
the street who have constantly answered surveys and questions for us.*

*The authors and publisher are grateful to those who have given
permission to reproduce the following extracts and adaptations
of copyright material*: p.34 Adapted extract from "Freegans:
The bin scavengers" by Liz Scarff, www.independent.
co.uk, 20 February 2006. Reproduced by permission of The
Independent. p.38 Adapted extract from "What price your
first step?" by Jane Phillimore, You Magazine, 27 March
2011. Reproduced by permission of Solo Syndication. p.40
Adapted extract from "The best Saturday job I ever had . . .",
The Times, 4 July 2012. p.43 Adapted extract from "Recycling
facts and figures", www.recycling-guide.org.uk, accessed
23 October 2013. Reproduced by permission of Fubra
Limited. Reproduced by permission of News Syndication.
p.46 Adapted extract from "House of Cards: what I learned
by watching the whole series in one sitting" by Gennady
Kolker, www.guardian.co.uk, 5 February 2013. Copyright
Guardian News & Media Ltd 2013. p.49 Adapted extract from
"Goodbye... and good riddance!" by Liz Jones, The Mail on
Sunday, 11 November 2012. Reproduced by permission of
Solo Syndication.

*Although every effort has been made to trace and contact copyright
holders before publication, this has not been possible in some cases.
We apologise for any apparent infringement of copyright and
if notified, the publisher will be pleased to rectify any errors or
omissions at the earliest opportunity.*

Sources: www.houseofcolour.co.uk,
www.marketresearchworld.net,
http://blog.notonthehighstreet.com, www.dailymail.co.uk,
www.techradar.com, www.guardian.co.uk,
www.nypost.com, http://online.wsj.com, http://nymag.com

*The Publisher would like to thank the following for their kind
permission to reproduce photographs*: Alamy pp.6 (Sony
logo/© Business), (Nike logo/Dorling Kindersley), 10 (shop/
Julian Eales), 18 (ticket/shinypix), (apples/incamerastock),
(Adele cd/Studio 101), (book/CBW), (iphone/Adrian Lyon),
21 (firehose/Imagebroker), 24 (Nick/I love images), 26 (teen
girl/Flickr Open), 28 (tower/Rebecca Johnson), 30 (Andes/
Friedrich Smeier), 43 (recycling/Alex Segre), 48 (Spanish
village/Robert Harding Picture Library), (English village/
nagelestock.com), 105 (Lauren/juanmonino), 114 (Sheila/
David J Green/Lifestyle), (Andrew/ONOKY/photononstop),
153 (make-up bag/YAY Media AS), (pyjames/Creative
Control), (swimsuit/Art Directors & TRIP), (toothbrush/
Danny Smythe), (phone charger/Metta digital), (repellent/
whiteboxmedia limited), (toothpaste/Richard Heyes),
(dinghy sailing/Joel Douillet), (sightseeing/Caro), snorkelling/
LOOK Die Bildagentur der Fotografen GmbH), (hiking/
superclic), 154 (stationers/Charles Stirling), (estate agent/
Ian Masterton), (drugs/Bonkers AboutPictures), (travel
agents/Radharc Images), newsagents/Gregory Wrona),
(butchers/RGB Ventures LLC dba Superstock), (bakers/Noble
Images), (fishmongers/Alex Segre), (craft stall/Steppenwolf),
(hypermarket/Peter Bowater), (off-licence/Jack Sullivan),
(GAP/Ben Molyeux Retail), (Zara/Lou- Foto), (health food
store/Richard Levine), (laundrette/reppans), 156 (jar/RT
images), (plastic bag/Mode Images), (tub/studiomode), (box/
B.A.E Inc.), polystyrene tray/Metta digital), (lid/RT Images),
(wrapper/Chris Haye), (sell-by date/David J Green), (coke
can/pumpkinpie), (packet/Carolyn Jenkins), (juice carton/
Nikreates), (yoghurt carton/studiomode), 158 (advertising/
Art Directors/TRIP), (weather/Mark Richardson), 159 (sticks/
ncamerastock), (path/Derek Croucher), (stones/Peter
Stone), (valley/Robert Harding World Imagery), (bush),
(pond/Ana Stowe), (farmhouse/Stephen Dorey); Mike Boyle
pp.31 (all bar b), 117, 155; Dairygoodness.ca; Arnos Design
Ltd pp.18 (DVD cover), (laptop box), 30; The Bridgeman Art
Library p.11 (Woman Embroidering 1812/Georg Friedrich
Kerstin); Abigail Bryans pp.20 (jar and sign), 21 (mugshot
and sign); Edwina Cooper pp.20 (cushions), 21 (mugshot);
Corbis pp.11 (butterfly/Horst Ossinger), 24 (Laura/Rick
Gomez), 37 (bottles/Andrew Brookes), 40 (Kane/Robbie
Jack), (Stafford/Colin Mc Pherson), 115 (grey haired woman/
Janusz Kawa), 154 (deli/cultura), (dry cleaners/Ocean); Elvis
and Kresse p.20 (firehouse bag); Fatface/PR Shots p.18 (T
shirt); Getty Images pp.6 (Google logo/Bloomberg), (Steve
Jobs/John G Mabanglo), 11 (dead salmon/Stockbyte),
16 (Caroline/Juanmonino), 18 (bread/stockbyte), 20 (wallet/
Barcroft Media), 21 (Kresse and Elvis Wesling/Barcroft
media), 24 (Sarah/Image Source), 26 (baby/photodisc/
Leanne Temme), (toddler/Shunyu Fan), (woman 30's/OJO
Images), (man at computer/Tara Moore), (noise/Don Bayley),

31 (blowing bubbles/Nathan Jones), 40 (Fiennes/Ton Shaw),
44 (all stills/Twentieth Century Fox televison), 45 (all stills/
Twentieth Century Fox televison), 48 (alps/Brian Lawrence),
51 (corn/stockbyte), (recording b/w/Fox Fotos), 104 (imac/
Handout), 105 (plane/Hans Neleman), 113 (pink room/
gerenme), (glitterball/Buenavista Images), 114 (Caroline/
Juanamonino), (Mark/Jena Ardell), (Haylee/Jay p. Morgan),
(Michael/Laflor), (Danielle/Mint Images/Tim Robbins), Sam
(Joshua Hodge Photography), 115 (child playing/thebang),
116 (Kate Lewis/Hero Images), 154 (greengrocers/Jason Todd),
158 (wildlife documentary/Sylvain Cordier/hemis.fr), (chat
show/CBS Photo Archive), 159 (rocks/Matthew p. Wicks),
(gate/Anne C. Dowie), (cliffs/David Henderson), (field/Image
Source), (hedge/Francois de Heel), (stream/Peter Unger),
(hill/Lok Photography); House of Colour p.9 (website); Ikea
pp.6 (logo); Istockphoto pp.6 (Samsung logo/George Clerk),
11 (tree/mb-fotos), 18 (trainers/Alec051), 26 (pensioner/Alex
Raths); Manchester News pp.49 (Liz Jones); Wendy Molyneux
p.45 (script writers); NB Pictures p.29 (Meryl Streep/Annie
Liebowitz); Chris O' Donovan p.39 (Rosie and Lauren); Oxford
University Press photobank p.18 (jeans/Gareth Boden); Press
Association Images pp.5, 6 (Jeff Bezos), 34 (freegan/Soeren
Stache/DPA), 51 (Camilla/Arthur Edwards/The Sun), (Timothy
Bentinck); Rex Features Ltd pp.40 (Ross/Richard Gardner),
(Parks/Geoffrey Swaine), 51 (Bentinck and cast/Denis Jones),
158 (cookery/Nils Jorgensen), (drama/MCT), (quiz) (sport/Back
Pages Images), (sitcom/CBS/Everett), (soap/TNT/Courtesy:
Everett Collection), (period drama//Everett Collection),
(news); Reuters p.19 (high street/Luke MacGregor), (boarding
up shop/StefanWermuth); Sam Richter p.113 (Ana); Roy
Ritchie p.36; Shutterstock pp.18 (oranges/Hamik), (flowers/
Kietr), 26 (boy on floor/Sergey Peterman), 153 (sunscreen/
Konstantin Faraktinov), (wash bag/Carlos Yudica) (hairdryer/
Nordlng), (comb/You Touch Pix of EuTotch), (adaptor/
exopixel), (razor/canonzoom), (beach towel/sergign),
(brush/Artur Synenko), (trunks/Karkas), (memory card/
Ilya Akinshin), (flip flops/dotshock), (nail scissors/Kostenko
Maxim), (scuba diving/C.K. Ma), (waterskiing/Valery V
Markov), (camping/Studio1 One), (windsurfing/Dima Fadeev),
154 (jewellers/Iakov Filimonov), (florists/Polia Shestakov),
156 (bottle/design56), (tin/Sebastien Crocker), 158 (TV stand/
Kitch Bain), (remote control/Andrzej Petelski), 159 (leaf/
Iurii Konoval), (fence/GQ), (mud/Matthijs Wetterauw), (grass/
digitalvox), (wood/Piotr Krzeslak), (cow/Supertrooper),
(sheep/Eric Isselee), (chickens/Anna Stowe), (lambs/Eric Lam),
(cockerel/Christian Musat); The Picture Desk pp.45 (still/
Media Rights Capital), 158 (The Simpsons/20th Century Fox/
Groeing, Matt); The Rough Guide p.153 (Sweden); Philippe
Tarbouriech p.115 (child in red); Brian Voce p.29 (all bar
Meryl Streep); Wikipedia Commons p.11 (paint pot); Mari
Yamazaki p.49 (Rob Penn).

Commissioned photography by: Gareth Boden pp.9 (Wendy), 50,
154 (DIY). Practical English stills photography by: Rob Judges

Photoshoot management and art editing by: Helen Reilly/Arnos
Design Ltd

Contents

G pronouns
V working out meaning from context
P vowel sounds

What's your first name?

It's Caroline, but most people call me Caro.

1A Why did they call you that?

1 SPEAKING & LISTENING

a Work with a partner. Talk about your names.
- My full name is…
- I'm named after…
- Some people call me… for short.
- I have a nickname. It's…
- I hate it when people call me…

b (**1 2**)) Listen to four people talking about their names. Write the names down, and tick (✓) the people who are happy with their names.

c Listen again and answer the questions for each person.
1 Why did their parents choose the name?
2 Do they have a nickname, or are they called something for short?
3 Do they like their name? Would they like to change it?

d Are *you* happy with your name? Would you like to change it?

2 PRONUNCIATION vowel sounds

a (**1 3**)) Look at the first names in the chart. Listen and circle the name which doesn't have the sound in the sound picture.

1	Chris Bill Olivia Brian
2	Peter Steve Emily Eve
3	Alex Adrian Andrew Ann
4	Sean George Paula Charlotte
5	Adele Ben Leo Jessica
6	Sam Grace James Kate
7	Tony Joe Robert Sophie
8	Ryan Liam Michael Simon

b With a partner, decide if they are men's names, women's names, or both. Write **M**, **W**, or **B** in the box. Are any of them short for another name?

c ▶ p.166 Sound Bank. Look at the typical spellings of the sounds in **a**.

d Look at some common British surnames. How do you think they are pronounced?

Adams   Evans   Harrison   Johnson   Jones
Mason   Murray   Taylor   Walker   Wright

e (**1 4**)) Listen and check.

3 READING & VOCABULARY
working out meaning from context

a You're going to read an article about names. Before you read, look at the title of the article. In what ways do you think a name can help or hurt you?

b Read the article and write the headings in the correct paragraphs. There is one heading you don't need to use.

A Life expectancy
B Names and careers
C How people see you
D Popular names in history
E Success at school

c Read the article again. Answer the questions with a partner.
1 How do people see you differently if you're called Elizabeth, or Sophie, or Ann?
2 What kind of names might help you to get better results at school?
3 Why might someone called Ellie choose to be an electrician?
4 When you are applying for a job, is it an advantage or a disadvantage to have an unusual name?
5 What kind of initials should you have if you want to live longer?

> 🔍 **Guessing the meaning of new words and phrases**
> When you are reading and find a word or phrase you don't know:
> 1 Decide if you think it's a noun, a verb, an adjective, etc.
> 2 Try to work out the meaning from the context (the other words around it).
> 3 If you still can't work out what it means, either ignore it and carry on reading, or use a dictionary to help you.

Is your name helping or hurting you?

Wendy Isabel Nichols

Most of us never think about our names. They're just names and they usually don't mean much – or do they? New research has come out which suggests that our names can affect everything from our emotional well-being to our career paths, and even how long we live.

1 _____

A recent survey asked 6,000 people in the UK to rank common names for men and women in three categories: successful, lucky, and attractive. The results showed a strong preference for certain names. People called James and Elizabeth were seen as the most successful, Jack and Lucy were the luckiest, and Sophie and Ryan were the most attractive. Overall, it seems that the best name for men is James, which came near the top in all three categories. The least desirable ones were George and Ann, which ranked near the bottom in all categories.

2 _____

The potential effects of your name go beyond perceptions. According to several studies, teachers give higher marks to children with attractive names. In the US, where grades are given on a scale from A (excellent) to D (poor), another study found that students with first names beginning with A or B received higher marks than students whose first names started with C or D.

3 _____

Some experts also believe that people are attracted to jobs that sound like their names. One study found that people called Dennis and Denise are more likely to become dentists. There are hairdressers called Harry, artists called Art, and even a lawyer called Sue Yoo*. Even if your name and job don't match, your name could affect your job prospects. A study found that American employers were more likely to consider the CVs of applicants who have 'normal-sounding' names. Researchers also say that companies are more likely to promote people if their names sound successful.

4 _____

It may seem incredible, but there is evidence that your name could affect how long you live. Researchers compared the death certificates of people with 'positive' initials (such as J.O.Y. or F.U.N.) and people with 'negative' ones (such as D.I.E. or S.A.D.). The results? People with positive initials live about four years longer than the average, while people with negative initials die about three years sooner.

So if you have an 'undesirable' name, should you change it to a new one? Most experts say no. For most people, having a positive attitude will help more than giving yourself a new name.

*The name Sue Yoo sounds like the phrase 'sue you', which means to make a claim against somebody in court.

Brian Adams Davies

---

d Look at the highlighted words or phrases in the article which are related to research. Try to work out what they mean, and how they are pronounced.

e Now match them with 1–9.

1 _____ *noun* people who study something carefully to discover new facts about it
2 _____ *noun* the facts that make you believe something is true
3 _____ *noun* an investigation of the opinions of a particular group of people
4 _____ *noun* the number you get when you add two or more numbers and then divide the total by the number of figures you added
5 _____ *noun* different levels or numbers used for measuring something
6 _____ *verb* to put in order according to quality, importance, etc.
7 _____ *adjective* probable or expected
8 _____ *adverb* generally
9 _____ *preposition* further than

f **1 5**)) Listen and check. Under<u>line</u> the stressed syllable.

g Do you think *your* name is helping or hurting you? Why?

4 SPEAKING

Do the questionnaire in groups.

Angelina Jolie and Brad Pitt with their children

WHAT'S IN A NAME?

- What are three first names you really like and three you don't like at all? Why do you like or dislike them?
- What are the advantages and disadvantages of...?
  - having a very common name
  - having a very old-fashioned name
  - having a very unusual name or a foreign name
  - being named after a celebrity or royalty
  - having the same first name as your father or mother
- Can you think of people who...
  - have a name that suits their appearance or personality? Why does it suit them?
  - have a name that doesn't suit them? Why doesn't it suit them?

5 **1 6**)) **SONG** *Rio* ♫

6 LISTENING & SPEAKING

a Look at the brand names. How do you pronounce them? What do these companies make?

b (1 7)) Listen to a radio programme about brand names. Which of the brands...?

1 is named after a Greek goddess _____
2 is named after the company's founder _____
3 has a name which means 'three stars' _____
4 is named after a very large number _____
5 has a name which means 'sound' plus 'boy' _____

c Listen again and answer the questions.

1 What do the 'I' and 'K' in IKEA stand for?
2 What did Samsung originally sell?
3 What was Nike's original name?
4 Why did Sony's founders choose its name?
5 What does the man say about the spelling of 'Google'?

d Look at the photos. What are the two products called? Do you know why?

e Work in pairs **A** and **B** and read about the two products. **B** ➤ **Communication** *p.104*.

f **A** read about how the Kindle was named. Find answers to the questions below.

1 Who named the product?
2 What instructions did the company's founder give for choosing a name?
3 What does the name mean?
4 Why is the meaning appropriate?

How was the Kindle named?

There were ebook readers before the Amazon Kindle, but the Kindle was the first to become popular around the world. Since it first appeared in 2007, millions of Kindles have been sold, and in fact Amazon now sells more ebooks than paper books.

When it was time to give the Kindle a name, Amazon's founder, Jeff Bezos, asked Michael Cronan to try to think of one. Cronan, who was an American designer, also had a business that created names for companies and products. Bezos told him that he didn't want a high-tech name. Amazon's customers loved traditional paper books and Bezos didn't want to annoy them.

Cronan and his wife talked a lot about reading, and about the warm, comfortable feelings people get from it. A lot of different names were considered, but he finally chose 'kindle', which means 'to light a fire'. Cronan thought that this would remind people of the excitement they feel when they are enjoying their favourite book. The name was also inspired by a line from the French novelist Victor Hugo: 'to read is to light a fire'.

g Tell **B** about how the Kindle was named, using questions 1–4 to help you.

h Now **B** will tell you about how the iMac was named.

i Talk to a partner.

1 What are some well-known brand names from your country? Do you know where the names came from?
2 What's the name of the brand and model of your computer, car, or phone? Why do you think they were given those names?
3 Can you think of a product name which you think is very clever? Why? Do you know one which doesn't suit the product well?

7 GRAMMAR pronouns

a Look at the sentences from the texts in **6**. What do the pronouns in **bold** refer to?

1 *Bezos told **him** that **he** didn't want a high-tech name.*
2 *Amazon's customers loved traditional paper books and Bezos didn't want to annoy **them**.*
3 *Jobs asked Segall for a new name that had 'Mac' or 'Macintosh' in **it**.*
4 *A few days after coming up with the name, Segall went to Jobs and suggested **it** to **him**.*

b ➤ **p.132 Grammar Bank 1A.** Learn more about pronouns and practise them.

c (1 9)) Listen and change the word order in the sentence. Change the direct object to *it* or *them*.

)) 1 ⟨ *Give me the book.*
   Give it to me.

)) 2 ⟨ *Give her the shoes.*
   Give them to her.

d Think of a couple you know well (friends or family). Tell your partner about them and try to get all of the pronouns right. Give the information below, and anything else you know about them.

names	jobs	how they met	pets	children
appearance	personality			

⟨ *I'm going to tell you about my neighbours. **His** name is Mario and **hers** is Sara. **She's** a writer and **he's** an accountant. **They** haven't got any children but **they** have a dog. **Its** name is Beppo...*

8 SPEAKING

a Read about three new products. Would you like to buy them? Why (not)?

b In pairs or groups, talk about what would make a good name for the products. Think about:

- the name's meaning, sound, and length
- things that the name could remind people of
- how you want people to feel about the product
- how easy the name would be to pronounce
- the names of similar products

c Make a list of possible names with your partner or group.

The car	The exercise machine	The translation app

A CAR THAT DRIVES ITSELF!

This amazing new car does all the driving for you while you read, relax, have a snack, or even have a nap! It's had zero accidents in thousands of hours of testing.
Target customers: Busy families, workers with long commutes

GET A 30-MINUTE WORKOUT IN 5 MINUTES!

This exciting exercise machine works nine major muscle groups and gets your heart working in just a few minutes.
Target customers: Men aged 18–30

You say it in your language... they hear it in theirs!

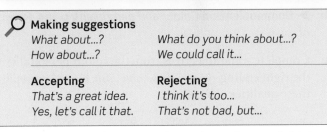

This smartphone app translates while you talk. Works for up to 12 languages.
Target customers: Business people

🔍 **Making suggestions**

What about...?	What do you think about...?
How about...?	We could call it...

Accepting
That's a great idea.
Yes, let's call it that.

Rejecting
I think it's too...
That's not bad, but...

---

d Decide on the best name for each product, and think about the reasons why the names are right.

e Present your best name to another pair or group.

⟨ *We suggest the name... for the car.*
  It's a perfect name because...

G adjectives
V adjective suffixes
P word stress

Are you getting the red shirt?

No, I prefer the green one. Green suits me better than red.

1B True colours

1 VOCABULARY adjective suffixes

a Take the colour personality test. Then compare your colour choices with a partner.

Colour personality test

What kind of person are you? Your preferences in colour may reveal the answer! Look at the colours quickly and write 1 on the colour that immediately attracts you the most. Then number the others 2–8. Don't think about fashion or whether the colour looks good on you, only on how they make you feel.

b ➤ **Communication** *Colour and personality p.104.* Read the results of the test.

c Complete some adjectives from the colour personality test with the right ending *-y, -ive, -less, -able, -ish.* How do people who have these qualities behave?

| mood____ | rest____ | self____ | sensit____ | soci____ |

d ➤ **p.152 Vocabulary Bank** *Adjective suffixes.*

2 PRONUNCIATION word stress

🔍 **Word stress on adjectives formed with suffixes**

When an adjective is formed from a root word and a suffix, the stress is always on a syllable of the root word, e.g. *rely – reliable.* The stress does not change when a negative prefix is added, e.g. *unreliable.*

a Under<u>line</u> the stressed syllable in the bold adjectives in the questions below. Remember it will never be on the prefix or suffix.

1 Who is the most **gla|mo|rous** person you know? What makes him / her like that?
2 Are you very **po|sse|ssive** of anything, e.g. your phone or your laptop? Why don't you like other people using it?
3 Were you a **re|be|llious** child or teenager? What kind of things did you do?
4 What are your most **comfor|ta|ble** clothes? When do you wear them?
5 Do you think you are a **cre|a|tive** person? Why (not)?
6 Have you ever been to a very **lu|xu|ri|ous** hotel or restaurant? Where? Was it worth the money?
7 Have you ever felt **en|vi|ous** of a brother or sister? Why (not)?
8 What's the most **im|pre|ssive** monument or building you've ever visited? Why did you like it so much?
9 What kind of **un|heal|thy** food do you really like eating?
10 What do you think is a **sui|ta|ble** present to take if somebody invites you for a meal in their house?

b **1 14**)) Listen to the adjectives and check. Then listen again and repeat them.

c Work with a partner. **A** ask **B** questions 1–5. Then **B** ask **A** questions 6–10.

3 LISTENING & SPEAKING

a Look at the website and the photos below. What do you think colour analysis is? Do you know anyone who has tried it?

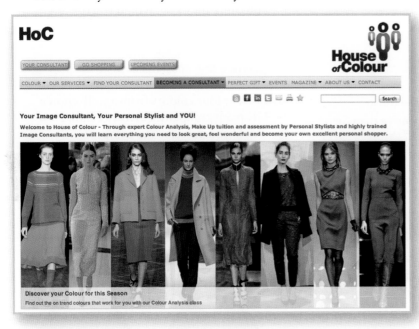

b (1 15))) Listen to an interview with Wendy Woodward, a woman who tried colour analysis. Answer the questions.

A

B

1 Which photo shows Wendy after she did colour analysis?
2 Why did she do colour analysis?
3 How did she feel after she had done it?

c Listen again. Mark the statements **T** (true) or **F** (false).

> 🔍 **Tip: True / False listening**
> • Read the questions before you listen.
> • Work on one question at a time.
> • Check your answers when you listen again.

1 A stylish colleague told Wendy about colour analysis.
2 Wendy went on her own to do colour analysis.
3 The colour analyst worked out her colours by making her try on a lot of different clothes.
4 Wendy learned that she was a 'winter' person.
5 Winter people should wear pale colours.
6 Wendy very rarely wears black nowadays.
7 Soon after the colour analysis she bought some cheap new clothes.
8 She exchanged clothes with her friends because they were different seasons.
9 People immediately told her that she looked more glamorous.
10 Wendy's mother and husband have also now done colour analysis.

d Listen again and correct the false statements in **c**.

e Talk to a partner.

1 Would *you* like to try colour analysis? Why (not)?
2 What colours do you prefer for these things? Why?
  • clothes (e.g. T-shirts, trousers, shoes, etc.)
  • cars
  • mobile phone cases
3 Do you know anyone who…?
  • wears one colour almost all the time
  • drives a bright red car
  • dyes his / her hair an unusual colour
  What are they like?
4 What kind of colours do these words remind you of? Can you explain why?

spring autumn summer winter angry relax money love holiday

4 GRAMMAR adjectives

a Complete each sentence with a word from the list.

as   in   more   most   much   ones   than   the

1 According to a paint company survey, the world's _____ popular colour is blue.
2 White meat is healthier _____ red meat.
3 Black tulips are much more expensive than pink _____.
4 The blue whale is the largest creature _____ the world.
5 Insurance for a red car can be a bit _____ expensive than for other colours.
6 White tigers are _____ less common than ordinary tigers.
7 Black tea isn't as good for you _____ green tea.
8 According to a survey, _____ most popular car colour in Europe is black.

b ➤ **p.133 Grammar Bank 1B.** Learn more about adjectives and practise them.

c Talk to a partner. Choose two topics or two questions from each section.

> **Compare them!**
> 1 restaurant food and home-made food
> 2 being an only child and having lots of brothers and sisters
> 3 the English and people from your country
> 4 walking or running outdoors and going to the gym
> 5 studying in the morning and studying at night
> 6 going on holiday abroad and going on holiday in your country

I think restaurant food is better than my home-made food because I'm not a very good cook, but it's much more expensive and it usually isn't as healthy...

> **Extremes!**
> 1 What is ▓▓▓▓ place you've ever been to? (hot)
> 2 Which sportsperson from your country do you think is ▓▓▓▓ role model? (positive)
> 3 Which is ▓▓▓▓ restaurant in your town? (popular) Which is ▓▓▓▓? (expensive)
> 4 Where are some places you often walk to? Which are ▓▓▓▓ to and ▓▓▓▓ from your home? (close, far)
> 5 Who is ▓▓▓▓ person you know? (clever) Why do you think so?
> 6 Where are you ▓▓▓▓: at home, at work, or somewhere else? Why? (stressed)

The hottest place I've ever been to was Rome in August. It was much too hot to go sightseeing...

5 READING

a Look at some names for colours from an online clothing website. What colours do you think they are? Would you use any similar words for colours in your language?

berry   ivory   melon   mint
morning sky   mushroom   wine

b Look at four colours from a well-known UK paint company, Farrow & Ball. How would you describe the colours?

1   2

3   4

c With a partner, try to match the colours to their names.

Arsenic   Cabbage White   Dead Salmon
Monkey Puzzle

d Read the article about the paint names. Check your answers to **c**.

FARROW&BALL

What colour is
Dead Salmon?

There was a time when you could tell what colour something was by its name. Red, green, even lemon yellow or royal blue immediately told us what something would look like. But, as anyone who has recently bought clothes, a car, or even children's crayons has probably noticed, the trend for giving colours bizarre names is now everywhere, and the image they create in our mind does not necessarily correspond with the actual colour.

One company which may have taken this trend the furthest is the popular UK paint company Farrow & Ball. They sell a wide range of beautiful colours with very unusual names. It is easy to laugh at these names, but in fact many of them have stories behind them.

Dead Salmon Why did the company give this attractive brownish-pink colour such a depressing-sounding name? In fact, the name has been used for this colour for more than 200 years. According to Farrow & Ball, the name comes from an 1805 bill for the painting of the library of an old English country house. 'Dead' actually referred to the paint finish, in the way matt or gloss might today.

Arsenic The name of this pleasant greenish-blue colour may surprise people who associate the name with a poisonous chemical and think of it as a white powder. However, in the late 18th century, arsenic was used to create a colour called Paris Green, which was commonly used in paint and wallpaper. Many people became ill as a result of living in houses with Paris Green walls or wallpaper, including, it is said, Napoleon.

Monkey Puzzle This dark greyish-green colour is named after a kind of pine tree found in Chile and Argentina. The tree got its English name in the 1800s after examples were brought to London, and somebody commented that it would be very difficult to climb, even for a monkey.

Cabbage White This subtle shade of white, which has a slight blueish hint, also gets its name from nature. It is named after the Cabbage White butterfly, so-called because the caterpillars feed on cabbages.

---

e Read the article again. Then cover the text and look at the colour names in **c**. In pairs, say what you can remember about the origin of the names.

f Look at the highlighted adjective and noun phrases. With a partner, try to work out what they mean.

g Would you use any of these colours to paint a room in your house? Are unusual colour names a trend in your country as well?

6 SPEAKING & WRITING

a You're going to describe your favourite room in your house to a partner. Think about these things:

- why it's your favourite room
- the decoration and furnishing, e.g. walls, curtains, blinds, cushions
- the furniture
- paintings, posters
- what else is in the room

While you listen to your partner, ask questions to help you imagine what the room is like.

b ➤ **p.113 Writing** *Describing a room.* Write a description of your favourite room.

1 🎥 VIDEO JENNY IS BACK IN LONDON

a (1 19)) Jenny works in New York for the magazine *New York 24seven*. She has just arrived in London. Watch or listen to her talking to Andrew. How does he help her? What problem does she have at the end?

b Watch or listen again. Mark the sentences **T** (true) or **F** (false). Correct the **F** sentences.

1 Jenny is in the UK for business and pleasure.
2 Andrew was on holiday in New York.
3 Jenny's husband (Rob) is working in San Francisco.
4 Andrew gives Jenny back her laptop.
5 He introduces himself, and says his surname is Paton.
6 Jenny's flight to London was delayed.

Why do you think a man was watching Jenny and Andrew? What do you think he is going to do?

2 🎥 VIDEO REPORTING LOST LUGGAGE

a (1 20)) Watch or listen to Jenny reporting her missing suitcase. Answer the questions.

1 How long is Jenny staying in the UK?
2 What does her suitcase look like?
3 What's in it?
4 How long will it probably take for Jenny to get her case back?

b Watch or listen again. Complete the **You Hear** phrases in the dialogue on p.13.

c (1 21)) Watch or listen and repeat some of the **You Say** phrases. Copy the rhythm and intonation.

d Practise the dialogue with a partner.

e 👥 In pairs, roleplay the dialogue.

A You are a passenger on flight BA1722 from San Francisco. You have just landed at London Heathrow Airport and your luggage hasn't arrived, so you go to Lost Luggage to report it. **B** works at the Lost Luggage counter. Use the **Useful language** to help you to describe your luggage.

B You work at the Lost Luggage counter at London Heathrow Airport. **A**'s luggage hasn't arrived. Take **A**'s details and give a reference number.

f Swap roles.

> 🔍 **Useful language: describing luggage**
> **Type of luggage:** *suitcase / case; sports bag; backpack / rucksack*
> **Colour:** *It's dark / light / greyish blue, etc.*
> **Material:** *It's made of hard plastic / canvas / synthetic material, etc.*
> **Size:** *It's small / medium size / large*
> **Extras:** *It has four wheels / a logo / a label, etc.*

))) You Hear	You Say 💬
Can I help you?	Yeah, my suitcase hasn't arrived.
_____ flight were you on?	Flight RT163 from JFK.
I'll take your _____ and then I can issue you with a reference number. Can I have your name, please?	My name's Jenny Zielinski. That's Z-I-E-L-I-N-S-K-I.
And you're a _____ to the UK.	That's right.
How _____ are you staying for?	Ten days.
OK. How many _____ are you missing?	Just one – a suitcase.
Can you _____ it for me?	Well, it's kind of greyish blue... and hard plastic, I think.
And what _____ is it?	Oh, it's medium size, like this. And it has wheels.
Anything else?	Yeah, there's a small lock and a label with my name and phone number on it.
And what was _____ the suitcase?	Just about everything! Clothes, toiletries, all my personal belongings, really.
Can I have your _____ in the UK?	Just a minute. It's The Grange, Marsh Lane, Long Crendon, Oxfordshire.
And a _____ number?	Yes, it's 001 202 494 012.
And finally, can you _____ this?	Of course. Do you have any idea where it is? I mean, do you think it's still in New York?
It's possible. We're very _____ for the inconvenience. Here's your reference number. You can track the progress of your luggage _____, or just give us a call. But we should be able to get it back to you within 24 hours.	That'd be great. Thank you.

3 🎥 AT HENRY'S HOUSE

VIDEO

a (1 22))) Watch or listen to the rest of Jenny's day. What other problem does she have?

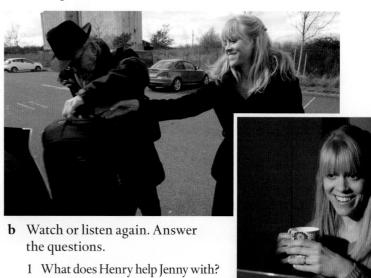

b Watch or listen again. Answer the questions.

1 What does Henry help Jenny with?
2 Is Rob having a good time in Alaska? Why (not)?
3 What is Jenny drinking?
4 Whose computer is she using?
5 Who is Luke?
6 When is Jenny going to see him? Why?
7 What is Henry going to lend Jenny?

Who is Selina Lavelle? Why do you think Grant (the man who was following them) is watching Henry's house?

c Look at the **Social English phrases**. Can you remember any of the missing words?

Social English phrases	
Henry	(And) it's _____ to see you.
Jenny	It's _____ to see you too.
Henry	No, no, _____ me take that.
Henry	You've had a hard journey. _____ me.
Jenny	It's weird, _____ it?
Rob	I really _____ you.
Jenny	Oh no! That's _____.
Rob	It's not your _____, is it?
Rob	Oh _____! You'll look great in those, Jenny!

d (1 23))) Watch or listen and complete the phrases.

e Watch or listen again and repeat the phrases. How do you say them in your language?

> **Can you...?**
> ☐ explain why you are travelling to a place
> ☐ report lost luggage
> ☐ greet someone you haven't seen for some time
> ☐ sympathize with someone about a problem

G present tenses
V holidays
P /s/ and /z/

2A Pack and go!

> **What time does your flight leave?**
>
> At 9.00. I'm getting the 7 o'clock train to the airport.

1 VOCABULARY holidays

a Look at the X-ray pictures of a backpack and a suitcase at airport security. Can you identify the 12 items inside them? Which item(s)…?
  1 do you have to take out of your bag when you go through security
  2 are you not allowed to take through security

b ➤ p.153 Vocabulary Bank *Holidays*.

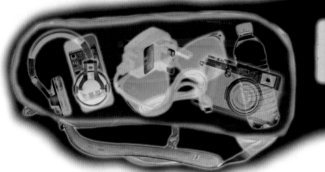

c Make a list of the ten most important things you make sure you take with you when you go on holiday.

d Compare with a partner. How many things are different?

e Read the introduction to an article. What do you think the top three things are that the British most often forget to pack?

Adapted from the Daily Mail

Home | News | Sport | TV | Health | Science | **Travel** | Money

Britons spend £118 million replacing forgotten holiday items

By TRAVEL REPORTER

Forty-one per cent of Britons forget to pack at least one essential item when they go on holiday, according to a survey.

In total, almost 15 million important holiday items are left behind each year, and Britons spend £118 million buying these things again once they reach their destination.

💬 Comment 🖨 Print

---

f (**1 27**))) Listen to the top ten items in reverse order, and write them down. Did you guess the top three correctly?

g Have you or has anybody you know ever forgotten something really important when they went on holiday? What happened?

2 PRONUNCIATION /s/ and /z/

a Look at the word below. What sound do the pink letters have, 🐍 or 🦓?

scissors

b (**1 28**))) Listen and check. Practise saying it.

c (**1 29**))) Listen and write the words in the correct column.

bags cruise flip flops holidays massage passport
pyjamas razor safari sunset swimsuit towels

🐍	🦓

d (**1 30**))) Listen and check. Practise saying the words.

e ➤ p.167 Sound Bank. Look at the typical spellings of the sounds. In what position is *s* never pronounced /z/?

f Practise saying the phrases.

some sunglasses   shoes and socks
summer clothes   striped pyjamas
bags and cases   see the sights

3 LISTENING

a (1 31)) Listen to five airport security screeners. Match them with pictures A–E.

b (1 32)) Listen to an interview with a US security screener. Does she feel mainly positive or mainly negative about her job?

c Listen again. Choose **a**, **b**, or **c**.

> 🔍 **Tip: Multiple-choice listening**
> • Read the questions carefully before you listen.
> • Don't choose an option just because it has a word you heard in the recording. Make sure *all* of the information is correct.

1 She mentions taking away people's _____.
  a food and drink
  b scissors and razors
  c perfume and shampoo

2 When she has to take things away from passengers she _____.
  a enjoys it
  b feels bad about it
  c thinks it's just a routine part of her job

3 What she likes best about her job is _____.
  a meeting all sorts of different people
  b keeping the things that she takes away from passengers
  c being able to get free flights

4 Some of her colleagues get angry with people who _____.
  a are rude
  b are trying to hide things
  c are slow

5 She thinks some screeners can be unfriendly because _____.
  a they work long hours
  b the job is very repetitive
  c the rules are always changing

6 One thing that annoys her about passengers is that _____.
  a they complain about travelling
  b they get aggressive
  c they don't know the rules

7 Passengers are most polite to the security screeners _____.
  a early in the morning
  b in the afternoon
  c late at night

d Have you ever had a problem going through airport security? What happened? Was the screener friendly?

4 SPEAKING & WRITING

a Look at the page from a website. Read some of the ideas for cheap holidays. Discuss the questions with a partner.

1 What do you think are the pros and cons of each idea?
2 Do you know anyone who has done these things? Were they a success?

🏠 | NEWS | SPORT | BUSINESS | **TRAVEL** | CULTURE

Want a cheap holiday? Try these ideas

1 **Go couch-surfing.** On websites like couchsurfing.org, local people will let you sleep on their sofa for free. It's not luxury travel, but you'll meet friendly locals and see how they really live.

2 **Swap houses.** Exchange houses with someone in the place you're going to visit. You stay in their place, and they stay in yours. Websites like homelink.org can arrange this for a small fee.

3 **Save on travel costs.** Book early for good offers with low-cost airlines. Use special services such as InterRail for travelling around Europe by train, or check out car-sharing websites like ridefinder.eu.

4 **Eat street food.** In many cities, even really expensive ones, you can find food which is both tasty and cheap at stalls in the street. For example, try crêpes in Paris, kebabs in Istanbul, tacos in Mexico City. Most places have their own delicious speciality.

5 **Try 'voluntourism'.** These holidays combine volunteer work and tourism. Help in an orphanage, work on an organic farm, and more – all for free. You'll save money and have experiences you'd never find on a package holiday.

b With a partner, write short paragraphs on three more ideas for saving money on holiday. Give reasons why each one is a good idea.

(*If you travel off-season, you'll save money on train and plane tickets, hotel rooms, and even food.*

c Show your three ideas to another pair. Which tips are the most useful?

5 GRAMMAR present tenses

a Caroline's going on holiday to Majorca. Circle the right verb form to complete her tweets. Tick (✓) if both forms are possible.

 Caroline   2h ago
Just arrived at the airport. ¹ *I wear / I'm wearing* a sunhat and flip flops and ² *I look like / I'm looking like* a typical tourist. # Majorcaherelcome!

 Caroline   1h ago
Oh no! I can't find my boarding pass! My flight ³ *boards / is boarding* at 11:00... 30 minutes from now... # Majorcaherelcome!

 Caroline   50m ago
Great news. Just found my boarding pass in the book ⁴ *I read / I'm reading.* ⁵ *I have / I'm having* a quick drink in the bar to celebrate! # Majorcaherelcome!

b Compare answers with a partner. Explain why you think each form is right.

c ➤ **p.134 Grammar Bank 2A.** Learn more about present tenses and practise them.

d ➤ **Communication** *Caroline's holiday plans* **A** *p.105,* **B** *p.106.*

e Make questions with the present simple or present continuous. Then ask and answer with a partner.

Holidays
- | you | prefer summer holidays or winter holidays? Why?
- | you | plan a holiday at the moment? Which places | you | think about? What | you | want to do there?

Weekends
- What | you | usually do at the weekend?
- What | you | do this weekend?

Today
- What time | this class | finish? Where | you | go after class today?
- What | you | do | this evening? Where | you | have dinner?

6 READING

a Think of some times when you have seen or met tourists from another country. Discuss the questions.

1 Where were the tourists from?
2 Where were they and what were they doing?
3 What was your impression of them?

b You are going to read an article about two tourism surveys. Before you read, discuss the questions with a partner. Choose answers from the nationalities in the list.

Which nationality or nationalities...?

the Americans	the British	the French	the Germans
the Greeks	the Italians	the Japanese	the Spanish

1 enjoy doing sport on holiday
2 love sunbathing
3 almost never sunbathe on holiday
4 drink more alcohol than usual on holiday
5 are the world's best tourists
6 are considered very polite
7 leave the worst tips
8 leave the most generous tips
9 make a lot of noise
10 dress well when they are on holiday

c Read the article once, and compare your answers to the findings in the surveys. How many did you guess correctly?

d Read the article again. Look at the highlighted words and phrases. With a partner, work out their meanings.

What different nationalities do on holiday...

A new survey of holidaymakers in Europe and the USA has found that the holiday you enjoy may depend on the country you come from.

Some holiday destinations were popular among all nationalities. The beach, for instance, was the undisputed leader among all destinations in the survey.

Activity holidays are also popular, for example, cycling, sailing, or trekking holidays. Even when their main aim is to relax, travellers said that they enjoyed seeing the sights and visiting places of interest in and around their holiday destination.

There are, however, country-specific differences:
- The Greeks are particularly keen on sport during their holidays, with 75% engaging in some kind of sporting activity.
- Sunbathing is extremely popular with the Germans. Almost 50% named it as their favourite holiday activity, especially on Spanish beaches – in fact 25% of high-income Germans are planning to go to Spain in the next 12 months. Going hiking and eating out in upmarket restaurants came second and third for Germans.
- Citing concerns about skin cancer, only one in ten Americans said sunbathing was something they would do on holiday. Eager to soak up the history and culture that they can't find at home, 46% of Americans prefer to go on tours of museums, historic buildings, and other places of interest.
- About 60% of UK travellers admitted drinking more while away than they would normally do, with 28% saying they had five or more alcoholic drinks every day.

Information from www.marketresearchworld.net, www.dailymail.co.uk, www.business-standard.com

... and what the locals think of them

Another survey, conducted by Expedia, an online travel company, has ranked the Japanese as the world's best tourists. The British and the Canadians rank second and third among the 27 nationalities in the survey. The survey also revealed that the French have the reputation for being the world's worst tourists.

Around 4,500 hoteliers across the globe gave their opinions on the best travellers overall, as well as on specific categories including politeness, generosity, behaviour, fashion sense, tidiness, and how much they complain.

The survey found that:
- The Japanese, British, Canadians, Germans, and Australians are considered the most polite tourists. The French were considered the most impolite.
- Hoteliers also found the French to be the most frugal and the meanest tippers. The biggest tippers were the Americans, followed by the British, the Germans, and the Japanese.
- The top three loudest nations were the Americans, the Italians, and the Spanish. The Japanese were ranked as the quietest.
- The Americans were at the bottom of the list for fashion sense, with the stylish Italians and French taking top prize.
- The Japanese, Germans, and British were considered the tidiest tourists. The Americans ranked at the bottom here as well.
- The Japanese were ranked as the least likely to complain, followed by the Canadians and the Swiss. The nationalities who complained the most were the Americans, the Germans, and the French.

e Talk to a partner.

1 What would you say are the favourite holiday destinations for people from your country? What do they like to do there?

2 How do you think people feel about tourists from your country in the categories from the survey (polite, generous, etc.)?

7 SPEAKING

a Choose two of the ideas below to talk about. Think about what you are going to say, and make notes.

- a place I'd really like to go to for a holiday
- a great winter holiday I once had
- things I do differently when I'm on holiday (clothes, tipping, activities...)
- a holiday I will always remember from my childhood
- things tourists do that annoy me
- a family holiday when everyone argued
- a holiday when I had a lot of problems
- a holiday when I did a lot of sport

b Work with a partner or in small groups. Talk about your topics, giving as much information as you can. Listen to the other student(s) and ask for more information.

> **Asking for more information**
> Ask questions about what people say to show interest and keep the conversation going.
> *Really? Why is / was that?*
> *What will / did you do next?*
> *What is / was it like?*
> *Would you do it again?*

8 WRITING

➤ **p.114 Writing** *Holiday tweets*. Write a series of holiday tweets.

9 ① 37⟩⟩ **SONG** *Destination: Anywhere* ♫

G possessives
V shops and services
P 's; linking

Where did you get your bag?

At a small shop a friend of mine recommended.

2B Opening up or closing down?

1 VOCABULARY shops and services

a Look at the photos. Do you usually buy these things…?

- online
- in a small local shop
- in a supermarket, hypermarket, or department store
- in another way

b ➤ p.154 Vocabulary Bank *Shops and services.*

c Talk to a partner. What's the difference between…?

1 a DIY store and a hypermarket
2 a stationer's and a newsagent's
3 a dry cleaner's and a launderette
4 an estate agent's and a travel agent's
5 'the shop's closing' and 'the shop's closing down'

2 LISTENING & SPEAKING

a Look at the photos. Do you see similar sights in any areas of your town?

b Read the article about high streets in the UK. Why have they changed so much? What are some towns trying to do?

Can anyone save the British high street?

The **high street** was once the heart of communities across the UK. The butcher's, baker's, and greengrocer's were all there, run by locals who knew their customers by name.

But today one in seven high street shops has closed down, or has been replaced by a café or a beauty salon, as shoppers drive to out-of-town hypermarkets or malls, or buy online. The recession doesn't help either. In the worst-hit towns, more than one-third of the small high street shops have disappeared.

To try to save their high streets, some towns now offer free parking nearby. Others plan to have live music and theatre performances in the town centre, and others are encouraging small businesses to move into empty shop spaces and open 'pop-up shops' (quirky, interesting shops that close or change after a few weeks). The towns are hopeful, but are these efforts too little, too late?

c 1 40)) Listen to four people talk about their local shopping street. Who is most optimistic about the situation of small shops?

d Listen again and complete the chart.

	Harry	Kate	Ken	Bea
1 Where do you live?				
2 What shops are there near you?				
3 What's happening to small shops in your area? Why? Do you think this is a good or bad thing?				

e Interview a partner with the questionnaire below.

My local shops

1 What kinds of shops are there near where you live?
2 Do you go to them much? If not, where do you buy things?
3 What shops have opened up or closed down near you? Are you pleased or sorry about it?
4 Are there any markets near you? Do you ever go to them? Do you have a favourite stall?
5 What chain stores are there near you? (H&M, Zara, etc.) Do you shop there? How do you feel about them? Are they in competition with local shops?
6 Are small shops in your country struggling? Do you think it's important to support them? Why (not)?

3 GRAMMAR possessives

a With a partner decide if the highlighted phrases are right (✓) or wrong (✗). Correct the wrong phrases.

1 Could you tell me where to find childrens' books?
2 What's Carlos's surname? I can never remember it.
3 I'm going to Marta's to study this afternoon.
4 Is this your new car's husband? It's lovely!
5 I mustn't forget it's the my mother's birthday tomorrow.
6 I'm sure you'll like Tony. He's a really old friend of mine.
7 I didn't like the film's beginning, but the end was good.
8 One day I'd love to have mine own flat.

b ➤ p.135 Grammar Bank 2B. Learn more about possessives and practise them.

4 PRONUNCIATION 's; linking

> 🔍 **The pronunciation of 's**
> The 's , like the s added to plural nouns and the third person of verbs, can be pronounced in three different ways:
> 1 /s/ after the unvoiced sounds /k/, /p/, /f/, /t/, and /θ/
> 2 /z/ after voiced sounds (most other sounds)
> 3 /ɪz/ after /s/, /z/, /dʒ/, /ʃ/, and /tʃ/

a (1 44)) Read the information box. Then listen and repeat the phrases.

1 🐍 my parents' house   my wife's brother
2 🦓 my friend's car   the men's toilets
3 /ɪz/ Charles's flat   my niece's husband

b (1 45)) Listen to the phrases. Is the 's 1 /s/, 2 /z/, or 3 /ɪz/?

☐ Maria's mother   ☐ Max's motorbike
☐ Philip's phone   ☐ Mr Smith's salary
☐ Tom's train   ☐ my neighbours' new dog
☐ my wife's work   ☐ George's job

c Practise saying the phrases.

d (1 46)) Listen and repeat the sentences, linking the marked words. Do you know why they are linked?

1 What's the name of the shop?
2 Jane's an ex-colleague of ours.
3 Some friends of mine are coming for dinner this evening.
4 Is that all your own work?
5 He lives at the top of the hill.
6 We're having lunch at Anne's.
7 They make their own bread.

e Practise saying the following sentences with a partner. Do you agree?

1 Mother's Day and Father's Day are just commercial opportunities for shops to sell more.
2 A chemist's should be open 24 hours a day.
3 It's safer to eat meat bought from a butcher's or a market than from a supermarket.
4 There's no point in spending much on children's clothes and shoes because they don't last for long.
5 If you don't like your friend's partner, it's better not to say so.
6 There should be a law against a boss's children being employed in his or her company.

5 READING

a You're going to read about a UK shopping site, *NotOnTheHighStreet.com*. Why do you think the founders decided to call it that?

b Now read **About us** and check.

Where everything has a story

ABOUT US

Award-winning entrepreneurs Holly Tucker and Sophie Cornish founded the website NotOnTheHighStreet.com from a kitchen table. Two working mothers, they loved discovering handmade and beautiful objects for themselves and as gifts, the kind of things that were sold in quirky markets, craft fairs or small boutiques. But finding these places took time.

So Sophie and Holly came up with an idea. What if there were one place which brought together unique and hard-to-find objects from all over the UK? From this idea, NotOnTheHighStreet.com was born. Launched with just 100 sellers, there are now thousands of talented and creative small businesses who sell here, with more joining every week. Each seller hand-makes their products, and sends them directly to the buyer. Happy shopping!

c Read about three of their sellers. Write the questions in the right place. There is one question you do not need.

A *What are your ambitions for the future?*
B *What sort of products do you make and sell?*
C *How does the place where you live influence your products?*
D *Do you also sell in shops or only from the website?*
E *How is your health now?*
F *Where did you start your company and where do you work now?*
G *When did you set up your business and why?*

d Read about the sellers again. Answer the questions with **KW**, **AB**, or **EC**.

Which seller…?

1 makes things that people specifically ask her for [ ]
2 gives some of the money she makes to a good cause [ ]
3 started her business after she moved house [ ]
4 would like her business to be more international [ ]
5 started working again after a period of not being able to [ ]
6 creates products out of unwanted things [ ]

e Look at the highlighted words related to crafts and work out their meanings.

f If you were able to buy one thing from one of the sellers, what would you buy? Who would you buy it for?

6 SPEAKING

Choose three of the topics and tell a partner about them. Give as much information as you can.

Talk about something you've bought which…

- was personalized for you
- you bought directly from the person who made it
- was a present for a friend or relative
- made you feel better
- you couldn't really afford, but you just had to have
- was made locally
- was eco-friendly
- you later had to take back to the shop

GIFTS   HOME   GARDEN   PICTURES & PRINTS   JEWELLERY   FASHION   BABY & CHILD   PETS   WEDDINGS   SEE MORE   [ ]   [FIND]

SOME OF OUR SELLERS

KRESSE WESLING

1 _____?
My husband and I have built our entire business around 'upcycling' – recycling old materials to make something new. We take old fire hoses* and create belts, wallets, phone cases, and bags from them.

What inspired you to start your business?
Recycling has always been a passion of ours. As soon as I saw some of the London Fire Brigade's old hoses, I instantly fell in love with them. We now collect old hoses across the country and 50% of the profits go to the Fire Fighters Charity.

2 _____?
It started in a single room where we lived in Brixton, London. Now we have a large workshop. We've recycled over 170 tonnes of hoses.

*hose = a long tube made of rubber used for putting water onto a fire, gardens, etc.

ABIGAIL BRYANS

Describe your product range. What makes it unique?
I make wooden signs with clever sayings. 'Champagne is the answer' is one of my most popular signs. I also get many fantastic requests for personalized signs from customers.

3 _____?
About ten years ago, I was on my own with three small children and no job. Over the years I had made small gifts like photo frames and sold them to friends, and it was a friend of mine who told me, 'Don't be frightened to fail'. Hearing those words inspired me to start the business. Now I'm working full-time at my kitchen table in south London.

4 _____?
I would just love my designs to be sold around the world. I'd also love a little workshop so that I didn't have to work in my kitchen!

EDWINA COOPER

What inspired you to create your business?
I'd always enjoyed painting, but about ten years ago I had a stroke*. I couldn't speak or move my right hand, which I used to paint. The doctors said I'd never paint again, but I slowly got better. A few years later, a friend asked me to do an illustration for her business. She liked what I did and it inspired me to start painting again.

5 _____?
Much better. I'm fully recovered now and I'm selling my hand-painted cushions on NotOnTheHighStreet.com. I'm so happy that people like what I do.

6 _____?
My husband, son, and I moved to the Isle of Wight about seven years ago, which is when I started painting cushions at home. I'm inspired by the island, and my customers say my paintings make them feel like they're on the island with me.

*stroke = a sudden serious illness when a blood vessel (= tube) in the brain bursts or is blocked

SWEET DREAMS ♡

GRAMMAR

Circle a, b, or c.

1 I emailed _____ the photos.
  a her   b she   c hers

2 What are _____ surnames?
  a them   b theirs   c their

3 He made _____.
  a for me coffee   b coffee for me
  c coffee to me

4 My sister _____.
  a lent them to us   b them lent to we
  c lent to we them

5 The red shoes are nice, but I prefer
  those _____.
  a blue one   b blues ones   c blue ones

6 He's _____ man I've ever met.
  a the bossiest   b the most bossy
  c the more bossy

7 She's _____ in her new job than she was
  before.
  a much more happy   b more happier
  c much happier

8 The film was _____ than the book.
  a a bit better
  b bit better
  c a bit more better

9 _____ a word he says.
  a I'm not believing   b I don't believe
  c I'm not believe

10 You look worried – what _____ about?
  a are you thinking   b you are thinking
  c do you think

11 Where _____ on holiday this summer?
  a do you go   b are you going   c you go

12 _____ our grandparents next weekend.
  a We're visiting   b We're visit   c We visit

13 I love looking at other _____ family photos.
  a people's   b peoples'   c people'

14 What's the _____ where you were born?
  a village's name   b village name
  c name of the village

15 We grow all _____ .
  a the own vegetables   b our own vegetables
  c ours own vegetables

VOCABULARY

a Complete the sentences with an adjective made from the **bold** word.

1 My grandmother is extremely _____. **glamour**
2 Teenagers can be very _____. **mood**
3 Don't be so _____! **child**
4 She's very _____. She won't do anything stupid. **sense**
5 He's always been _____ – he loves painting. **create**
6 Their car's not really _____ for a family of four. **suit**
7 Our hotel room was _____. **luxury**
8 Work is very _____ at the moment. **stress**
9 It's a bit _____ to carry so much money. **risk**
10 Her Russian is very _____. **impress**

b Complete the words.

1 There are lots of mosquitoes – where's the **i**_____ **r**_____?
2 We're going on a **s**_____ in Kenya – I hope we see elephants!
3 It's a **p**_____ holiday, so everything's included.
4 He stayed in the sun for too long and he got **s**_____.
5 It always takes me ages to **p**_____ my bags.
6 I need a new **m**_____ **c**_____. The one in my camera is full.
7 Free **g**_____ tours of the museum leave every hour.
8 I can't go swimming. I don't have my **s**_____.

c Where can you buy these things? Write the name of the shop.

1 meat _____
2 a newspaper _____
3 bread _____
4 flowers _____
5 aspirins _____
6 a house _____
7 fish _____

PRONUNCIATION

a Circle the word with a different sound.

1 🐍 toothpaste   safari   expensive   baker's
2 ⬆ sunbathe   butcher's   brush   fishmonger
3 ☎ raincoat   comb   memory   overall
4 🦓 possessive   clothes   bizarre   sights
5 🍸 delicious   envious   chemist's   healthy

b Underline the stressed syllable.

1 im|pul|sive   3 pro|fi|ta|ble   5 news|a|gent's
2 sight|see|ing   4 am|bi|tious

CAN YOU UNDERSTAND THIS TEXT?

a Read the article once. Do you agree that the kind of holiday you enjoy depends on your personality?

Make sure your holiday matches your personality

'Choosing the right holiday is more than just picking a place or experience that sounds fun or interesting,' says Arthur Hoffman of Expedia Asia Pacific. 'Travellers should think carefully about what they and their travel companions are like, and then research travel destinations,' he says. 'This will help ensure the right holiday for the right person and their personality.'

So here's some advice on what different personality types should look for when picking their next holiday.

Extrovert / introvert

Extroverts enjoy holiday experiences that provide high levels of excitement, novelty, risk-taking, and social interaction. ^{1}_____, restaurants, and crowded cafés rather than art galleries and temples or churches. They love action-packed holidays that never stop.

Introverts are the opposite: they like activities that promote reflection and intellectual or spiritual experiences.

Nervous / relaxed

Nervous individuals tend to prefer destinations, cultural activities, and food types that remind them of home or of past travel experiences. When travelling overseas, they often choose restaurants that serve food similar to their country of origin. Unusual experiences tend to worry them. ^{2}_____, they can find resorts or holiday experiences with high levels of socialising and activities stressful.

Relaxed people are just the opposite. They are OK with trips involving unknowns, and take new challenges in their stride.

Open / closed

Open people will rarely go back to the same destination unless they have fallen in love with the place and want to explore it further. They enjoy big cities that offer lots of variety, such as Mumbai, London, Paris, New York, or Sydney.

Closed people visit places they have fond memories of, such as their hometowns. ^{3}_____.

Conservative / eccentric

Conservative types will often take holidays that others will be impressed by within their immediate social circles. ^{4}_____ and showing them their latest holiday photos.

Eccentrics take holidays that might not win them much social approval, such as bird-watching in Siberia!

Careful / spontaneous

Careful people like to plan well in advance – way before a holiday even begins. They want to know the exact where, when, and why of their holiday, and often have a long list of must-sees. ^{5}_____ and will spend a lot of time researching on the internet and reading travel guides. They often record their holidays through photos, videos, travel diaries, or blogs.

Spontaneous people don't make plans and will go along with the flow.

b Read the article again and complete it with phrases A–F. There is one sentence you do not need.

A They tend to have strict time and money budgets
B They often go back to the same holiday destination again and again
C They tend to prefer busy, lively places
D They love telling others where they have been
E They often go on holiday with large groups of friends
F Although they prefer not to travel alone

CAN YOU UNDERSTAND THESE PEOPLE?

1 47))) In the street Watch or listen to five people and answer the questions.

Diarmuid   Edisha   James   Sean   Elayne

1 Diarmuid's mother chose his name to help him to remember _____.
   a a person   b a city   c a country
2 Edisha's names were chosen by _____.
   a her father   b her mother   c her aunts
3 Two colours James says he likes, or used to like are _____.
   a red and green   b green and blue   c red and blue
4 What Sean remembers about the holiday is _____.
   a watching the rain   b playing in the rain
   c arguing in the rain
5 Elayne prefers to shop online because _____.
   a it's more convenient for her
   b she doesn't like all the people in the malls
   c she likes the choice you have online

CAN YOU SAY THIS IN ENGLISH?

Do the tasks with a partner. Tick (✓) the box if you can do them.

Can you…?

1 ☐ agree or disagree with this statement, and say why: *Our names can affect how successful we are in life.*
2 ☐ talk about what makes a successful brand name
3 ☐ compare how different nationalities behave on holiday
4 ☐ ask and answer these questions:
• What do you usually take on holiday? Have you ever forgotten anything important?
• What shops are there where you live? How are they changing? Where do you usually do your shopping?

Short films A farmers' market
VIDEO Watch and enjoy a film on iTutor.

G past simple, past continuous, or *used to*?
V stages of life
P *-ed* endings; sentence rhythm

> What were you like as a teenager?

> Very different! I used to have long hair, and I played in a rock group.

3A The generation gap

1 GRAMMAR past simple, past continuous, or *used to*?

a Look at the picture of a school playground. Which child or children do you think is / are…?

> a tomboy   a 'girly' girl   a bookworm
> a well-behaved child   quarrelling
> being naughty

b 2 2)) Listen and check. Do you identify with any of them? Which one? Why?

c Read the posts on a blog where people write about what they were like as children. Who thinks they have changed the most / the least?

d With a partner, circle the correct form of the **highlighted** verbs. Why is the other form not possible?

e ➤ **p.136 Grammar Bank 3A.** Learn more about the past simple, the past continuous, and *used to*, and practise them.

What kind of child were you... and have you changed?

Nick   I'd say I was a pretty well-behaved child. I loved toy cars, and ¹ *I was spending / I used to spend* hours lining them up to create traffic jams. I was an only child so I didn't have as much opportunity to be naughty as other kids! I think I'm still someone who avoids conflict but sadly I don't have as much of an imagination as I used to.

Laura   I was a good mix between girly girl and tomboy. I loved playing outside – but I didn't like jeans, I liked pretty clothes. For example, I remember once when I climbed a really high tree but I couldn't get down, because ² *I was wearing / I used to wear* a pink frilly dress and it got caught in the branches! In that sense I haven't changed much. I still love wearing pretty clothes and I still love going for walks in the country.

Sarah   As a child ³ *I used to be / I was being* very shy. My dad was in the army so my family moved around a lot, a different school almost every year. I became a lot more confident after ⁴ *I started / I used to start* university. A lot of the people at uni didn't know anybody else, so it was easier to make friends. In fact nowadays many people see me as outgoing!

2 PRONUNCIATION & SPEAKING
-ed endings; sentence rhythm

a **2 5)))** Listen to the three different pronunciations of the *-ed* ending.

1 I used to be shy. I liked animals.

2 I've changed a lot. I enjoyed exams.

3 /ɪd/ I started school. It ended in tears.

b **2 6)))** Listen to some more regular past simple verbs. How is the *-ed* ending pronounced? Tick (✓) the right box.

	/t/	/d/	/ɪd/
1 I hated eating vegetables.	☐	☐	☐
2 We looked alike.	☐	☐	☐
3 I tried everything.	☐	☐	☐
4 We lived abroad.	☐	☐	☐
5 I hoped to pass.	☐	☐	☐
6 We decided to move.	☐	☐	☐

c Practise saying the sentences.

> **Past or present?**
> When the *-ed* ending is pronounced /t/ or /d/, it can often be difficult to hear whether a regular verb is in the past or present tense. Use the context to help you.

d **2 7)))** Listen to six more sentences. Are the verbs in the present or past? Write **Pr** or **Pa**.

1 ☐ 2 ☐ 3 ☐ 4 ☐ 5 ☐ 6 ☐

e **2 8)))** Listen to the rhythm of the conversation below. Then practise it with a partner. Copy the rhythm, and try to pronounce the *-ed* endings correctly.

> A **When** was the **last time** you **stayed** at a **hotel**?
>
> B **Last year**. We were **driving** to the **south** for a **holiday**, and we **stopped** at a **hotel** for the **night** on the **way**.
>
> A Did you **use** to **go** to **hotels** when you were a **child**?
>
> B **No**, we **used** to **spend** the **holidays** at my **grandparents'**. They **lived** in a **village** in the **country**.

f Talk to a partner.

> **Events in your life**
> Take it in turns to ask and answer the questions with the past simple form of the verb.
> 1 Where ▆ you born? (be)
>   Where ▆ you ▆ when you ▆ a child? (live, be)
> 2 How old ▆ you when you ▆ primary school? (be, start)
>   ▆ you ▆ your first day? (enjoy) What ▆ you ▆?(do)
> 3 When ▆ the first time you ▆ abroad? (be, travel)
>   Where ▆ you ▆? (go)
> 4 When ▆ the last time you ▆ a meal for friends? (be, cook)
>   What ▆ you ▆? (make) ▆ your friends ▆ it?(like)
> 5 When ▆ the last time you ▆ relatives? (be, visit)
>   Who ▆ you ▆? (visit) What ▆ you ▆? (do)

> *Where were you born?*
>
> *I was born in a small town called Morella.*

> **When I was younger**
> Do you agree with these statements? If you do, explain why. If you don't, change them so that they're true for you.
>
> **When I was younger...**
> 1 my town **used to have** better shops and services than it does today.
> 2 children **used to spend** more time playing outside than they do now.
> 3 people **used to cook** more, and eat out less.
> 4 the weather **didn't use to be** as changeable.
> 5 more young people **used to go** to university. Now they all want to get a job when they finish school.
> 6 people **didn't use to watch** so much TV.

> *I don't agree with 1. I think there used to be fewer good shops. We now have a new shopping mall outside the centre of town.*

> **What was happening?**
> Add two more times and dates that you remember well to the list. Where were you then? What were you doing?
> • at midnight on 31 December of last year
> • at 9.00 last night
> • at lunchtime on your last birthday
> • _____
> • _____

> *At midnight on 31 December of last year, I was at a friend's house. We were playing music and dancing...*

3 VOCABULARY stages of life

a Which stage of life is each person in? Match the people and the photos.

- ☐ a baby
- ☐ a toddler
- ☐ a child
- ☐ a pre-teen
- ☐ a teenager
- ☐ in his / her early twenties (= 20–23)
- ☐ in his / her mid-thirties (= 34–36)
- ☐ in his / her late forties (= 47–49)
- ☐ a pensioner

> 🔍 **middle-aged**
> The word *middle-aged* means different things to different people, but usually refers to a person in their forties or fifties.
> *I'm not sure how old he is, but he looks middle-aged.*

b (2 9)) Listen and check.

c Which stages of life do you associate with…?
- nursery school / primary school / secondary school
- learning a language / learning to swim / learning to drive
- going to bed early / staying up late / sleeping late
- having your first boyfriend or girlfriend / your first job / your first grandchild
- going to work abroad / being self-employed / being retired

d Think of three people you know who are in different stages of life in **a**. Tell your partner about them.

> *My sister Ana is in her mid-thirties, but she looks younger. She's married and has a six-month old baby called Mario. She used to work as a nurse but now she's at home looking after Mario.*

4 LISTENING

a Can you always tell how old someone is from their appearance? What other ways are there of telling a person's age, e.g. the kind of music they like?

b (2 10)) Listen to **Part 1** of a local radio news report on teenagers and answer the questions.
1 Who is able to hear the Mosquito Tone?
2 Were both the presenters able to hear it?
3 Were you able to hear it? How did it make you feel?

c (2 11)) Listen to **Part 2** of the news story. What is the Mosquito Tone being used for? Does everybody think it's a good idea?

d Listen to **Part 2** again. Complete the information in your own words.
1 Some shop owners think that teenage gangs can…
2 Shop owners think that the Mosquito Tone… for them.
3 They say that it doesn't…
4 Some groups of people are trying to… because they think it's harmful and unfair.
5 The Mosquito Tone has been released as…
6 This allows teenagers to…

e Do you think the shop owners and teenagers are using the Mosquito Tone in an appropriate way? Why (not)?

5 READING & SPEAKING

a Look at the headlines of three news stories. In groups of three, say what you think each one is about.

> # Under 16? This is no place for you!

> ## Babies at the movies

> # Airline's new child rules cause controversy

b You are going to read one of the three articles and tell each other about it. Work in groups of three.
➤ **Communication** *News stories* **B** *p.105.* **C** *p.106.*

c **A** read the article below and find answers to the questions.
1 What new idea is being tried? Where?
2 What problem is this idea meant to solve?
3 Who will be affected by it?
4 What good points about this idea are mentioned?
5 What problems with the idea are mentioned?

Home | **News** | Sport | TV&Showbiz | Health | Science | Travel | Money

Under 16? This is no place for you!

As from today, teenagers under 16 will be banned from the centre of the Welsh town of Bangor at night. This is the first time a town in the UK has banned children from an entire city centre.

The aim of the new rule is to reduce crime and anti-social behaviour in the town centre. In the last year, the area has seen a large number of robberies committed by young people.

The new curfew, which applies between 9 p.m. and 6 a.m., means that any person under 16 who is caught in the centre of town without a parent or adult guardian could go to jail for three months or pay a £2,500 fine.

Both parents and some politicians have criticized the rule, which they say treats all young people like criminals. Sports groups, youth centres, and even churches could be affected, they say.

One mother said: 'My son is 16, and he wouldn't be allowed to walk home from the bus stop with these rules.'

Another resident said: 'The idea is simply crazy.'

Adapted from the Daily Mail

Glossary
1 _____ /ˈkɜːfjuː/ *noun* a time after which people are not allowed to go outside their homes
2 _____ /ˈænti ˈsəʊʃl bɪˈheɪvjə(r)/ *noun* a way of acting that is not considered acceptable by other people
3 _____ /bæn/ *verb* said officially that something is not allowed
4 _____ /faɪn/ *noun* a sum of money that you have to pay for breaking a law or rule

d Read the article again. Work out the meaning of the highlighted words and phrases, and then complete the glossary. Check the pronunciation of the words and phrases.

e Work in groups with **B** and **C**. Tell each other your stories. Try to use the words from the glossary and explain them to **B** and **C** if necessary.

f Discuss the questions with your group.
1 Do you think these are good ideas? Why (not)?
2 Are there any places in your town where babies, children, or teenagers aren't allowed?
3 Are there any places where you *don't* think babies / small children, teenagers, adults, or old people should be allowed? Why?

> I don't think children should be allowed in spas. It's a place to relax, and children make a noise in the pool.

6 SPEAKING & WRITING

a What were you like as a child, or as a teenager? Tell a partner. Talk about three of the topics in either When I was a child… or When I was a teenager… . Say how you're different today.

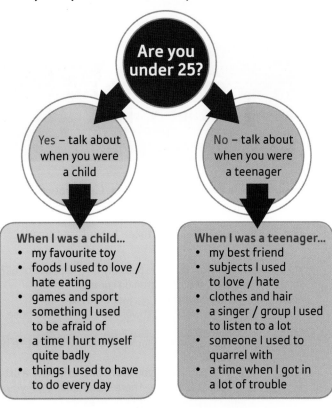

Are you under 25?

Yes – talk about when you were a child

No – talk about when you were a teenager

When I was a child…
- my favourite toy
- foods I used to love / hate eating
- games and sport
- something I used to be afraid of
- a time I hurt myself quite badly
- things I used to have to do every day

When I was a teenager…
- my best friend
- subjects I used to love / hate
- clothes and hair
- a singer / group I used to listen to a lot
- someone I used to quarrel with
- a time when I got in a lot of trouble

b Write a paragraph for the blog in **1** about what you used to be like as a child (or as a teenager) and if you have changed.

7 ②12») SONG *Young folks* ♫

Who's this picture of?

It's me when I was a child. It reminds me of all the wonderful family holidays we had.

3B In the picture

1 VOCABULARY photography

a Look at the photo. Where was it taken? Do you have any photos of yourself in front of a famous monument?

b Simon and Alice are tourists in Pisa. Complete the dialogue with the words below.

right   background   blurred   take   behind   automatic

Alice	Excuse me, could you possibly ¹____ a photo of us?
Man	Yes, sure. Which button do I press?
Alice	This one here. It's ²____, just press it.
Man	Right. You want the tower in the ³____, I suppose.
Alice	Yes, please.
Simon	Can you take it so it looks, you know, as if we're holding up the tower?
Man	All right, I'll try. Can you move back a little ... a little to the ⁴____ ... Just a minute. There's someone ⁵____ you. OK, I think that's OK. Do you want to have a look?
Alice	Oh, that is so great. But I moved. It's a bit ⁶____. Could you take just one more?
Man	Oh, all right...

c **2 13**⟩⟩ Listen and check.

d ➤ p.155 Vocabulary Bank *Photography*.

2 PRONUNCIATION word stress

a **2 16**⟩⟩ Under<u>line</u> the stress in the words beginning with *photo*. Listen and check. Practise saying the words.

1 pho|to|graph
2 pho|to|gra|pher
3 pho|to|gra|phy
4 pho|to|gra|phic
5 pho|to|ge|nic
6 pho|to|co|py

b Now under<u>line</u> the stressed syllable in the multi-syllable words in 1–7 below.

> 1 There's a tree in the **back|ground**.
> 2 In the **fore|ground** there's a girl.
> 3 You can see a house in the **dis|tance**.
> 4 There's a man be**|hind** her.
> 5 It's a **close-|up** of a watch.
> 6 It's out of **fo|cus**.
> 7 Is your **cam|era au|to|ma|tic**?

c **2 17**⟩⟩ Listen and check. Practise saying the sentences.

d ➤ **Communication** *Spot the differences* **A** *p.107,* **B** *p.108.* Describe the picture to each other and find the differences.

3 LISTENING & SPEAKING

a How do you feel about having your photo taken? Do you think you're photogenic? Why (not)?

b **2 18**⟩⟩ Listen to **Part 1** of an interview with Brian Voce, a professional portrait photographer. Make notes under the questions below.

1 How did he first become interested in photography?

_____

2 What kind of people does he photograph and where?

_____

3 Which famous person did he have an embarrassing experience with? What happened?

_____

4 What's the favourite photo he mentions?

_____

portrait by Brian Voce

portrait by Brian Voce

portrait by Annie Leibovitz

portrait by Brian Voce

c In **Part 2** of the interview, Brian explains how to look good in a portrait. Before you listen, read sentences 1–8. With a partner, decide whether you think they are **T** (true) or **F** (false).

1 Most people enjoy being photographed.
2 It's easier to relax if you are on your own with the photographer.
3 A professional photographer won't take long to get good photos.
4 What you wear is not really important.
5 Most people, including men, will look better with make-up on.
6 It's better to pose standing up than sitting down.
7 It's important to be in a comfortable position.
8 It's better not to look at the camera until just before the photographer shoots.

d 🔊 2 19)) Listen and check your answers.

e Listen again and correct the false statements.

f Talk to a partner.

1 Are there any tips you've learned that you might put into practice next time someone takes a photo of you?
2 Do you think you're good at taking photos? Why (not)?
3 What do you normally take photos with?
4 Do you prefer taking photos of scenery or portraits of people? What else do you take photos of?

4 WRITING

➤ **p.115 Writing** *An article.* Write an article with tips on how to take good holiday photos.

5 GRAMMAR prepositions

a With a partner, complete the gaps with a preposition from the list.

> at (x2)   from   in   of (x2)   over   next to

I took this photo when we were flying ¹____ the Andes – I was going ²____ Argentina to Chile. Luckily, I was sitting ³____ the window, so I had a perfect view. I'm not usually very good ⁴____ taking photos, but I think this one is beautiful, and I'm quite proud ⁵____ it. Later on during the flight, we had a lot of turbulence, and by the time we finally arrived ⁶____ Santiago I was feeling quite nervous. But when I look ⁷____ this photo it reminds me ⁸____ the feeling of calm that mountains always give me.

b Which preposition(s) in the text…?

1 show where a person or thing is
2 show where a person or thing is moving
3 are examples of prepositions used after certain verbs
4 are examples of prepositions used after certain adjectives

c ➤ **p.137 Grammar Bank 3B.** Learn more about prepositions and practise them.

d Complete 1–10 with a preposition. Then choose four topics to talk to a partner about.

1 A photo you took that you are very proud ____
2 Someone in your family that you really like talking ____
3 Something you're really looking forward ____ at the moment
4 Something your country is famous ____
5 Someone you often argue ____
6 A beautiful sight that you once flew ____
7 What you have ____ the walls of your bedroom
8 Someone you could rely ____ in a crisis
9 Something you usually ask ____ when you eat out
10 Somewhere you had to walk ____ a large number of steps

6 READING

a What do you do with the photos you've taken? Tell a partner. Which of these do you usually do?

- store them on your computer, phone, tablet, etc.
- back them up on a separate hard drive or CD-ROM
- email them to friends and family
- upload them to an online photo site
- print them out

b Read the article about storing digital photos and complete 1–5 with a heading from the list. There is one heading you don't need to use.

A Safe in the cloud?
B Hard drives don't hold enough photos
C Digital files can deteriorate
D Photo sites come and go
E Technology becomes obsolete
F How long will they last?

How safe are your digital photos?

In the past, your grandmother probably kept her photos in a box, or in an old album, and sadly, over time these memories faded or disappeared. But with today's technology, that shouldn't be a problem. A digital photo lasts forever, right?

Actually, think again. Though it is still a good idea to preserve all of your photos as digital computer files, there are plenty of things that can damage or even destroy those high-tech memories.

1 _____
Very few people realize this can happen, but if you store your photos as .jpgs (the most common file format), the file will actually deteriorate every time you copy or resave it. Experts disagree about how much damage this can do, but the damage is real.

2 _____
Your files may be safe on your hard drive, but how long will your hard drive last? The average is just five years. Before then, one big magnet could erase your drive in an instant. You could back up your photos on a CD-ROM, but they don't last much longer: about 10–20 years at most, experts say.

c Read the article again. Match the storage method with the problem it has.

1	.jpg files	a	only last for about five years
2	hard drives	b	only last for 10 to 20 years
3	CD-ROMs	c	are damaged when they're copied
4	CD-ROM drives	d	can go out of business
5	'the cloud'	e	may not exist in the future
6	photo sites	f	can be damaged by storms

d Look at the highlighted words in the text related to digital photos and computers, and work out their meaning from the context.

e What do you think is the biggest threat to your own digital photos? After reading the article, will you do anything differently to protect your photos?

3 _____

Let's say all goes well and your CD-ROM full of photos lasts for 20 years. By then, will there still be any CD-ROM drives in the world that can read the disc? This is also true for flash drives, memory cards, and the rest. Today's high-tech storage solution is tomorrow's useless floppy disk.

4 _____

People talk about saving their files in a magical place on the internet, like Apple's iCloud or Dropbox. But this just means your files are in a company's data centre on – guess what? – a whole load of hard drives, which could die or go bad just as easily as your own. Just recently, a summer thunderstorm hit a cloud storage centre in the US, and major sites like Netflix, Pinterest, and Instagram were knocked offline for almost a whole day. Thousands of files were lost.

5 _____

Websites like Flickr and Instagram let you quickly upload photos and share them with others. But bear in mind that a photo site which is popular now could one day go out of business, taking your photos with it.

So what should you do? Experts say to make lots of copies of your photos and save them in many different ways – on your computer, on a backup drive, online, and even as traditional printed photos. It may be too late to save Grandma's photos, but you can still preserve yours.

7 LISTENING & SPEAKING

a (2 23)) Listen to three people talk about their favourite childhood photos. Number the photos 1–3. There is one photo you don't need to use.

b Listen again. Which speaker…?

1 wanted to have the photo on his / her wall, but couldn't ☐
2 doesn't think he / she looks very good in the photo ☐
3 says the photo makes him / her feel better when he / she is a bit sad ☐
4 only saw the photo many years after it was taken ☐
5 likes the photo because of the emotion you can see in it ☐
6 used to keep the photo in his / her kitchen ☐

c Think of an interesting photo of yourself as a child. Tell a partner about it. Include the information below or your own ideas.

- How old are you in the photo?
- Who are you with?
- What's happening, or what has just happened?
- When and where was the photo taken?
- Why do you like it? Does it remind you of anything special?
- Where do you keep or display it?

d Show your partner some more photos on your phone and tell him or her about them.

1 ◼️◀ HENRY'S CAR
VIDEO

a **(2 24)》** Watch or listen to Jenny and Henry. Where does Henry want to take her? Why can't he? How is Jenny going to get there?

b Listen again and ⟨circle⟩ the correct answer.

1 Jenny's suitcase *still hasn't been found | has been found*.
2 Henry thinks Jenny *will like Luke | won't understand Luke*.
3 Henry's car *has a flat tyre | has two flat tyres*.
4 He thinks the car was damaged by *neighbours | vandals*.
5 Jenny *doesn't know | knows* Luke's address.
6 Jenny had previously decided *to travel by public transport | to rent a car*.
7 She offers to *make dinner for Henry | take Henry out to dinner*.
8 Jenny *waits | doesn't wait* while Luke looks at her laptop.

> **Glossary**
> **a spare (tyre)** /speə ˈtaɪə/ = an extra tyre in a car
> **the AA** = a breakdown service in the UK

> 🔍 **British and American English**
> *rent a car* = American English
> *rent a car* OR *hire a car* = British English

Who do you think vandalized Henry's car?
Who is the man who arrives as Jenny leaves?

2 ◼️◀ RENTING A CAR
VIDEO

a **(2 25)》** Watch or listen to Jenny renting a car. Answer the questions.

1 How long does Jenny rent a car for?
2 What car does she rent?
3 Where does she want to leave the car?

What do you think is significant about the news on the TV? Do you think Jenny noticed it?

b Watch or listen again. Complete the **You Hear** phrases in the dialogue on p.33.

c **(2 26)》** Watch or listen and repeat some of the **You Say** phrases. Copy the <u>rhy</u>thm.

d Practise the dialogue with a partner.

e 👥 In pairs, roleplay the dialogue.

   A You're a visitor to the UK who wants to rent a car for a week. Talk to the assistant and choose the car you want. Use **Useful language** to help you.

   B You're the assistant at a car rental company. Help **A** choose a car and get all of **A**'s details. Use **Useful language** to help you.

f Swap roles.

> 🔍 **Useful language: describing cars**
> **Kinds of drive:** *automatic* or *manual*
> **Car types:** *economy (small cars)*
> *compact (small, but larger than economy)*
> *family (medium size)*
> *luxury (large cars, 4x4s, sports cars)*
> *convertibles (open-top cars)*
> *people carriers (for more than five people)*
> **Extras:** *air conditioning, satnav*

»)) You Hear	You Say 💬
Hello. Can I help you?	Oh, hi. I'd like to rent a car, please.
Have you _____ from us before?	No.
OK, could I _____ your driving licence, please? Great. So what _____ of car are you looking for?	Oh, nothing too big. It's just for me.
OK, so a compact. _____-door?	Yeah, that'll be fine.
For how long?	Nine days.
Automatic or _____?	An automatic, please.
Any additional _____?	No, just me.
Great. Well, we have several _____ I can show you, but I'd recommend the Vauxhall Corsa. It's £_____ per day and that includes insurance.	That sounds promising. Can I take a look?
Of course, but first I'd like to run through some of the basics. The _____ tank is full when you start, so if you return it with a full tank, there's no extra _____.	Great.
But if you get any _____ tickets or speeding fines you have to pay for them yourself.	Fair enough! Would it be possible to leave the car at the airport?
No problem, but that's a one-way rental so there's an additional charge of £_____.	OK.
And one last thing – have you driven in _____ before?	Yes, I have. So driving on the left's not a problem.
That's good. OK, let's go out and take a look at the car. We can go through the paperwork afterwards.	Great.

3 WHERE IS HENRY?

VIDEO

a (2 27 »)) Watch or listen to Jenny's afternoon and evening. What has happened to a) her laptop? b) her suitcase? What does she hear on the news?

b Watch or listen again and mark the sentences **T** (true) or **F** (false). Correct the **F** sentences.
1 Henry is in his study when Jenny comes back.
2 Jenny reminds Henry about the dinner.
3 She isn't surprised by Luke's news about her computer.
4 Luke thinks that Henry has probably gone to the university to work.
5 Henry is always late for everything.
6 Jenny is feeling tired because of jet lag.
7 When she wakes up, Henry is back.
8 She phones Rob to say goodnight.

Who do you think was responsible for what happened on the news? What do you think Jenny is going to do next? What do you think has happened to Henry?

c Look at the **Social English phrases**. Can you remember any of the missing words?

Social English phrases
Henry   I'm _____ I can't take your call at the moment.
Henry   Please leave your message after the _____.
Luke   Hi, Jenny. What's _____?
Jenny   _____ on... my suitcase has arrived!
Jenny   Well, at _____ it's back.
Jenny   I'm _____ tired.
Jenny   Thanks, Luke. See you _____.

d (2 28 »)) Watch or listen and complete the phrases.

e Watch or listen again and repeat the phrases. How do you say them in your language?

👤 **Can you...?**
☐ talk about transport options
☐ rent a car
☐ record a voicemail greeting and leave a message

G future forms: *will / shall* and *going to*
V rubbish and recycling
P /ɪ/, /aɪ/, and /eɪ/

When are they going to collect the rubbish?

They'll be here on Tuesday, I think.

4A That's rubbish!

1 LISTENING

a How often do you or your family throw away food? What kind of things? How do you feel about it?

b Look at the photo below. What do you think the woman is looking for? Why?

c You're going to listen to a journalist, Liz Scarff, talking about her experiences of living as a 'freegan'. Read the beginning of an article she wrote about freegans. Who are they? What do they do?

NEWS VOICES | SPORT | TECH | LIFE | PROPERTY | TRAVEL | MONEY

My three days as a freegan

By Liz Scarff

They're not poor or homeless, but they look in rubbish bins for food to eat. They call themselves 'freegans' – a combination of the words 'free' and 'vegan' – and they are upset about how much food people waste. Around seventeen million tons of food is thrown away in Britain every year, four million of which is perfectly good to eat. This is especially disturbing since four million people in Britain can't afford a healthy diet.

Their ideas are admirable, but taking and eating food from the rubbish sounds disgusting, embarrassing, and possibly unsafe. So, just how easy is it to live on food from bins? My challenge is to live as a freegan for three days. Too embarrassed to go on my own, I've brought my friend Dave. But first, we meet up with two London freegans, Ash and Ross, for a quick lesson in freeganism.

Adapted from The Independent

d (2 29)) Listen to Liz Scarff talk about trying to live as a freegan. Mark the sentences **T** (true) or **F** (false).

Sunday

1 You should take gloves and a torch with you before going to look in bins. ☐

2 Large shops are better than small or medium size ones. ☐

3 In the first bin they found frozen chicken soup and *chilli con carne*. ☐

4 They also found some eggs, but they were past their sell-by date. ☐

5 Ross says you don't need to worry if the packaging is broken or if something is past its sell-by date. ☐

6 He says you should wash everything you find before eating it. ☐

Monday

7 Liz and Dave found the unlocked bin behind a large supermarket. ☐

8 They found fruit and vegetables in the bin behind the supermarket. ☐

9 They didn't feel embarrassed looking in the bins. ☐

10 They had soup and bread and baked apples for dinner. ☐

e (2 30)) Listen to the second part of Liz's challenge. Answer the questions.

Tuesday

1 How did Liz feel on Tuesday morning?

2 What did they have for breakfast?

3 What did they find in the bins on Tuesday?

4 How does she feel about what people had thrown away?

5 What did they have for dinner on Tuesday evening?

6 Did all the ingredients come from the rubbish?

Wednesday

7 What was wrong with the bins in the farmer's market on Wednesday?

8 What did they find in them?

9 What did Liz learn from trying freeganism?

f What do you think are the advantages and disadvantages of being a freegan? Can you imagine ever trying it?

2 VOCABULARY rubbish and recycling

a Look at three sentences from the listening. Can you remember any of the missing words?

1 Ash and Ross walk confidently to the _____, lift the _____, and start looking for food.
2 At the bottom is a _____ of eggs.
3 If the _____ is open or it's past the _____ - _____ _____, don't take it.

b (2 31)》 Listen and complete the sentences.

c ➤ p.156 Vocabulary Bank *Rubbish and recycling.*

3 PRONUNCIATION /ɪ/, /aɪ/, and /eɪ/

a Look at the sound pictures. What are the words and sounds? Write the words from the list in the right column.

away bin date diet garbage lid lifestyle packaging reapply recycle tray waste

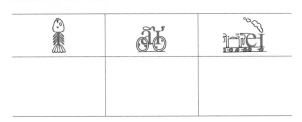

b (2 36)》 Listen and check. Practise saying the words.

c ➤ p.166 Sound Bank. Look at the typical spellings for the three sounds in **a**.

4 SPEAKING

a Read the questionnaire and think about your answers.

b Discuss the questions in groups of three or four.

What a waste!

You

What three things could you and your family do in order to throw away less food?

What kind of things do you recycle? Do you ever feel guilty about not recycling enough? Why (not)?

Have you ever eaten anything that was past its sell-by date? Why (not)? Did anything happen?

Have you ever taken something that someone else has thrown away? What was it? What did you do with it?

What do you do with clothes, books, or furniture that you don't want but could still be used?

Is there anything you are going to do differently now?

Other people

What could your local council do to make it easier to recycle where you live?

What do you think restaurants or supermarkets in your town should do with unused food? Do you know if any of them ever do it?

What kind of things do you think have too much packaging? When do you think packaging is really necessary?

Which of the things you've discussed do you think would make the most difference to your environment?

5 READING

a How long have you had your mobile phone? When do you think you'll get a new one? What will you probably do with your old phone?

b Read the article about mobile phone recycling. Find two reasons why recycling mobiles is better than throwing them away.

Home   Reviews   Videos   **Phones**   Tablets   Cameras   Components   Computing   Car Technology   News   Deals

Got a new mobile? Think twice before you throw the old one away!

Recycling our old mobile phones is something we often mean to do. But by the time we remember to do it, we decide that they're so old they're worthless, and we throw them away. But are they really?

1 _____ 'Only about 3–4 per cent of the phones we receive can't be repaired,' says Simon Walsh, Sales and Marketing Director for a British phone recycler.

As a phone arrives at a recycling centre, it goes through a rigorous testing process, which starts with a check to ensure that it's not been lost or stolen.
2 _____ Many phones are then passed to specialized repair centres.

Even mobiles that can't be repaired are valuable. 3 _____ Batteries contain nickel which can be used to make stainless steel for saucepans. The plastics in phones can be melted down to be made into traffic cones.

Of the phones that can be reused, about 20% stay in the UK. The rest of them are sent to places in Asia and Africa where they are specially needed because there are few landlines.

But there's more to it than that. It's good to recycle and reuse second-hand mobiles from the UK, but the countries which receive the mobiles also need to recycle them. 4 _____

This is a growing problem because some mobile phone parts contain dangerous chemicals. 5 _____. The phone's electrical circuits contain lead, which can cause brain damage.

It's estimated that there are more than 500 million used mobile phones around the world. If we send all of them to landfills, over 130,000 kilos of lead will be released into the soil. 6 _____.

The even greener alternative to recycling seems almost unthinkable. It's to keep your current phone for more than the usual twelve months!

Adapted from www.techradar.com

> **Glossary**
> **nickel** /'nikl/ a hard, silver-white metal
> **lead** /led/ a soft, heavy, grey metal used in the past for water pipes or to cover roofs

c Read the article again and complete it with **A–F**.

> A They contain small quantities of metals such as platinum, which are used to make jewellery.
> B If they don't, the phones will still end up in landfill.
> C As demand for mobiles and smartphones increases, the problem is going to get even worse.
> D Some phone batteries have cadmium, a metal which can cause lung cancer.
> E Then components such as the keypad are checked.
> F In fact, most mobiles can be repaired and sold again.

d Look at the highlighted words and phrases connected with recycling and the environment. Work out their meaning from the context.

e What other electronic gadgets and appliances do you think people could recycle? Do they do it where you live?

6 GRAMMAR future forms: *will / shall* and *going to*

a Complete the dialogues with *will | shall* or *be going to* and the correct form of the verb.

1 **A** Could you take the rubbish out? It's beginning to smell.
   B I _____ it as soon as this programme finishes, I promise. (do)

2 **A** _____ I _____ your plate now, madam? (take)
   B Yes, thanks. It was delicious, but I couldn't finish it all.

3 **A** What _____ you _____ when you finish school? (do) I know you've made plans.
   B I _____ a gap year, and work on a conservation project in Peru. (have)

4 **A** I'm a bit worried about the picnic. I think it _____ this afternoon. (rain)
   B Well, on the internet it says it _____ sunny. (be) I wouldn't worry if I were you.

5 **A** Don't put bottles in the rubbish. We need to take them to the bottle bank.
   B OK, OK. I _____ it again. (not do)

b (2 37)) Listen and check. Practise the dialogues with a partner.

c ➤ p.138 Grammar Bank 4A. Learn more about future forms and practise them.

d Talk to a partner. Choose two topics from each group to talk about, or use your own ideas.

Talk about a plan you have…
- for this evening
- for the weekend
- for your next holiday
- to save money or spend less
- to improve your diet
- to learn something new

Make a prediction about…
- the environment
- your favourite sports club
- the economy and unemployment
- an actor, singer, or group you like
- your friends' or family members' careers
- the characters in a TV series you watch

🔍 **Responding to plans and predictions**
Plans
I'm going to…
Are you? So am I.
What a good idea! How nice!

Predictions
I don't think… will / is going to…
I think so too.
I don't think so either.
I hope so. I hope not.

G first and second conditionals
V study and work
P word stress

Why do you want to study business?

Because if I get a good degree, I'll be able to find an interesting job.

4B Degrees and careers

1 VOCABULARY study and work

a Read the job adverts. Would you like to do either of the jobs?

b Complete the adverts with a word from the list.

> covering CV experience degree
> references qualifications vacancy

c ➤ p.157 Vocabulary Bank *Study and work.*

2 PRONUNCIATION & SPEAKING
word stress

a Under<u>line</u> the stressed syllable in these words.

a|ttend de|gree di|sser|ta|tion P|h|D
post|gra|du|ate pro|fe|ssor qua|li|fi|ca|tions
re|fe|ree re|si|dence scho|lar|ship se|mi|nar
tu|to|ri|al un|der|gra|du|ate va|can|cy

b **2 42**)) Listen and check.

c Work in pairs. What is the difference between…?

1 an undergraduate and a postgraduate
2 a master's degree and a PhD
3 a campus and a hall of residence
4 a professor and a tutor
5 a seminar and a webinar
6 a tutorial and a lecture
7 qualifications and skills
8 a covering letter and a CV

d Talk to a partner. Look at the points below. When you choose a subject to study, how important do you think these factors should be? How important were they for you?

- future career prospects
- how much you like the subject
- how learning the subject will allow you to help others
- your parents' wishes and dreams
- how hard you have to study
- the quality of the teaching
- other factors: _____

Bird Keeper
New
★ Add to shortlist

Bristol | £ Competitive

Bristol Zoo Gardens is hiring an Animal Keeper for our Bird Section. The successful applicant will be a bird keeper with at least two years' experience of working with a variety of bird species. Applicants should have [1]_____ such as an A-level in English or Biology. A [2]_____ in Zoo Management would also be an advantage.

To apply, please send a [3]_____ letter and [4]_____ to…

Art Handler
New
★ Add to shortlist

London | £27,000–£30,000

A fine-art mover is seeking to fill a [5]_____ for the position of Art Handler. The ideal candidate will have a minimum of two years' [6]_____ of moving and handling very expensive art and antiques for museums and galleries. Excellent [7]_____ from previous employers are also required, as well as a driving licence.

3 LISTENING

a Would you ever consider doing a job for no pay? Why (not)?

b You're going to listen to three people talking about their internships. First read the information below. What is an internship? What do you think the advantages and disadvantages are?

'It's slave labour,
Real interns speak out

For many young graduates, starting out in a new career means taking an unpaid internship, with no guarantee of a permanent job at the end. While internships can provide graduates with useful experience, referees, and skills for their CVs, they also require a lot of hard work. Many interns feel exploited by employers, who treat them as cheap labour. In fact, nearly 40% of internships are unpaid, especially in industries such as fashion, PR, the media, and politics. Legally, most interns in the UK are entitled to the minimum wage. However, few employers realize this. Many interns have to work in bars or restaurants at night to pay for their rent, food, and expenses, while others end up in debt.

We spoke to three recent interns about their experiences…

Adapted from the Daily Mail

c (2 43)) Listen to Rosie, Joe, and Lauren talk about their experiences of internships. Who had a positive experience? Who had the most negative experiences?

d Listen again, and make notes in the chart.

	Rosie	Joe	Lauren
The kind of company			
The good side			
The bad side			

e Discuss the questions.

1 Have you ever done an internship? Do you know anyone who has worked as an intern? Did they have a good experience?
2 Do you think unpaid internships are fair? Why (not)?

4 GRAMMAR
first and second conditionals

a (2 44)) Listen to the ends of two job interviews. Complete the conditionals. Which person do you think has a real possibility of getting the job?

1 If we _____ you the job, when _____ you _____ to start?
2 If we _____ you the job, you _____ a lot of training.

b ➤ **p.139 Grammar Bank 4B.** Learn more about first and second conditionals and practise them.

c (2 47)) Listen and write five first conditional sentences giving advice to people looking for work. Do you agree with the advice?

d Imagine you were in these situations. What would you do? Say why using a second conditional.

> If I was offered a great job abroad, I'd probably take it, because...

1 You are offered a great job abroad.
2 Your partner is offered a job abroad in a country that you wouldn't like to live in.
3 You have to choose between a well-paid but boring job and a very interesting but badly paid job.
4 You are offered a job while you are still in the middle of your studies.
5 You have to choose between working at night or working at weekends.

Rosie Norman

but it teaches you a lot'

Joe Kenyon

Lauren O'Connor

5 READING

a In your country, do young people sometimes do part-time jobs in the evening or at weekends, or while they're at university? What sort of part-time jobs are common where you live?

b Read the newspaper article about Saturday jobs. Who is most positive about the job they did?

c Read the article again. Answer with A–E.

Which person…?

1 _____ felt that the job was badly paid

2 _____ liked the parts of the job where he / she could rest

3 _____ started very early and finished very late

4 _____ enjoyed spending time with the other workers

5 _____ was very unsuccessful in one of his / her jobs

6 _____ learned the importance of enjoying the work that you do

7 _____ learned the importance of punctuality

8 _____ got practice in something that later became his / her job

9 _____ and _____ aren't sure if they learned anything

10 _____ stopped getting any weekly money from his / her parents after starting his / her first part time job

The best Saturday job I ever had…

Shelf-stacker, dog-walker, and baby-sitter — most of us would have one of these classic Saturday jobs at the bottom of our CVs, if we were being strictly accurate. For the teenagers of today, however, it is far more difficult to find part-time work.

A Sir Ranulph Fiennes, explorer

When I was 16, I wanted to buy a canoe and needed £85. I washed the buses at Midhurst bus station between 3 a.m. and 7 a.m. during the week. Then I washed the dishes at the Angel Hotel from 6 p.m. to 10 p.m. I was paid £11 per week in all, and that's how I got the cash. It is too long ago to know if I actually learnt anything from the experience.

B Russell Kane, comedian

I did two humiliating Saturday jobs. The first was selling vacuum cleaners door to door. I didn't sell a single one. The other job was working with my granddad for a frozen-food delivery service. I doubt that a Saturday job really teaches you anything. Where I come from, it's automatic: at age 11 you get a job. It wasn't, 'Hey man, I'm really learning the value of work.' It was, 'If I want money, I must work for it.' My dad never gave me a penny of pocket money after the age of 11.

C Tony Ross, illustrator and author

In the fifties, when I was a boy, I used to work at the Post Office over Christmas. Many of us did it, and it was fantastic fun. I earned enough to buy an old motor scooter. My favourite part was going in the lorry to collect the mail bags from the station, because you didn't have to walk the streets all day. The other good thing was doing a round with your own house in it, because then you could stop for a cup of tea. I learnt the basics of working for money like arriving on time, and enjoying it no matter what. It was a good introduction because very few people work for fun. I think I'm probably the only one.

D Clive Stafford Smith, lawyer

I worked for a sand and gravel* company when I was 16. It was cold, damp, and so boring that I cried. I've learned various important things from that job. First, I know I'm very lucky to have a job now that I truly love. I also learned that it's crazy to pay bankers millions while paying minimum wage to people at gravel companies. It's terrible work and no one should have to do it. Anyone who says differently should be forced to work at that gravel company for a year.

E Adele Parks, author

When I was 16, I worked in our local supermarket, stacking shelves for two years. In a job like that you make the decision whether this is what you want to do for the rest of your life. I was doing my A-levels, and the other guys and girls were really quite pleased for me, as they were living through my experiences. I am good at talking and telling stories, and I think I learnt it there, because one of the things about stacking shelves or being at the checkout is that you get to pass the time with people. That's what I liked best.

*Very small stones often used on paths or roads

d Look at the highlighted words and phrases related to jobs, and work out their meaning from the context. Then match them with the definitions.

1 _____ *noun* a regular route that someone takes when collecting or delivering something

2 _____ knocking on people's doors to try to convince them to buy something

3 _____ *noun* taking things directly from e.g. a shop or business to people's homes

4 _____ *noun* a job which involves putting things on shelves, usually in a supermarket

5 _____ *noun* the place where you pay, e.g. in a supermarket

6 _____ *noun* the smallest amount of money a job can pay you according to the law

e Which of the jobs mentioned do you think sounds the best / the worst?

6 SPEAKING

In groups of three, discuss the questions about work and studies. Follow the arrows to ask the questions that are most relevant to you / your partners.

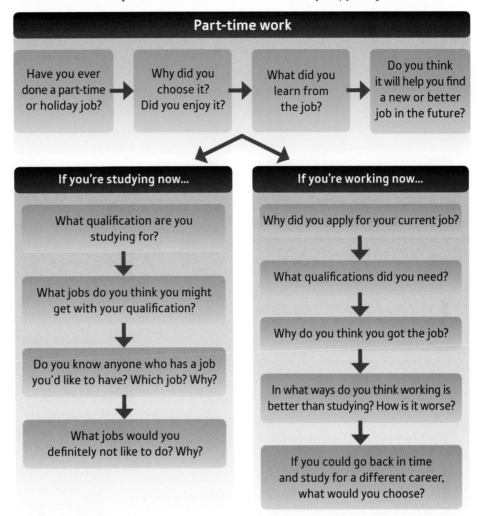

Part-time work

Have you ever done a part-time or holiday job? → Why did you choose it? Did you enjoy it? → What did you learn from the job? → Do you think it will help you find a new or better job in the future?

If you're studying now...

What qualification are you studying for?

↓

What jobs do you think you might get with your qualification?

↓

Do you know anyone who has a job you'd like to have? Which job? Why?

↓

What jobs would you definitely not like to do? Why?

If you're working now...

Why did you apply for your current job?

↓

What qualifications did you need?

↓

Why do you think you got the job?

↓

In what ways do you think working is better than studying? How is it worse?

↓

If you could go back in time and study for a different career, what would you choose?

7 WRITING

➤ **p.116 Writing** *A LinkedIn profile.* Create your own profile for *LinkedIn* or a similar site.

8 ② 48)) SONG *5 o'clock world* ♫

GRAMMAR

(Circle) a, b, or c.

1 I couldn't answer my phone because
   I _____.
   a drove   b used to drive   c was driving

2 We _____ to a lot of different shops
   yesterday.
   a went   b used to go   c were going

3 She _____ get up so late.
   a didn't use   b didn't use to
   c didn't used to

4 When I was young I _____ playing football.
   a love   b was loving   c used to love

5 We're very pleased _____ our holiday
   photos.
   a with   b to   c of

6 A Are we going out?
   B It _____ the weather.
   a depends   b depends on   c depends of

7 _____ the steps until you get to the bottom.
   a Go down   b Go   c Be down

8 A These bags are so heavy!
   B _____ you with them.
   a I help   b I'm going to help   c I'll help

9 A I've made an appointment to see my
      dentist.
   B When _____?
   a do you go   b will you go   c are you going

10 I'm really sorry. I promise _____ late again.
   a I'm not   b I won't be
   c I'm not going to be

11 This job looks interesting. _____ I apply?
   a Shall   b Do   c Will

12 I _____ to work abroad unless the pay was
   very good.
   a don't want   b won't want
   c wouldn't want

13 I might get the job if I _____ more experience.
   a will have   b had   c would have

14 If you _____ to earn some money, you
   shouldn't become an intern.
   a will need   b need   c needed

15 You won't get into university _____ harder.
   a unless you don't study   b if you study
   c unless you study

VOCABULARY

a Write a word or phrase connected with age.
   1 15 years old _____   4 over 65 _____
   2 21 or 22 _____   5 58 _____
   3 18 months old _____

b (Circle) the right word or phrase.
   1 My sister's a very good *photographer | photographic*.
   2 It's very dark in here so you'll need to use *zoom | flash*.
   3 I always *upload | download* my photos onto Facebook.
   4 There's my dog, in the *bottom right-hand | right-hand bottom* corner.
   5 What *document | file* format did you save the photo as?
   6 Here's a photo of us on the beach – you can see our hotel in the
      foreground | background.

c Write words for the definitions.
   1 a person whose job is to take the rubbish away   _____
   2 the material often used to make boxes   _____
   3 the top of a jar   _____
   4 a large plastic bag for putting rubbish in   _____
   5 a plastic or paper cover for a chocolate bar   _____
   6 a large area of land where waste is put   _____ _____

d Complete the words.
   1 Don't forget to include a **c**_____ letter with your CV.
   2 I'm living in a hall of **r**_____ in my first year at university.
   3 He won't get the job. He doesn't have enough **q**_____.
   4 You need to **a**_____ for a work permit to work in the US.
   5 Most students attend **l**_____ every day.
   6 I'm trying to get a job, but there very few **v**_____.
   7 Her new job has a **t**_____ period of six months.
   8 The **m**_____ wage in the UK is about £6.50 an hour.

PRONUNCIATION

a (Circle) the word with a different sound.

1	blurred	hoped	changed	saved
2	behind	opposite	skills	lid
3	recycle	apply	file	faculty
4	reapply	waste	replay	data
5	photo	front	overseas	focus

b Under<u>line</u> the stressed syllable.
   1 pho|to|gra|pher   3 re|cy|cle   5 qua|li|fi|ca|tions
   2 pho|to|co|py   4 un|der|gra|du|ate

CAN YOU UNDERSTAND THIS TEXT?

a Read the article once. Is it positive or negative about recycling in the UK?

Recycling facts and figures

UK households produced over 30 million tonnes of waste last year, of which 25% was collected for recycling. This figure is still quite low compared to some other EU countries, some of which recycle over 50% of their waste. There is still a great deal of waste which could be recycled that ends up in landfill sites.

Some interesting facts
- Up to 60% of the rubbish that ends up in the dustbin could be recycled.
- On average, 16% of the money you spend on a product pays for the packaging, which ultimately ends up as rubbish.
- Up to 80% of a vehicle can be recycled.
- Nine out of ten people would recycle more if it were made easier.

Aluminium
- 24 million tonnes of aluminium is produced annually, 51,000 tonnes of which ends up as packaging in the UK.
- £36,000,000 worth of aluminium is thrown away each year.
- Aluminium cans can be recycled and ready to use in just six weeks.

Glass
- Each UK family uses an average of 500 glass bottles and jars annually.
- Glass is 100% recyclable and can be used again and again.
- Glass that is thrown away and ends up in landfills will never decompose.

Paper
- It takes 70% less energy to recycle paper than to make it from raw materials.
- 12.5 million tonnes of paper and cardboard are used annually in the UK.
- The average person in the UK throws away 38 kg of newspapers per year.
- It takes 24 trees to make one ton of newspaper.

Plastic
- 275,000 tonnes of plastic are used each year in the UK – that's about 15 million bottles per day.
- Most families throw away about 40 kg of plastic per year, which could otherwise be recycled.
- The use of plastic in Western Europe is growing by about 4% each year.
- Plastic can take up to 500 years to decompose.

b Read the article again. Mark the sentences **T** (true) or **F** (false).

1 The UK recycles more than most other EU countries.
2 Most of the rubbish that is thrown away could be recycled.
3 More than half of an old car can be recycled.
4 Most people think that recycling is easy.
5 Aluminium is an easy material to recycle.
6 Glass can only be recycled a few times.
7 Recycling paper uses less energy than making it.
8 The UK uses more plastic than paper and cardboard.
9 UK families recycle all their plastic.
10 Plastic doesn't last forever in landfill.

CAN YOU UNDERSTAND THESE PEOPLE?

2 49))) In the street Watch or listen to five people and answer the questions.

Jo   David   Paul   Marc   Kaley

1 Jo thinks children shouldn't be allowed in restaurants sometimes because _____.
   a they can be noisy b they don't appreciate the food
   c they shouldn't be out late
2 What kind of photos does David like taking?
   a photos of buildings b portraits of people
   c holiday photos
3 Paul _____.
   a buys a new phone every two years
   b is given a new phone every two years
   c changes his phone contract every two years
4 Which of these did Marc <u>not</u> study?
   a American history b British history
   c European history
5 In which of these places has Kaley worked?
   a a school and an office b an office and a restaurant
   c a laboratory and a shop

CAN YOU SAY THIS IN ENGLISH?

Do the tasks with a partner. Tick (✓) the box if you can do them.

Can you…?

1 ☐ talk about what you were like when you were a child or teenager
2 ☐ describe the different stages of a person's life
3 ☐ describe a favourite photograph of yours
4 ☐ say what you think about recycling
5 ☐ talk about your education, and about your work or your work plans

Short films A New York sanitation worker
VIDEO Watch and enjoy a film on iTutor.

G present perfect simple
V television
P /w/, /v/, and /b/

5A What's on?

How long has that quiz show been on TV?

It's been on for a long time, for at least three years.

1 VOCABULARY television

a How many hours of TV do you watch a day? Tell a partner about one TV programme you love and one you hate. Give reasons.

b (3 2)) Listen to the excerpts from six TV programmes. Match each excerpt to a programme.

____ a	chat show	____ d	sitcom
____ b	documentary	____ e	sport
____ c	drama series	____ f	the news

c ➤ p.158 Vocabulary Bank *Television.*

2 PRONUNCIATION & SPEAKING
/w/, /v/, and /b/

a (3 5)) Listen and repeat the three sound pictures and words.

we switch weather	TV volume over	be button celebrity

b (3 6)) Listen to the pairs of words. Can you hear the difference? Practise saying them.

1 a why	b buy
2 a ban	b van
3 a vet	b wet
4 a boat	b vote
5 a bake	b wake
6 a wine	b vine
7 a fiver	b fibre
8 a very	b berry

c (3 7)) Listen and circle the word you hear.

d Practise saying the sentences.

Let's buy a wide-screen TV.
I never watch live sport.
Switch over to channel five.
It won't be over before eleven.

e Ask and answer with a partner.

1 Do you watch TV programmes…?
  – on a TV (where? what kind?)
  – on your computer, tablet, or phone
2 Are there any TV programmes that…?
  – you always switch off as soon as they start
  – you watch although you know they are awful
  – you only watch because the rest of your family like them
3 Which channel do you usually watch…?
  – when there is a big news story
  – for live sport
4 Do you ever…
  – turn the volume right down (or off) during a programme? What kind of programme?
  – get bored halfway through a programme but still carry on watching? Why do you carry on watching?

3 LISTENING

a Do you watch any cartoon series on TV? Which one(s)? What do you think of them?

b (3 8)) Listen to **Part 1** of a chat show where the guests are two sisters who write for a new US animated series called *Bob's Burgers*. Tick (✓) the topics they discuss.

1 ____ who the series is for
2 ____ what the series is about
3 ____ how they got the job
4 ____ how much money TV writers earn
5 ____ their daily routine
6 ____ how many episodes they write in a year
7 ____ how long it takes to create an episode
8 ____ the process of creating an episode
9 ____ the actors in the series
10 ____ their favourite episodes in the series

c Listen again for more details about the topics they discuss, and make notes.

44

d **3 9**)) Listen to **Part 2** of the programme. Why do they mention the following?

1 Loren Bouchard
2 baked potatoes
3 Jon Hamm
4 their other sisters
5 *Game of Thrones* and *Homeland*
6 *The Real Housewives of Beverly Hills*

e How important is a good script in a TV series? Think of examples of programmes that you think are well written or badly written.

4 GRAMMAR present perfect simple

a Complete the questions with a word from the list.

already ever for just since yet

1 Have you _ever_ watched a UK or US period drama series? What was it? Did you like it?

2 Are there any programmes that have been on TV in your country _____ five years or more? Do you ever watch them?

3 Do you sometimes re-watch an episode of a series that you've _____ seen?

4 What TV actors or presenters did you like when you were a child? Have they made any good programmes _____ then?

5 Is there anything that has _____ happened in the news today?

6 Is there a new TV series that everyone is watching? Have you seen it _____?

b Ask and answer the questions with a partner.

c ➤ p.140 Grammar Bank 5A. Learn more about the present perfect simple and practise it.

d Tell your partner about…

• a series you've just finished watching
• a film you've seen more than three times
• a DVD or film download that you've had for over a month but not watched yet
• a film or TV programme that everyone you know has seen but you haven't

5 READING

a Read the Wikipedia entry about Netflix. Does anything similar exist in your country? Would you like it to?

b Now read the article below. Is the journalist positive about…?

1 the series *House of Cards*
2 Netflix
3 both

Article Talk   Read Edit View history

Netflix

From *Wikipedia, the free encyclopedia*

Netflix Inc. is an American provider of on-demand internet streaming media, available in North and South America, the UK, and several other European countries. In its simplest form, video is streamed to the user's computer. TV series and films can be paused or restarted at will. According to a 2011 report, Netflix is the biggest source of North American web traffic.

ALL IN ONE SITTING

We have all been there: you settle in to watch one episode of a TV show, and eight hours later you've watched the whole season…

On the day when Netflix released the entire 13-episode first season of its political drama series *House of Cards* in one go, it reminded viewers on Twitter to #watchresponsibly: 'Don't forget to shower, eat something, get up and walk around!' All through that day, people were tweeting: 'What episode are you on?' Netflix's strategy was to encourage subscribers to 'binge-watch' the show – the TV equivalent of binge-eating.

House of Cards of course is not rubbish; it is a highly praised political drama. Originally a novel by Michael Dobbs, it follows the congressman Francis 'Frank' Underwood (Kevin Spacey), his scary wife, Claire, and young reporter, Zoe Barnes, as they struggle for power and influence in Washington. At 2 a.m., two episodes into the series, I simply couldn't stop. It was going to be a long night.

The show is clearly and cleverly structured for binge-consumption. Each episode is called a 'chapter'. There are no introductory flashbacks, common in traditional series. And at the end of nearly every episode, the cliffhanger makes the temptation to find out what is going to happen unbearable. By 10 a.m. the next day, and minutes away from the end of the final episode, I was searching for a release date for season two.

Initial reviews of Netflix's strategy and the show were mixed. Liz Shannon, a fellow binge-watcher, was sceptical. 'I'm not convinced that substituting the buzz that traditional shows acquire during a whole season for the buzz of binge-watching will be a success.' Laura Hudson was slightly more critical. 'It's not a great show; it's debatably a good one, but more importantly, it was just good enough to make me press "next" every time the episode finished.' That's precisely the point.

What's clear is that with DVDs and on-demand video, consumers have never had more choice in their own media consumption habits. Why pay the very expensive monthly cost for cable service when you're only watching three or four shows on as many channels? And why wait each week or months at a time for your favourite show? And with Netflix another advantage is that there are no commercials.

Netflix knows that it's already succeeded, at least in the US. *Breaking Bad*, for example, another good show for binge-watching, has been a hit. According to the *Wall Street Journal*, '73% of members who started streaming season one of *Breaking Bad* finished all seven episodes. Seasons two and three were longer – thirteen episodes each – but the number of viewers jumped to 81% and 85% respectively.'

As for me, I've heard great things about *Friday Night Lights*. Netflix, here I come.

Whether it's *Downton Abbey* or *The Big Bang Theory* – tell us about your TV binge experiences…

Adapted from The Guardian

c Read the article again. Choose a, b, or c.

> 🔍 **Tip: Multiple-choice reading**
> - Read the text first to get an idea of what it's about and how it's organized.
> - Read the questions and try to eliminate any options that you know are wrong.
> - Finally, re-read the parts of the text that go with the other options and try to choose the correct one.

1 *Binge* + a verb means ____.
   a to share your experience of doing something with other people
   b to do something too much in a short period of time
   c to do something late at night

2 *House of Cards* is ____.
   a an addictive sitcom
   b a soap opera about politics
   c a drama series based on a book

3 One of the features of *House of Cards* is that each episode ____.
   a ends making you want to watch the next one
   b begins with some scenes from previous episodes
   c is based on one chapter of the book

4 The first reviewers ____.
   a made both positive and negative comments about the show and Netflix's strategy
   b thought the series was good but Netflix's strategy was irresponsible
   c thought that people would return to watching shows weekly

5 According to the article, nowadays ____ than before.
   a more TV series are being made
   b people have more choice as to how to watch TV series
   c people watch more channels

6 In the series *Breaking Bad* ____.
   a the first season was longer than the second one
   b the second season was nearly twice as long as the first one
   c fewer people finished watching the third series

d Look at the highlighted words related to TV. With a partner work out their meaning from the context.

e Talk to a partner.

1 Do you think you would enjoy *House of Cards*? Why (not)? Have you seen any of the other series mentioned in the article?

2 What was the last TV series you got 'addicted' to?
   • Did you watch it in weekly episodes, on DVD, or online?
   • How many seasons did you watch?
   • How many episodes did you usually watch in one sitting?

3 Have you ever 'binge-watched' any other series? Why (not)? Do you know anyone who has?

6 SPEAKING

a Look at the statements and decide if you agree or disagree with them. Think of reasons why.

1 You enjoy a series more if you watch it weekly and don't binge-watch.

2 Children under the age of five shouldn't watch any television at all.

3 TVs should be banned from bars and restaurants.

4 Violent programmes shouldn't be shown before 10 p.m.

5 There aren't enough good programmes to fill all of the channels available today.

6 Families shouldn't have the TV on while they are having meals.

7 The news on TV is not objective, as most channels are controlled by the government.

b Work in small groups. Choose statements from **a** where you don't all agree. See if you can persuade the other students to agree with you.

> *I agree with **1**. There's more suspense when you have to wait a week for the next episode...*

G present perfect continuous
V the country
P vowel sounds; sentence stress

How long have your parents been living in the country?

For two years. They moved back to their village when they retired.

5B The country in other countries

1 VOCABULARY the country

a Look at photos from three different places in Europe. With a partner, answer the questions.

1 Which country do you think they were taken in?
2 What do you think it would be like to live in each of these places? Which would you prefer?
3 Can you name at least three things in each photo?

b ➤ p.159 **Vocabulary Bank** *The country.*

A
B
C

2 PRONUNCIATION vowel sounds

a Look at the pairs of words below. Are the vowel sounds the same or different? Write **S** or **D**.

1 leaf	wheat	
2 bush	mud	
3 plant	grass	
4 grow	cow	
5 pick	chicken	
6 pond	stone	
7 lamb	farm	
8 sheep	field	

b (3 14)) Listen and check. Practise saying the words.

3 LISTENING & SPEAKING

a (3 15)) Listen to Melisa from Turkey who used to live in the country and Eric from the USA who lives there now. Answer the questions.

	Melisa	Eric
1 What's the countryside like where they live / used to live?		
2 How do / did they entertain themselves?		
3 What disadvantages do they mention?		

b Talk to a partner.

1 Do either of the two places described attract you? Why?
2 Does the countryside they describe sound like the countryside near you? Why (not)?
3 Do you ever go to the country? Why do you go? Do you enjoy yourself there? Why (not)?
4 Answer the questions below.

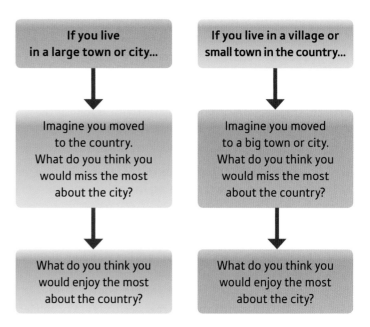

If you live in a large town or city...

Imagine you moved to the country. What do you think you would miss the most about the city?

What do you think you would enjoy the most about the country?

If you live in a village or small town in the country...

Imagine you moved to a big town or city. What do you think you would miss the most about the country?

What do you think you would enjoy the most about the city?

48

4 READING & SPEAKING

a Read the introduction to the article. Why do you think people move from the city to the country? Why do some people move back?

From the city to the country

(and sometimes back again)

Not everyone who moves to the country ends up staying there. In fact, for the first time in years, as many people are moving back to cities as are moving out to the country.

b Work in pairs **A** and **B**. **A** read about Liz Jones, **B** read about Rob Penn. Answer questions 1–5.

Liz Jones

'I was just divorced, and bored with my easy, if super-busy, London life. I wanted to live somewhere quieter, simpler, more beautiful, so I sold my house and bought a big farmhouse with 50 acres of land. I'll look after horses, I thought, I'll get a dog. I'll grow all my own food. It will be idyllic and friends will come to stay and tell me how lucky I am to live here.

But even from the first week, it was a nightmare. When I moved in, the house was cold and absolutely filthy, and the cooker didn't work. I discovered everything in the countryside is more expensive: you have to drive miles to find a shop where everything costs twice as much as in my local supermarket in London. I never fitted in. I think that in the country, if you are a woman, you will never be accepted unless you are a full-time mum. Another thing I hated was the shooting! I just couldn't pass a group of men with guns, shooting rabbits and deer, without getting out of my car and saying: "Do you really have nothing better to do on a Saturday morning?" That didn't make me very popular. I became so lonely, I often used to sit in my car and listen to the kind voice of the satnav lady.'

After five years Liz decided to go back to London. 'On my last night in the country, I sat outside underneath millions of stars and I thought to myself: "I've come to the end of a five-year prison sentence."'

1 Why did Liz move to the country?
2 What was she dreaming of doing there?
3 What problems did she have at the beginning?
4 Why does she think people didn't accept her?
5 How long did she stay? What did she compare living in the country to?

Glossary	
1 _____	*phrasal verb* leaving a car
2 _____	*phrasal verb* started to live in a new home
3 _____	*phrasal verb* was able to live and work well with other people
4 _____	unit of land, equivalent to 4,050 square metres

Rob Penn

Rob Penn, a writer, left London for some peace and quiet in the Black Mountains in Wales. 'I've been living here in a small farmhouse for eight years now,' says Penn. 'It wasn't easy at first. The fact that I ride a bicycle every day caused suspicion. In the countryside you only use a bike if something is wrong. A local farmer said to me, "I see you on the bike. How long have you lost your driving licence for, then?"'

Over time, however, Penn has managed to fit in with his new neighbours. 'I'm lucky. I live in a place with a strong sense of community. My local pub is an active part of that. We have two village halls as well. Between them, they put on activities or meetings every night of the week – singing workshops, the garden club, zumba, as well as monthly films and occasional quiz nights.

'In the city, you choose your community. It may be through work, your football team, or your kids' school or your colleagues,' says Penn. 'In the country, your neighbours are your only community.'

Penn has no plans to move back to London. 'I stood in a field this week, listening to the first sounds of spring. I love to hear the birds singing in the sunshine. I wouldn't live anywhere else. The rural sights, sounds and, above all, communities beat the city any day.'

1 Who is Rob Penn? Where did he move to?
2 Why did he move?
3 How long has he been living there?
4 What problems did he have at first? Did he solve them?
5 Why did he decide to stay?

Glossary	
1 _____	*phrasal verb* organize an event e.g. a play, a workshop
2 _____	*phrasal verb* integrate, be able to live and work well with other people
3 _____	*phrasal verb* go to live in a place where you lived before

c Read your article again. Work out the meaning of the highlighted words, and then complete the glossary.

d Cover the articles and use your answers to questions 1–5 to tell each other about Liz and Rob in your own words. Try to use the phrasal verbs from the glossary, and explain them to your partner if necessary.

e Answer the questions in small groups.

1 What was one problem that both Liz and Rob had? Do you think this would be the main problem for people moving from the city to the country in the area where you live? Why (not)?
2 Why do you think one of them succeeded and the other failed?
3 Do you know anyone who's moved from the city to the country? Did they stay? Why (not)?
4 Do you know anyone who's moved from the country to the city? Did they stay? Why (not)?

5 GRAMMAR present perfect continuous

a Look at the photos and speech bubbles. Circle the correct verb form.

I'm planting / I've been planting potatoes right now. Can I call you back?

①

②

Take those boots off! They're covered in mud!

What do you expect? I'm working / I've been working in the garden all day.

b Compare answers with a partner. Explain why you chose each answer.

c ➤ **p.141 Grammar Bank 5B.** Learn more about the present perfect continuous and practise it.

6 PRONUNCIATION & SPEAKING
sentence stress

a Complete sentences 1–10 with the present perfect continuous of the verbs.

1 I _____ really hard this week. (work)
2 I _____ well lately. (not sleep)
3 My neighbours _____ a lot of noise recently. (make)
4 I _____ about getting a new phone for a while. (think)
5 I _____ with my family a lot recently. (argue)
6 I _____ TV at all lately. (not watch)
7 I _____ very stressed for the last few weeks. (feel)
8 I _____ a lot of exercise this month. (do)
9 I _____ a lot recently. (go out)
10 I _____ a lot of time on Facebook this week. (spend)

b **3 17))** Listen and check. Then listen and repeat, copying the rhythm.

c Work with a partner. For each sentence in **a** say if it is true for you or not, and give reasons.

1 is true for me. I've been working really hard this week because I have exams soon.

d Now think of two things you have or haven't been doing this week or recently. Work in pairs **A** and **B**. **A** tell **B** what you've been doing. **B** show interest by asking for more details. Then swap roles.

I've been eating out a lot recently.

Oh really? Why?

Because some friends of mine are visiting, so we've been going out together.

7 READING & LISTENING

a Are there any radio or TV programmes you know that have been running for a long time in your country? Do you watch them? What do you think of them? Why do you think they've been so successful?

b (3 18)) Read and listen to an article about *The Archers*, a BBC programme that is the world's longest-running radio soap opera. Answer the questions.

1 What is the programme about?
2 What was its original aim?
3 Who were the original main characters?

1954
1994

A British Institution

Just before 7 o'clock every evening, people all over Britain, from Camilla, Duchess of Cornwall (a major fan, who actually appeared on the show) to students, housewives, and farmers, tune in to BBC Radio 4, and listen to an introductory tune that has been playing every night for more than 60 years. It is the theme tune to *The Archers*, the longest running radio soap opera in the world, and a British institution. *The Archers*, which is about life in the fictional village of Ambridge, was conceived by the Ministry of Agriculture as a way of providing information about new farming methods to British farmers and smallholders in order to increase productivity after the Second World War, during the years of food shortages and rationing. It was originally about the lives of three farmers: Dan Archer, who farmed efficiently with little cash, Walter Gabriel, who farmed inefficiently with little cash, and George Fairbrother, a wealthy businessman who farmed for a hobby. The programme was hugely successful – at the height of its popularity it was estimated that 60% of adult Britons were regular listeners, and today its listeners number over a million. The involvement of the Ministry of Agriculture ended in the 1970s, but *The Archers* still contains many storylines and discussions about farming, and has a separate 'agricultural story editor'.

Glossary
smallholder /'smɔːlhəʊldə/ a person who owns or rents a small piece of land for farming
rationing /'ræʃənɪŋ/ the policy of limiting the food, fuel, etc., that people are allowed to have, when there is not enough for everyone to have as much as they want; it started in the UK in the Second World War in 1940 and ended in 1954.

c (3 19)) You are going to hear an interview with an actor who plays one of the main characters in *The Archers*. Do these statements describe (**A**) the actor, (**C**) his character, or (**B**) both?

1 His name is David Archer. ____
2 He's very honest and dependable. ____
3 He was born on a sheep station in Tasmania. ____
4 His father worked as a farmer. ____
5 He lives in Ambridge. ____
6 He has a cottage in Norfolk. ____

d Listen again and make notes. What does he say about these things?

1 how long he's been working on the programme
2 his character's grandfather
3 why his father went to Devon
4 what the other actors know about the country
5 what city and country people like about *The Archers*
6 where he lives now and why

e Are there any radio or TV programmes in your country about farming or the countryside? Have you ever watched them? How popular are they?

8 WRITING

➤ **p.117 Writing** *An informal email.* Write an email about things you've been doing recently.

9 (3 20)) SONG *Country boy* ♫

1 🎥 A WORRIED PHONE CALL
VIDEO

a (3 21)) Watch or listen to Jenny talking to Rob on the phone. In the end, what does Rob say she should do?

b Watch or listen again. Answer the questions.

1 Is Jenny sure the man in the news is the man she met on the plane? Why (not)?

2 What time were Jenny and Henry planning to have dinner?

3 What time is it now? Why is Rob worried about this?

4 How does Jenny describe the house?

5 What doesn't she think she'll be able to do?

If you were Jenny, would you stay in Henry's house alone?

2 🎥 MAKING A POLICE REPORT
VIDEO

a (3 22)) Watch or listen to Jenny and Luke at the police station. What information does the police officer ask for about Henry? How do Luke and Jenny describe him?

b Watch or listen again. Complete the **You Hear** phrases in the dialogue on p.53.

c (3 23)) Watch or listen and repeat some of Jenny's **You Say** phrases. Copy the rhythm and intonation.

d 👥 In groups of three practise the dialogue.

e ➤ **Communication** *Reporting a missing person* **A** *p.107,* **B** *p.108.*

)) You Hear	You Say 💬
... You also said that your father-in-law – Henry Walker – hasn't returned home yet. How long has he been _____?	He was supposed to be home three hours ago.
OK. It's a bit early to report him missing but I'll _____ a statement. So, your name's Jenny Zielinski.	That's right.
And you're staying at The Grange, Marsh Lane, Long Crendon.	Yes.
OK. Can you _____ Mr Walker?	He's 62, I think. He's average height and build. He has grey hair and glasses. I don't know what colour his eyes are. *They're brown. Here is a photo of him.*
When did you _____ see him?	This morning. Around ten.
Where were you?	At his house in Long Crendon.
And do you remember what he was _____?	Oh, just a brown jacket, a dark green shirt, and jeans.
Do you remember anything _____ about the last time you saw him?	Yes, actually. We were going to go to Oxford but Henry's two front tyres had been punctured.
Really? So you left for Oxford and he stayed to fix the car?	Yes.
Do you know what his _____ were for the rest of the day?	No.
Can you give me some idea of his normal _____?	Not really... *Well, he's an academic. He teaches at the university a few days a week but he often works from home. He takes a lot of long walks, but never this late.*
And Jenny, do you _____ seeing anything unusual when you got back to the house this afternoon?	Well, there was my suitcase. The airport had returned my lost luggage and the lock was broken.
Is there anything _____?	There were some books on the floor. *Really? That's weird. Henry's normally really tidy.*
OK. Try not to _____, we'll look into this. In the meantime, perhaps you should stay with Luke, and if you think of anything else, or he turns up, give me a call.	

3 🎥 A THREATENING MESSAGE
VIDEO

a (3 24)) Watch or listen to Jenny and Luke talking the next morning. What's the good news? What's the bad news?

b Watch or listen again. (Circle) the correct phrase.

1 Jenny feels *safer | less safe* in Luke's house.
2 The username on the laptop *is | isn't* Jenny's.
3 When Luke opens a file he finds *a photo | a formula*.
4 Jenny receives *a text message | a video message* from Henry.
5 Henry says the people who are holding him want her *laptop | suitcase*.
6 Henry shows them *today's | yesterday's* newspaper.
7 He asks Jenny and Luke *to go | not to go* to the police again.
8 He asks them *to give Rob a message | not to say anything to Rob*.

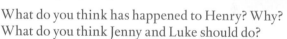

What do you think has happened to Henry? Why? What do you think Jenny and Luke should do?

c Look at the **Social English phrases**. Can you remember any of the missing words?

Social English phrases
Jenny Thanks for _____ me stay.
Jenny What does it _____?
Luke I have _____ idea.
Jenny It's a _____ from Henry!
Henry As you can see, I'm _____.
Henry Listen _____.

d (3 25)) Watch or listen and complete the phrases.

e Watch or listen again and repeat the phrases. How do you say them in your language?

> 👤 **Can you...?**
> ☐ describe someone's appearance and routine
> ☐ report a problem to the police
> ☐ thank someone for helping you

Communication

1A HOW WAS IT NAMED?
Student B

f Read about how the iMac was named. Find answers to the questions below.

1 Who named the product?
2 What instructions did the company's founder give for choosing a name?
3 What does the name mean?
4 Were any other names considered?

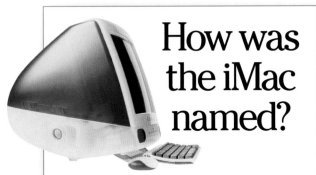

How was the iMac named?

First produced in 1998, the bright turquoise iMac computer was a huge success for Apple and started a range of other 'i' products like the iPod, the iPad, and the iPhone. But who put the 'i' in iMac?

The answer is Ken Segall, an advertising executive in New York City. He had known Steve Jobs, the founder of Apple, for many years before he named the iMac. There was already a range of Macintosh computers, so Jobs asked Segall for a new name that had 'Mac' or 'Macintosh' in it. He also wanted the name to show people that they could go online more easily with the new computer.

Segall and his team thought of dozens of names before they chose 'iMac'. The 'i' was for 'internet', but it could also mean 'individual' or 'imagination'. A few days after coming up with the name, Segall went to Jobs and suggested it to him, together with four other names. Unfortunately, Jobs hated all of them. He preferred a name that he had thought of on his own: 'MacMan'.

A week later, Segall suggested more names to Jobs, including 'iMac' again. 'Well,' said Jobs, 'I don't hate it this week.' The rest is history.

g Listen to **A** tell you about how the Kindle was named.

h Now tell **A** about how the iMac was named, using questions 1–4 to help you.

1B COLOUR AND PERSONALITY

a Read about the colours you have chosen in first and second place, and in seventh and eighth place. <u>Underline</u> the things that apply to you.

Colour personality test

RED: If you put red in 1st or 2nd place, you are energetic and assertive – you say what you think, and people listen to you. However, you are also impulsive, and sometimes make decisions without thinking enough. If you put red in 7th or 8th place, you have lost some of your enthusiasm for life.

YELLOW: If you put yellow in 1st or 2nd place, you are hard-working and ambitious. You are often good at business, and are optimistic about the future. If you put yellow in 7th or 8th place, you may feel a bit isolated at the moment. You need to make an effort to meet new people.

BLUE: If you put blue in 1st or 2nd place, you are very loyal and reliable. You never panic, and are in control of your life. You are also sensitive, however, and your feelings can be easily hurt. If you put blue in 7th or 8th place, you may feel unsatisfied with your life, and want to make changes.

GREEN: If you put green in 1st or 2nd place, you are persistent, and don't give up easily. You want to be recognized, and you probably don't like change. However, you can also be selfish and quite possessive. If you put green in 7th or 8th place, you are probably quite stubborn, and can be very critical of other people.

PURPLE: If you put purple in 1st or 2nd place, you are a bit immature, and can be moody. You dream of the perfect relationship or the perfect job. If you put purple in 7th or 8th place, you are mature and responsible.

BLACK: If you put black in 1st or 2nd place, which is unusual, you are rebellious, and don't accept your current situation. If you put black in 7th or 8th place, you feel in control of your life, and are calm and self-confident.

BROWN: If you put brown in 1st or 2nd place, you are restless and insecure. You worry about your health, and may be a bit of a hypochondriac. Security is very important to you. If you put brown in 7th or 8th place, it means you don't look after yourself enough, and may have health problems.

GREY: If you put grey in 1st or 2nd place, you are very independent and afraid of commitment. You don't like doing things in groups, and prefer watching to doing. If you put grey in 7th or 8th place, you are sociable and ambitious.

b Tell your partner about the results. What do you agree with? What don't you agree with?

🔍 **Talking about findings and results**
According to the personality test, I'm...
It says that I'm...
That's quite accurate. / That's definitely me.
That's not me. / That isn't accurate at all.

2A CAROLINE'S HOLIDAY PLANS
Student A

a Ask and answer questions with **B** to complete Caroline's holiday itinerary. Use the information in the calendar and the correct form of the verb, present simple or present continuous.

A *What time does she leave London?*

B *At five past eleven in the morning. What time does she arrive in Palma?*

A *At two forty in the afternoon.*

Calendar

Thursday
11.05 a.m.   leave London (Gatwick) flight EZ8629
2.40 p.m.   arrive in Palma, Majorca

Friday
_____   have yoga class
10.00 a.m.   go waterskiing with Emma (meet at rental shop)
Afternoon   go sightseeing in _____

Saturday
8.30 a.m.   go on guided tour of Palma
_____   have dinner at *Tristán* (table booked in Emma's name)

Sunday
8.00 a.m.   go on boat trip round Pollensa Bay
6.00 p.m.   _____

Monday
5.30 a.m.   get bus to airport
_____   leave Palma, Majorca flight EZ 8630
10.50 a.m.   arrive London Gatwick

b Check your answers by comparing your calendars.

3A NEWS STORIES Student B

c Read *Babies at the movies*. Find answers to the questions below.

1 What new idea is being tried? Where?
2 What problem is this idea meant to solve?
3 Who will be affected by it?
4 What good points about this idea are mentioned?
5 What problems with the idea are mentioned?

| Home | News | Sport | TV&Showbiz | Health | Science | Travel | Money |

Babies at the movies

In family-friendly Brooklyn, New York, where going for a walk involves pavements full of mothers pushing buggies and toddlers on scooters, cinemas have now also become a part of baby culture.

Three cinemas in the area have agreed to put on early afternoon sessions so that parents can watch the latest films with their young children and avoid calling the babysitter.

The cinemas are open to anyone at these times, though the experience may not be suitable for the average film fan. To avoid waking up sleeping babies, the sound of the films is softer than usual. Films with loud, surprising noises, such as gunshots, are usually not shown.

One mother, Rhonda Walsh, 32, described her visit with her four-month-old daughter, Madeleine. 'There was a chorus of crying,' she remembered.

But in spite of the screaming babies, she managed to enjoy the experience. 'Of course I don't remember what the movie was,' she added.

Adapted from the Daily Mail

Glossary
1 _____ /'sku:təz/ *noun* child's toys with two wheels that you stand on and move by pushing one foot against the ground
2 _____ /'skri:mɪŋ/ *verb* crying loudly in a high voice
3 _____ /'bʌgiz/ *noun* chairs on wheels that you use for pushing a baby or young child in
4 _____ /'gʌnʃɒts/ *noun* sounds of a gun being fired

d Read the article again. Work out the meaning of the highlighted words, and then complete the glossary. Check the pronunciation of the words.

e Work in groups with **A** and **C**. Tell each other your stories. Try to use the words from the glossary and explain them to **A** and **C** if necessary.

Communication

2A CAROLINE'S HOLIDAY PLANS
Student B

a Ask and answer questions with **A** to complete
Caroline's holiday itinerary. Use the information
in the calendar and the correct form of the verb,
present simple or present continuous.

> A *What time does she leave London?*
>
> B *At five past eleven in the morning.*
> *What time does she arrive in Palma?*
>
> A *At two forty in the afternoon.*

Calendar

Thursday

| 11.05 a.m. | leave London (Gatwick) flight EZ8629 |
| *2.40 p.m.* | arrive in Palma, Majorca |

Friday

7.30 a.m.	have yoga class
10.00 a.m.	go water skiing with _____ (meet at rental shop)
Afternoon	go sightseeing in Palma Old City

Saturday

| 8.30 a.m. | _____ |
| 9.00 p.m. | have dinner at *Tristán* (table booked in Emma's name) |

Sunday

| 8.00 a.m. | _____ |
| 6.00 p.m. | have massage at hotel spa |

Monday

| _____ | get bus to the airport |
| 8.30 a.m. | leave Palma, Majorca flight EZ 8630 arrive London Gatwick |

b Check your answers by comparing your calendars.

3A NEWS STORIES Student C

c Read *Airline's new child rules cause controversy*. Find
answers to the questions below.

1 What new idea is being tried? Where?
2 What problem is this idea meant to solve?
3 Who will be affected by it?
4 What good points about this idea are mentioned?
5 What problems with the idea are mentioned?

| Home | News | Sport | TV&Showbiz | Health | Science | Travel | Money |

Airline's new child rules cause controversy

It is a decision that adult air passengers will love – but it could annoy families who are travelling together. Malaysia Airlines has decided to ban children under 12 years of age from the first class cabin and the top deck of its A380 planes, so that adult travellers can relax without hearing crying and screaming.

Malaysia Airlines CEO Tengku Azmil said that the company received 'many' complaints from passengers who buy expensive tickets, but then can't sleep because of crying children.

The decision means families travelling with children will only be able to sit in the economy section on the lower deck. While some have called the decision discriminatory, others agree with it. Travel writer Suzanne Rowan Kelleher said: 'My guess is that many parents would opt for kid-free zones on planes when they're travelling without their children.'

Adapted from the Daily Mail

Glossary
1 _____ /ˈskriːmɪŋ/ *verb* crying loudly in a high voice
2 _____ /dɪˈskrɪmɪnətəri/ *adj* unfair; in a way that treats one group of people worse than others
3 _____ /dek/ *noun* one of the floors of a ship, bus, or plane
4 _____ /bæn/ *verb* say officially that something is not allowed

d Read the article again. Work out the meaning of the
highlighted words, and then complete the glossary.
Check the pronunciation of the words.

e Work in groups with **A** and **B**. Tell each other your
stories. Try to use the words from the glossary and
explain them to **A** and **B** if necessary.

3B SPOT THE DIFFERENCES Student A

Describe the photo to your partner. Your partner has a very similar photo. Find ten differences between the photos.

A *In my photo, there's a... in the foreground.*

B *There isn't one in my photo.*

PRACTICAL ENGLISH 3 REPORTING A MISSING PERSON Student A

a You are going to report a missing person. Read your role and decide on the details.

> You are sharing a flat in London with a friend from your country. The address is 23 Barrow Street, London W2 7EG.
> • *Decide which of your friends it is.*
> You saw each other in the morning.
> • *Decide what time and where.*
> You had arranged to have dinner together at home.
> You got home at 5 o'clock, but it is now 10 p.m. and he / she hasn't turned up, and isn't answering his / her phone. You are worried and go to the police.
> • *Decide what your friend's normal routine is.*

b **B** is a police officer. He / she will ask you questions about your friend, and make a report. **B** will start.

c Swap roles. You are now a police officer. **B** is going to report a missing person. First, think what questions you need to ask.

MISSING PERSON INFORMATION

Reported by	
Name	
Address	
Phone	

Missing person	
Name	
Address	
Description (age and appearance)	
Last seen	
Wearing	
Expected to see at	for
Plans for rest of day	
Normal routine	

d Interview **B** and fill in the form. Finally, tell **B** not to worry and that you are sure the person will turn up soon. You start:

> *Come in and take a seat. Now, you want to report a missing person, is that right?*

e Together decide what happened to your friends!

Communication

3B SPOT THE DIFFERENCES Student B

Describe the photo to your partner. Your partner has a very similar photo. Find ten differences between the photos.

A *In my photo, there's a... in the foreground.*

B *There isn't one in my photo.*

PRACTICAL ENGLISH 3 REPORTING A MISSING PERSON Student B

a You are a police officer. **A** is going to report a missing person. First, think what questions you need to ask.

MISSING PERSON INFORMATION

Reported by	Name	
	Address	
	Phone	

Missing person	
Name	
Address	
Description (age and appearance)	
Last seen	
Wearing	
Expected to see at	for
Plans for rest of day	
Normal routine	

b Interview **A** and fill in the form. Finally, tell **A** not to worry and that you are sure the person will turn up soon. You start:

Come in and take a seat. Now, you want to report a missing person, is that right?

c Swap roles. Now you are going to report a missing person. Read your role and decide on the details.

You are sharing a flat in London with a friend from your country. The address is 15 Vine Road, London EC1 9AJ.
• *Decide which of your friends it is.*
You saw each other at lunchtime.
• *Decide what time and where.*
You had arranged to go to the cinema together.
The film started at 7.00 but your friend didn't turn up.
It is now 11p.m., and he / she isn't answering his / her phone. You are worried and go to the police.
• *Decide what your friend's normal routine is.*

d **A** is a police officer. He / she will ask you questions about your friend, and make a report. **A** will start.

e Together decide what happened to your friends!

Writing

1 DESCRIBING A ROOM

a Read Ana's description of her room. Does it sound comfortable to you? Why (not)?

b Read the description again. Number the topics in the order she mentions them.

- ☐ The colour of the walls, door, etc.
- ☐ What furniture there is
- ☐ Where the room is
- ☐ Why she likes it

c Complete the gaps in the text with a preposition from the list. Some prepositions are used more than once.

---

above ~~at~~ from in inside on with

---

d You're going to write a description of your favourite room. **Plan** the description.

1 Say which room it is and where.
2 Describe the room, the furniture, and the decoration.
3 Say if the room has changed at all.
4 Explain why it is your favourite room.

e **Write** the description of the room, in **four** paragraphs. Use **Vocabulary Bank** *Adjective suffixes p.152* to help you with vocabulary.

f **Check** your description for mistakes (grammar, vocabulary, punctuation, and spelling).

◀ *p.11*

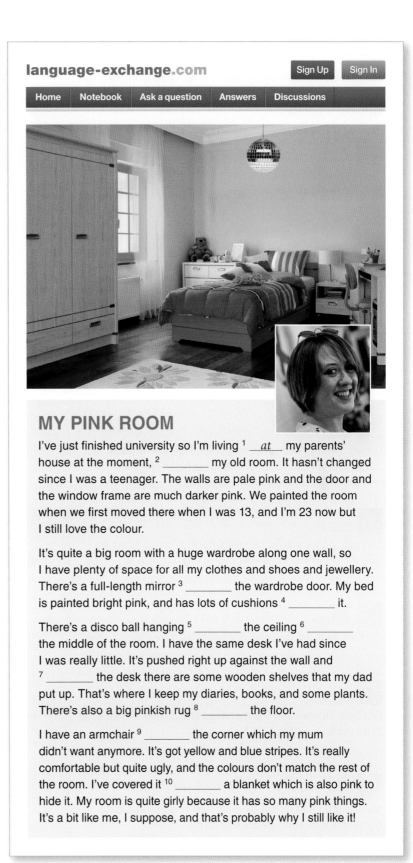

language-exchange.com [Sign Up] [Sign In]

| Home | Notebook | Ask a question | Answers | Discussions |

MY PINK ROOM

I've just finished university so I'm living ¹ __*at*__ my parents' house at the moment, ² _____ my old room. It hasn't changed since I was a teenager. The walls are pale pink and the door and the window frame are much darker pink. We painted the room when we first moved there when I was 13, and I'm 23 now but I still love the colour.

It's quite a big room with a huge wardrobe along one wall, so I have plenty of space for all my clothes and shoes and jewellery. There's a full-length mirror ³ _____ the wardrobe door. My bed is painted bright pink, and has lots of cushions ⁴ _____ it.

There's a disco ball hanging ⁵ _____ the ceiling ⁶ _____ the middle of the room. I have the same desk I've had since I was really little. It's pushed right up against the wall and ⁷ _____ the desk there are some wooden shelves that my dad put up. That's where I keep my diaries, books, and some plants. There's also a big pinkish rug ⁸ _____ the floor.

I have an armchair ⁹ _____ the corner which my mum didn't want anymore. It's got yellow and blue stripes. It's really comfortable but quite ugly, and the colours don't match the rest of the room. I've covered it ¹⁰ _____ a blanket which is also pink to hide it. My room is quite girly because it has so many pink things. It's a bit like me, I suppose, and that's probably why I still like it!

Writing

2 HOLIDAY TWEETS

a Read the holiday tweets once. Who is on holiday now? Who is going to have a holiday soon? Who has just finished a holiday?

 Caroline
Having the most amazing experience in Majorca! Met fantastic people but have put on 3 kilos in 4 days!

 Mark
Another hard day: reading, having a nap by the pool, eating, and sunbathing. ☺

 Haylee
48 hours until I'll be in Rio sipping a piña colada – or is it a caipirinha? Can't wait!

 Michael
Oh no! 3 noisy children sitting behind me on my plane to LA. This is going to be the longest flight of my life.

 Sheila
Just got to Uganda! So beautiful here! After 13 hours on bus, am ready for a shower!

 Andrew
Packing bags. Holidays so stressful! Not sure I want to go!

 Danielle
Got back an hour ago – plants dead and no milk in fridge. ☹ Send me back to the beach.

 Sam
Making the most of last glorious morning in sun. Going home this p.m. and to work tomorrow.

b Read the tweets again. How does each person feel? What words and phrases or symbols do they use to express their feelings?

c Read the **Useful language** box. Then rewrite the last four tweets using full sentences.

> **Useful language: writing tweets**
> Because tweets are short messages and can only have a maximum of 140 characters (including letters, spaces, icons, and punctuation), people frequently leave out words in sentences, often pronouns and auxiliary verbs like *I'm, I've, it's,* and *there is / are*. This is acceptable in tweets and text messages but not in formal writing.
> *Having the most amazing experience = I'm having the most amazing experience*
> *Another hard day = It's been another hard day*
> *3 noisy children sitting behind me = There are three noisy children sitting behind me*

d Imagine you're having a four-day holiday. **Write** a tweet for each of the situations below. Use the **Useful language** and **Vocabulary Bank** *Holidays p.153* to help you with vocabulary.

- the evening before your holiday
- the first morning of your holiday
- the second and third days
- the last evening of your holiday
- the day after your holiday is over

e **Check** your tweets to make sure they are not more than 140 characters.

◄ *p.17*

3 AN ARTICLE

a Look at the photos in the article from a photography magazine. Which of them do you like? How are they different from ordinary portraits of people?

b Read the article and write the headings in the correct place. (There are two headings you don't need to use.) Which tip do you think is the most useful? Have you ever used any of these tips yourself?

> **Don't make them pose**
> Try different angles
> **Move away from the centre**
> Take a close-up
> **Don't look at me!**

c You are going to write three tips for how to take good holiday photos. With a partner, **plan** the content of each tip and think of three headings.

Use the **Useful language** and **Vocabulary Bank** *Photography p.155* to help you with vocabulary.

Useful language: tips and instructions

Imperatives
Get up high and look down on your subject.
Don't make people pose.

Possibilities
You could sit on the floor...
You might ask the person to look at something outside the photo.
One good idea is to photograph people while they are working...
Another possibility is to...

---

d **Write** your article explaining why each tip is useful.

e **Check** your article for mistakes (grammar, vocabulary, punctuation, and spelling).

◀ *p.29*

THREE TIPS FOR TAKING GREAT PORTRAIT PHOTOS

1 _____

In most photos, the subject is looking at the camera. This is often a good idea, but there are other things you can try. You might ask the person to look at something outside the photo. This can make a photo more interesting – viewers want to know what the person is looking at. Or the person could be looking at something (or someone) that is in the picture.

2 _____

Many people are very uncomfortable when people are taking photos of them and don't know how to relax. One good idea to help them is to photograph them while they are doing something, for example, working, or with their friends or family, or doing something that they enjoy. This will help them relax, and you will get better pictures. This is an especially good idea if you are taking pictures of children.

3 _____

If you change the angle or the perspective of your photos, you can make them more interesting and unusual. Get up high, for example, stand on a table or chair, and look down on your subject. Or you could sit on the floor and look up. Both of these angles will make the photo more original.

4 A LINKEDIN PROFILE

a LinkedIn is a website where you can connect with colleagues and former school or university friends, who might be able to help you to find a new job. Read the beginning of Kate Lewis's profile. What kind of company do you think Shopping Spy is? What do you think Kate is studying?

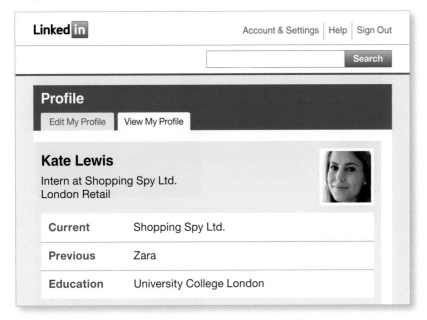

b Now read the rest of Kate's profile and check if you were right.

c Read the profile again. The computer has found eight spelling mistakes. Can you correct them?

d **Plan** your own profile. Use the **Useful language** and **Vocabulary Bank** *Study and work p.157* to help you.

1 Include a summary of your present situation.
2 Give details about your education and previous work experience.

e **Write** your profile for a site like LinkedIn. (Or go to linkedin.com and create a profile.)

> 🔍 **Useful language: writing a CV, covering letter, or LinkedIn profile**
> *I am currently working at / a student at…*
> *I am seeking a position in the … industry*
> *I have … years' experience -ing*
> **Punctuation**
> Use Capital letters for company names, countries, cities, languages, and school subjects.
> Use a full stop (.) after company abbreviations like Ltd. and Inc.

f **Check** your profile for mistakes (grammar, vocabulary, punctuation, and spelling).

◀ *p.41*

Summary

I am currently studying at University College London and will gradaute in June with a degree in Comunications and Marketing. I am looking for a position in retail or marketing in the fashion industry. I am enthusiastic and hard-working, and keen to start in my new profesion.

I already have some expierence working in fashion. At present, I am working part-time as an intern at Shopping Spy Ltd., which is a website that helps shoppers find great shops and sales in London. I work in the online team, which provides essential information to customers and colleges. I have direct contact with customers.

I have also had a part-time sales job at the Zara store in Covent Garden.

Experience

Intern
Shopping Spy Ltd., London
September – present (9 months)

Sales assistant and cashier
Zara, London
June – September 2013 (4 months)
I greeted customers and asisted them with purchases. I brouhgt out new stock, and worked at the till.

5 AN INFORMAL EMAIL

a Read an email from Louisa to her daughter, Maria, who is studying in Boston. What is the main subject of her email? How does she feel about it?

b Read the email again and complete it with a verb from the list in the present perfect continuous. Use contractions.

clear do (x2) watch read snow study

c Imagine you are replying to a similar email from a friend or family member. **Plan** what you're going to write.

1 Thank him / her for writing, and react to the news in his / her email.
2 Say what you've been doing lately.
3 Think of at least three questions to ask in your email.
4 Ask him / her to reply to the email.

d **Write** the email. Use the **Useful language** to help you, and follow 1–4 in **c** above.

> 🔍 **Useful language: informal emails**
>
> **Thanking someone for an email**
> *Thanks for your email / message.*
> *It was great to hear from you.*
> *Glad to hear you're well.*
>
> **Mentioning previous emails**
> *I'm so pleased / happy / sad / sorry to hear that...*
>
> **Asking someone to reply**
> *Write (back) soon!*
> *Looking forward to hearing all your news.*
> *I can't wait to hear from you.*

e **Check** your email for mistakes (grammar, vocabulary, punctuation, and spelling).

◀ *p.51*

From: Louisa and Eric Barton
To: Maria Barton
Subject: May 1st – what happened to spring?

Hi Maria,

Thanks for your email. Glad you're well, and hope that it's not too cold in Boston.

When your father and I woke up this morning, this is what we saw! The calendar says it is May 1st, but the weather doesn't agree. It ¹_____ for about 12 hours non-stop now. Your poor father ²_____ the snow all morning so that we can drive to the supermarket and buy some food. I ³_____ the news on TV. They say the storm will be over by tomorrow, so don't worry too much about us.

Besides the weather, nothing is new here. Dad ⁴_____ a lot of repairs around the house over the past few weeks. He finally fixed the freezer – just in time for the snowstorm!

I ⁵_____ a great novel for the book club: It's 'The Bostonians' by Henry James. It made me think of you there in Boston – have you read it? I'm sure you'd enjoy it.

Well, good luck with your exams. ⁶_____ you _____ hard? I hope so.

Miss you lots. What ⁷_____ you _____? Write soon!

Much love

Mom

Listening

1 2))

Interviewer Excuse me, I'm doing a survey. Can I ask you some questions about your name?
Sean OK.
Interviewer So, what's your name?
Sean Sean Gibson.
Interviewer Is that S-E-A-N or S-H-A-U-N?
Sean S-E-A-N.
Interviewer Why did your parents call you that?
Sean I think I'm named after the actor Sean Connery, who played James Bond in the 60s. He was very famous at the time when I was born.
Interviewer Do you have a nickname?
Sean Actually, at school they used to call me 'Brains'. Um, it was meant to be a joke, I think, because I wasn't a particularly good student.
Interviewer And are you happy with your name?
Sean Mmm, I like it. I was usually the only Sean at school, which I think was quite a good thing. But people find it quite difficult to spell, especially as there are two possible spellings, and most foreign people find it really difficult to pronounce.
Interviewer Would you like to change it?
Sean No, I definitely wouldn't change it.
Interviewer So, what's your name?
Deborah Deborah.
Interviewer Is that with an h at the end?
Deborah Yes, D-E-B-O-R-A-H.
Interviewer Why did your parents call you that?
Deborah Ah, I'm actually named after the hospital where I was born, Deborah Hospital in New Jersey – near New York. My dad thought of that.
Interviewer Do you have a nickname?
Deborah No, but everyone calls me Debbie or Deb.
Interviewer Are you happy with your name?
Deborah Not really.
Interviewer Would you like to change it?
Deborah I don't know. When I was little, I renamed myself April and then Caroline, but now I don't like those names either.
Interviewer So what's your name?
James James.
Interviewer Is that spelt in the usual way?
James Yes. J-A-M-E-S.
Interviewer Why did your parents call you that?
James I'm not sure. I think they just liked the name. I'm not named after anyone or anything like that.
Interviewer Do you have a nickname?
James Not exactly. At university some of my friends called me Jim for short, but I didn't like it very much. I've always introduced myself as James.
Interviewer Are you happy with your name?
James Yes. I've always liked it.
Interviewer Would you like to change it?
James No. I can't imagine being called something different. But I don't think it really matters anyway – a name is just a name.
Interviewer So what's your name?
Philippa Philippa.
Interviewer How do you spell it?
Philippa P-H-I-L-I-P-P-A.
Interviewer Why did your parents call you that?
Philippa My parents are Scottish, but they were living in England when I was born. They heard the name Philippa – it isn't a common name in Scotland – and they decided that they liked it.
Interviewer Do you have a nickname?
Philippa Well, when I was growing up everyone called me Pippa for short, which I didn't like at all!

Interviewer Are you happy with your name?
Philippa I hated it when I was growing up because it was different. And not one single person spells it right! But now I don't mind it, because it is a bit different.
Interviewer Would you like to change it?
Philippa No, I like it for me.

1 7))

Interviewer Good afternoon. This is *Uncommon Knowledge*, the programme that looks at everyday things from unusual angles. Today we're talking to the Creative Director of a company that names companies and products. Welcome, John.
John Hello, Sarah.
Interviewer Now, tell us. How do companies choose their names? Are they usually named after the people who start them?
John Well, sometimes. Many companies are named after their founders, for example the Swedish furniture company IKEA. The first two letters in IKEA – the I and the K – are the initials of Ingvar Kamprad, the company's founder.
Interviewer And what about the last two letters, the E and the A? What do they stand for?
John The E is for Elmtaryd, which is the name of the farm where Ingvar Kamprad grew up.
Interviewer And the A?
John The A is for the name of a village near his hometown, called Agunnaryd. I'm not quite sure exactly why this village was important to him, but obviously it was.
Interviewer I always assumed that 'ikea' was a Swedish word with some sort of special meaning.
John Ah, I'm afraid not. But many other companies choose names which have specific meanings. For example, Samsung, the big Korean electronics company.
Interviewer What does Samsung mean?
John In Korean, Samsung means 'three stars'. The name was chosen back in the year 1938, and at that time three stars was the most impressive rating that people could imagine for hotels and things like that.
Interviewer So if they'd started the company today they would probably have called it 'five stars' – whatever that is in Korean.
John Absolutely. In any case the company was very different in its early days. For instance, in the beginning, in 1938, Samsung wasn't an electronics company. It was a company which sold fish, vegetables, and fruit to China. It didn't start selling electronics until the 1970s.
Interviewer Oh really? I didn't know that.
John And another brand name with a special meaning is Nike, the American company which is famous for its trainers and sports clothes.
Interviewer I think I know this one. Nike is the Greek goddess of victory. Is that right?
John Yes, that's right. What's interesting is that 'Nike' wasn't the company's original name. When it started in 1964, its original name was Blue Ribbon Sports. They changed their name to Nike a few years later in 1971.
Interviewer Very interesting.
John And another company with an interesting name is Sony, the Japanese electronics company. Sony is a combination of 'sonus', the Latin word for sound, and 'sonny', an American slang term that means 'boy'.
Interviewer 'Sound' plus 'boy'.

John That's right. They chose it because it has an interesting meaning and it's easy for people all over the world to pronounce. Obviously that's an important thing for a business name.
Interviewer One more question, this time about the American internet company, Google. The name has something to do with numbers, I think.
John That's right. 'Googol' is a word for a very large number: a one followed by 100 zeroes.
Interviewer Really? That's quite hard to visualize!
John The name shows that there is a huge amount of information online, and you can find it all by Googling it.
Interviewer Yes. It's a really good name for a search engine.
John Yes, indeed. Now, of course, the spelling is different. 'Google' the company is G-O-O-G-L-E, but the number is spelled G-O-O-G-O-L. But that's where the name comes from.
Interviewer Fascinating. Thanks very much for speaking with us this afternoon.
John You're very welcome.

1 15))

Interviewer Why did you decide to try colour analysis, Wendy?
Wendy Well, I was sharing an office with a lady who always looked incredibly stylish and well-dressed. And when I asked her what her secret was, she told me that she'd done colour analysis. Another reason was that I was really bored with black. I felt like I wore black too often, and I wanted to wear new colours that were more suitable for me. I didn't know what was wrong with the way I dressed, but I wasn't happy about it. So I brought two friends along and we went to see a colour consultant.
Interviewer What was she like? It was a woman?
Wendy Yes, she was a woman. Just wonderful, very friendly and helpful. She put loads of scarves on me that were in different colours and shades. They just drape the scarves around the front of you, like when you go to the hairdresser's, and see which ones look best for your skin tone. Once she'd done all the colours for me, then she put me in the right make-up as well.
Interviewer What colours did she say were best for you?
Wendy Well, I learned that I'm a 'winter person'. There are four sorts of people: spring, summer, autumn, and winter. The winter colours are all very strong, for example dark purple, a dark blue, fuchsia, and a light purple colour called lobelia, which is named after a flower. Another colour winter people should wear a lot is emerald green. And she said I shouldn't wear yellow or orange, or shades of colours which have a lot of yellow in them, like lime green.
Interviewer Do you still wear black?
Wendy Yes. Winter people are the ones who can wear black. I still do wear it once or twice a week.
Interviewer What changes did you make after your colour analysis?
Wendy The first thing I did was get a couple of affordable T-shirts in my new colours, to sort of try it out. I've got a little book with a set of swatches in my colours that I carry with me, absolutely everywhere, so I can be sure I'm buying the right colours. Also, my two friends were both autumn people, so we did a big clothes swap. I gave them all of my autumn colours and they gave me all of their winter colours.

Interviewer Did people notice a change in you?

Wendy They definitely noticed. And the most frequently used word was 'glamorous'. 'Wendy, you look so glamorous!' And after a while I really felt more glamorous. I might just be wearing a T-shirt and a pair of jeans, but in the right colour, and it makes a great difference. Now I feel more confident as a person, in the workplace, and socially. I feel more confident when I go shopping too – before I never knew what to buy and was just hopeless, really.

Interviewer Would you recommend colour analysis to others?

Wendy Absolutely. In fact, about four or five people in the office saw me and did the same thing. My mother's done it too. I told my husband to do it – they do it for guys as well – but he hasn't agreed yet. But he will!

1 19))

Andrew Are you all right? I'll carry that for you.

Jenny Oh yeah, that'd be great. Thank you.

Grant We've just arrived on the flight from New York. He's talking to someone. I'll follow them.

Andrew And have you been to the UK before?

Jenny A few times, actually. I work for a magazine in the States – New York 24seven – and we have a sister company in London.

Andrew I see. And are you here on business this time?

Jenny Sort of. I'm here for a few meetings, but I have a couple of days off beforehand. I'm visiting my father-in-law in the countryside. How about you? How was your holiday in New York?

Andrew It wasn't really a holiday. I was doing some research there.

Jenny That sounds interesting.

Andrew It was, but I didn't have much time for sightseeing! Is your husband coming too?

Jenny No, he's working.

Andrew What does he do?

Jenny He's a journalist. He's on assignment in Alaska at the moment.

Andrew In Alaska? Wow!

Jenny I know, right? I've never been, but he says it's incredible.

Andrew I can imagine. A bit different from the English countryside!

Jenny That's true.

Andrew I'd better go. Oh, before I forget, here's your laptop.

Jenny Oh yeah! Thanks a lot. Sorry, I didn't ask your name.

Andrew Andrew Page. And yours?

Jenny Jenny Zielinski. It was nice meeting you.

Andrew You too.

Jenny And thanks again for helping with my bags.

Andrew No problem. Have a great time at your father-in-law's.

Jenny I will... if I ever get through here!

Andrew Bye then.

Jenny Yeah bye. Take care.

Jenny Henry?... Hi, yeah, I'm here at last. The flight was late taking off... I'm so sorry you've had to wait for me... I know, I know. And you won't believe this – it looks like my suitcase didn't get here... I'm not sure, it's turning out to be a nightmare! I can't wait to just get back to your house and – oh, hang on, I have to go – it's my turn. Bye.

1 22))

Jenny ...and we landed on time but then I couldn't find my suitcase so then I had to go to lost luggage and report it missing.

Henry You poor thing! What a journey!

Jenny Well, I'm here now.

Henry And it's lovely to see you.

Jenny It's great to see you too.

Henry No, no, no, let me take that.

Jenny It's OK.

Henry You've had a hard journey. Allow me.

Jenny Thanks, Henry.

Grant We've got a problem.

Rob I can't believe I'm not there with you, Jenny.

Jenny Neither can I. It's weird, isn't it?

Rob I really miss you.

Jenny Me too. How's Alaska?

Rob Not great. It's been snowing all day! I haven't left the hotel.

Jenny Oh no! That's awful.

Rob What are you drinking? Is that coffee?

Jenny No, it's tea.

Rob Tea?

Jenny It's good. Really!

Rob Where's Dad now?

Jenny I think he's getting me something. I'm not sure what.

Rob So why are you using his computer?

Jenny Oh, it's crazy. You know my laptop?

Rob Yeah?

Jenny This screen keeps popping up and asking me for a password. I've never seen it before. I'm worried I have a virus.

Rob It's not your day, is it? First your suitcase and then your laptop!

Jenny No, but your dad's being so nice. And he says your cousin Luke will be able to fix my computer for me. Apparently he's kind of a computer geek.

Rob Kind of? He's a genius. If he can't do it, nobody can.

Jenny Well, I'm going to go see him tomorrow.

Henry Here's a pair of my pyjamas you can use, Jenny.

Rob Oh wow! You'll look great in those, Jenny!

Selina Selina Lavelle.

Grant Selina? It's Grant. She's in the house, but she isn't alone. I could come back tomorrow with...

Selina No. Stay there. All night if you have to.

Grant Yes, boss.

1 27))

So, in reverse order, the list of things that the British most often leave behind when they go on holiday.

At number ten we have – their passports. Yes, believe it or not many Brits only realize when they get to the airport that they've left their passports at home.

At number nine, flip flops. An easy solution there – they can buy some new ones at their holiday destination.

Number eight, their mobile phone. This is bad news, as it's not easy to replace when you're on holiday, but maybe it's a good thing as it makes it easier to really disconnect, without calls or emails.

At number seven, toothbrushes, and at number six, toothpaste. Another easy thing to buy though, at any local chemist's.

At number five, sunglasses. Yes, Brits have them, but because we don't use them very often we forget to pack them, and we end up buying another pair, which we will then forget again next time.

Number four, a good book. But nowadays if you've forgotten a book but you have a Kindle or iPad, it's easy to buy some more wherever you are.

At number three, sunscreen. This is something we really ought to try to remember to take, because sunscreen is often much more expensive in holiday resorts. And you really can't sunbathe or do water sports without putting some on.

At number two, phone chargers. So you remembered your phone – but you forgot the charger. Well, it is possible to buy chargers when you're away, or you might even be able to buy one online and get it delivered to wherever you're staying.

Finally, the number one thing people forget to bring is... comfortable shoes! We seem to forget that when you go sightseeing or even shopping, not to mention going for walks, comfortable shoes are a must. So next time you pack, make sure all these things are on your checklist!

1 32))

Interviewer How long have you been an airport screener?

Screener Two years.

Interviewer What's the most difficult part of the job?

Screener Definitely the repetition. You say and do the same things again and again... and again. I mean, it's so boring. It eats away at you. I also don't like taking and throwing away people's things. But there are certain things you can't bring through security. I often have to take away big bottles of sunscreen and expensive perfume, home-made food, uh, also, you know, razors and scissors and other things and throw them in the trash, usually in front of the passenger. They look so sad and confused. It makes me feel a little sad for them, too.

Interviewer What do you like about the job?

Screener The only thing that keeps it interesting is the variety of people you meet. I enjoy talking with people and wondering where they're travelling to and things like that. It really tells you something about society.

Interviewer What are your colleagues like?

Screener Um, some are great, but some are terrible. Like, if a passenger is moving too slowly, they can be really unkind. Even if it's an elderly traveller, or just a businessman with too many electronic gadgets. The bad ones, um, they shout at people to push their bags through the belt. I mean, they don't have to be rude about it. One of my colleagues refuses to say 'please' and 'thank you'. Can you believe that? He tells people to lift their arms, show their feet, take off their belt, and things like that, in a very unkind way.

Interviewer Why do you think some screeners are so unfriendly?

Screener Well, I think that it really is, as I said before, because of the repetition. I mean, you try standing in the same place and repeating the same instructions to people and watch them make the same mistakes again and again. It's emotionally exhausting.

Interviewer What are some things that annoy you about passengers?

Screener I always find it surprising when people don't know they have to take off their coats or boots, or take out their laptops, or that they can't take bottles of water through. Sure, not everyone has the opportunity to travel, but I mean, have these people not picked up a newspaper, or watched TV, or spoken with someone else who has flown in the last ten years?

Interviewer How do passengers treat you generally?

Screener Some are nice and courteous. Especially in the morning, people seem either cheery and warm or, you know, simply tired and indifferent. They're rarely rude in the morning. By the afternoon, people become more stressed, and they become less friendly and sometimes angry. They get so upset at us personally. But, I mean, we don't make the rules. Someone else does.

1 40))

Harry I live in Hereford, which is a small town in the UK very near Wales, and our local shopping street, our high street, it has all the normal chains like McDonald's and WHSmith the stationer's. There are also some smaller shops that are independently owned – there's a butcher's, a hardware store, things like that. There used to be a department store that was owned by a local family, but it closed down last year.

The local shops are already having problems, I'd say. And now they're going to develop a new shopping centre outside town, and that'll kill the high street. Also, more people are shopping online now. It worries me because if there are no shops, then the centre of town will just die and become really depressing, maybe just with pound shops or empty stores.

Kate In Toronto, where I live in Canada, the shopping street near my house has everything, from delicatessens and pharmacies to restaurants and clothing stores. There are also corner shops, grocery stores, and chains like Starbucks as well.

The smaller, independently owned shops are definitely struggling because people are going to big indoor shopping malls or supermarkets, especially in winter when it's too cold to be walking around outdoors. Online shopping is still not very common due to the long distances between cities and towns in Canada. Postal delivery and overnight delivery aren't really practical.

Ken I'm from Kobe, a city in Japan, and near the train station we have little shops like a baker's, a café, a greengrocer's, and lots of corner shops.

But people there shop at department stores, mainly. You know, Japanese department stores have everything – clothes, TVs, fruit and vegetables. I don't often go to small independent shops, because I usually need to buy a lot of different things. So it's a lot more convenient to go to a department store. I know the small shops are disappearing and that's a little sad, but better things are replacing them. They're just responding to the customers' needs. It's what the shoppers want.

Bea I live in the centre of Valencia in Spain, and my nearest big shopping street is called Calle Colón. I almost always go shopping there as it's so close. It has pretty much all the shops I like and a big department store too called El Corte Inglés – it's a Spanish institution!

I'd say the small local shops are doing quite well. Of course some places close down, but then new ones open up – a Japanese chain called Muji, for example, that sells stuff for your house. There are quite a few shopping centres round Valencia but I never go to them, as they tend to be out of town, so you need a car or bus to get there, and I think the same is true for a lot of people round here, and also tourists like the small shops. Even though I do use them, for me there are two problems with small shops in Spain. One is that they often close at lunchtime, which I find really impractical. The other thing is that small shops don't offer the same sort of service that a big store can. For example, it's more difficult to have things delivered, or to change something and get your money back.

2 10)))

Interviewer Welcome back. Up next, age and the generation gap. We know how hard it can be to tell someone's age, but in fact it turns out there may be a way that's quite simple. It's called the 'Mosquito Tone Test', and Mark is here to tell us more.

Mark Thanks, Sue. The Mosquito Tone is a sound – a very high pitched, very annoying sound, which is why it's named after the insect. What's interesting is that apparently as we age, we slowly lose our ability to hear this sound. According to scientists, almost everyone under the age of 25 can hear the Mosquito Tone, but almost no one over 25 can hear it!

Interviewer Really! Is that right?

Mark Yes. And to test this out, I actually played the tone for my family last night. My wife and I heard absolutely nothing at all, but our teenage daughters could hear it, and in fact they complained that it was an irritating sound that was quite painful to hear.

Interviewer Oh no! Well, at the risk of irritating some of our younger listeners' ears, why don't we play the tone briefly now?

Mark OK, here goes. I'm playing the tone in 3, 2, 1…

Interviewer Have you played the tone yet?

Mark I just did. Or, at least, I think I did.

Interviewer Well, I suppose that just confirms that neither of us are under 25!

2 11)))

Interviewer Now Mark, apart from testing a person's age, what is the Mosquito Tone being used for?

Mark This has actually become an interesting controversy. Because the sound is so annoying, and because only the young can hear it, the Mosquito Tone is being used to keep teenagers away from certain places.

Interviewer What kinds of places?

Mark Well, for example, from shopping centres. As you know in some towns you get large groups of young people hanging around shopping centres and causing trouble. And some shop owners say that these gangs can annoy other customers, or frighten them away, which is obviously not good for business. So now these centres can play the Mosquito Tone over their audio system, and the groups of teenagers will feel uncomfortable and leave the area. But of course the sound won't annoy the other customers at all, as they don't hear it.

Interviewer Have you spoken to any of these shop owners?

Mark Yes, I have, and they said that the Mosquito Tone has worked very well for them. And they also said that although it's true that the Mosquito Tone is certainly very annoying, it doesn't hurt the teenagers.

Interviewer It sounds like rather a good idea to me. But you said this was a controversy. Who's against it?

Mark Well, there are some groups of people who are trying to ban the Mosquito Tone. They've pointed out a number of problems with it. Firstly, they worry that the sound really is harmful, but more to the point they say that the Mosquito Tone affects all young people, some of whom are well-behaved and just want to go shopping. And finally they say that the Mosquito Tone doesn't actually stop the problem of teenage gangs, it just drives them from one place to another.

Interviewer Those do seem like good points.

Mark Yes, indeed. And there's also an interesting twist. Some teenagers have discovered an advantage to the Mosquito Tone.

Interviewer Oh yes?

Mark Well, the Mosquito Tone has also been released as a ringtone for your mobile. So in secondary schools that don't permit mobile phones, teens can use their phones in class. They can receive calls and messages during lessons and teachers don't have any idea what is happening.

Interviewer Because the teacher can't hear it! That must really annoy them.

Mark That's right. And if they can't hear it, they can't…

2 18)))

Interviewer What inspired you to become a photographer?

Brian My cousin, who was ten years older than me, built a darkroom in his house which I used to visit. From the moment I saw a developing photograph appearing like magic on a piece of paper under the red light, I was completely hooked. At the same time my school started a photography club, so I joined it. I soon knew it was what I wanted to do, and later I went on to study photography and film-making at university.

Interviewer What sort of people do you usually photograph, and where?

Brian I've mainly photographed classical musicians and their ensembles and orchestras. I usually photograph them at work and they often perform in wonderful buildings, which are also great for photography, so I've had the chance to work in palaces and churches in Rome, Vienna, Salzburg, Paris, and other places.

Interviewer Have you had any other famous clients?

Brian Yes, several. I was once asked to photograph Prince Charles, for example.

Interviewer Oh, and how did that go?

Brian In fact, it was a bit embarrassing. He was visiting a mosque, and though there were many other press photographers there, I was the only one who was given permission to enter the mosque at the same time as the Prince. When I got to the door, I was asked to take my shoes off, and I realized that I had an enormous hole in one of my socks! I was so embarrassed, all I could think about was this hole as I tried to get shots of Prince Charles. And then he left through a different door, and I had to follow him, still in my socks.

Interviewer Do you have a favourite portrait of a celebrity?

Brian I have lots, but for example there's a portrait of Meryl Streep by Annie Leibovitz, where she's wearing a face-mask. It's absolutely wonderful.

2 19)))

Interviewer What are some tricks to taking a good portrait?

Brian Each situation is different and what works for one person may not work for another. The most important thing is to get people to relax. Being photographed makes most people nervous and insecure, so, assuming they're not professional models, generally it's best not to have other people around, watching the photo shoot. Once people relax they can even enjoy the process but it does take a long time, so another important thing if you want to have a good photo taken of you is not to be in a hurry. I often need between three and four hours.

Interviewer What else can the person who is being photographed do to improve the picture?

Brian To start with they should wear comfortable clothes, and if they can, if it's a studio photo, bring some different clothes with them – things that they feel good in.

Interviewer What about make-up?

Brian If people are used to wearing make-up, then they should use it, because again it will make them feel good. Actually make-up is often a good thing – and in fact, even for men, a little powder can make them look better under studio lights.

Interviewer What about how to pose?

Brian Well, standing up straight isn't usually a good pose. You can get much more interesting pictures of people, for example, sitting on the floor, leaning against the back of a chair, or sitting just on the edge of a chair. Interestingly, sometimes it's a good thing for people to feel a bit uncomfortable, because the more uncomfortable people are the less they think about their expression and the better the pictures can be. It also helps if people look away and only turn to the camera at the last moment.

Interviewer Brian, thank you very much, and I'll try to remember those tips.

2 23)))

1 I really love this photo, even though I look a bit strange in a dress that was obviously too big and a coat that was too small! But it's the way that my grandfather and I are looking at each other that I love about it. We were about to go for a walk, and are standing just in front of the door of his house, on the steps. It was a really cold day so he'd lent me his fur hat. I don't know who took the photo, probably my grandmother, but it's a lovely reminder of my grandfather, who died a few years ago. I have it in a frame on my desk, and both my mother and my grandmother have a framed copy of the same photo – we all love it.

2 My favourite photo ever – not just from my childhood but in my whole life – is this one that my dad took when we went camping. I'm standing in the mountains and on a rock in front of me is this animal called a marmot – it's like a big mouse, and they're quite common round here. The marmot was standing incredibly close to me and it almost looks as if it's smiling at the camera! It wasn't shy at all. A strange thing is, I always remembered the day the photo was taken, but I actually didn't see the photo with my own eyes until last year, when I turned 35. My parents found a load of old photos and scanned them for me so that I'd have them in digital form. I wanted to enlarge this one and make it into a poster, but the file wasn't big enough.

3 Er, there are loads of childhood photos to choose from, but one of my favourites is this one which was taken by my dad – he was always the family photographer – and I think it was a day when we went for a picnic with my brothers and cousins. In the picture, I'm the little blonde one in the front. I think I was about seven or eight, er, and the two boys on the right are my brothers, and the rest are my cousins.

It reminds me of how close I am to my extended family. So, er, I look at it when I miss home – and it cheers me up. I used to have it stuck on my fridge but now it's packed away in a box somewhere. But my mum uploaded it onto Facebook so now I can look at it any time.

2 24))

Jenny Hello?… Yes, it is… Oh, that's great news. Thank you… Later today? Great. Now I won't have to buy new clothes… Yeah, that's the right address. Bye.
Henry Good news?
Jenny Great news! They found my suitcase, and they're bringing it over later today.
Henry Excellent. Right, I'll take you to my nephew's house so he can fix your computer.
Jenny I'm looking forward to meeting Luke.
Henry You'll like him. He's a bright boy. Not that I understand a word he says.
Jenny I'll bet he doesn't know much about Greek mythology either!
Henry You're probably right.
Henry That's funny.
Jenny What's wrong?
Henry The tyre's flat.
Jenny Do you have a spare?
Henry Well, yes, but it shouldn't be flat, it's new and…
Henry I don't believe it!
Jenny What is it?
Henry They're both flat! They've been punctured!
Jenny What? Somebody did that on purpose? In the English countryside?
Henry You get vandals everywhere these days. Well, I'll just have to stay here and see if I can get the AA to bring out another spare tyre. I'll call you a taxi.
Jenny Isn't there a bus I could catch?
Henry Well, there's a bus stop on the main road. You could get the bus to Oxford from there, I suppose.
Jenny How do I get to the bus stop?
Henry The quickest way is the footpath at the back of the house.
Jenny I think I'll do that then.
Henry Are you sure you want to get the bus? How will you find Luke's house?
Jenny You gave me the address. I can look it up on my phone if I get lost.
Henry Yes, of course. But, this is really inconvenient for you. You were going to borrow my car, weren't you?
Jenny No, don't worry, Henry. I'd actually decided to rent a car anyway. I'll need it for work and it'll probably be cheaper to rent here than in London. I can get one while Luke is working his magic.
Henry Well, if you're absolutely sure. Just go to the back door and you'll see the path. Follow that – takes you to the bus stop.
Jenny OK. Oh, and I'd like to cook dinner this evening to thank you for having me.

Henry You don't need to do that!
Jenny I want to.
Henry Well, if you're sure. What time?
Jenny How about seven o'clock?
Henry Great! And I'll keep my phone on in case you need me.
Jenny See you later, Henry.
Henry Bye!
Henry Who's that?
Jenny Luke?
Luke You must be Jenny. Hi.
Jenny Nice to meet you.
Luke You too. Come in. Would you like some coffee? I've just made some.
Jenny I'd love to, but I'm running a bit late. We had trouble with the car and then the bus took forever. And I really need to get to a car rental place. I'm really sorry, but could I just leave the computer with you?
Luke Yeah, no problem.
Jenny That's great. I feel awful just leaving it here like this.
Luke Honestly, don't worry about it.
Jenny Are you sure?
Luke Yeah, it's cool. I love doing this kind of thing. I'll send you a text and let you know how I'm getting on.
Jenny That's nice of you, Luke. Thanks. See you later.
Luke See you later.

2 27))

Jenny Henry? Henry? Henry?
Henry This is Henry Walker. I'm afraid I can't take your call at the moment. Please leave your message after the tone.
Jenny Hi, Henry, it's Jenny here. I just wanted to let you know everything went fine. I got my car and I'm back home. Remember I'm making dinner. See you soon.
Jenny Hi Luke, it's Jenny.
Luke Hi Jenny, what's up?
Jenny I just wanted to apologize for running off this morning.
Luke You really don't need to! I should apologize, actually. It's going to take me longer than I thought to unlock your computer. It's like there's an extra security code or something.
Jenny That's really weird.
Luke Don't worry, I'm sure I can crack it.
Jenny I just have no idea how it got there. Hang on.
Luke What is it?
Jenny My suitcase has arrived!
Luke Hey, that's great!
Jenny Oh, look at that. The lock's broken.
Luke Must have been the baggage handlers!
Jenny Well, at least it's back.
Luke So, how's uncle Henry?
Jenny He isn't here. I called him but he didn't answer.
Luke He probably went for a walk. He often does that. He thinks about his research and stuff.
Jenny Well, I hope he's back in time for dinner!
Luke He will be. He's always on time.
Jenny Yeah, Rob told me Henry's very punctual.
Luke Unlike Rob!
Jenny Exactly.
Luke Is that the jet lag catching up with you?
Jenny Yeah, I'm pretty tired.
Luke You should have a nap. Don't worry, I'll get this computer working as soon as I can.
Jenny Thanks, Luke. See you later.
Luke Bye!
Jenny Oh no, dinner! Henry? Henry? That's strange.
Henry This is Henry Walker. I'm afraid I can't take your call at the moment. Please leave your message after the tone.
Newsreader The victim of last night's assault at Heathrow Airport has been named as Andrew Page. Mr Page is a research scientist from Oxford. Police believe he was attacked as he left the airport. He is now in hospital in a critical

condition. Police are appealing to anyone who may have seen Mr Page to contact them immediately. Mr Page had just returned from New York where he was conducting research on renewable energy.
Rob Hi, Jenny.
Jenny Rob, I need to talk to you.

2 29))

Sunday
Liz Dave and I meet Ash and Ross, two London freegans who will train us how to find food in the rubbish. Ash is 21, and his friend Ross is 46. This is Ash.
Ash First, you need the right equipment. Take gloves and a torch. Also, you have to know where to go. Small to medium size shops are probably best. The larger shops lock their bins.
Liz We're in the car park behind a supermarket. It's 5 p.m. and dark, so people don't notice us. Ash and Ross walk confidently to the bins, lift the lids, and start looking for food.
The first bin bag we open contains frozen meals, including chicken curry and chilli con carne. The meals haven't been opened and the sell-by date is today. Underneath are ten tubs of ice cream, with the same sell-by date. At the bottom is a carton of eggs. The sell-by date is next week. Ross says this isn't surprising.
Ross We get a lot of eggs. Sometimes, if one breaks, they just throw away all of them. But, er, you know, just be careful when choosing what to eat. If the packaging is open or it's past the sell-by date, don't take it. Oh, and wash everything you find before you eat it.

Monday
Liz Now it's time for Dave and me to try freeganism on our own. As we begin, it's freezing cold. After an hour and a half of searching, we still haven't found one unlocked bin. Eventually, we go behind a smaller supermarket and… success! The bins are open. There's a plastic bag full of vegetables at the bottom. So, while Dave holds the lid open, I reach in. A couple of people are watching us, and I'm so embarrassed. But the bag's full of potatoes, apples, and carrots, and there's nothing wrong with them. We'll make a nice soup with them. Now, we just need bread. We look inside a coffee shop's bin and there is some. But we're right outside the station and it's rush hour. We're too embarrassed to take it. So we go to the bins outside a nearby supermarket, where we find a plastic bag of sliced bread. The bag is unbroken and the sell-by date is today. At home, after washing the vegetables, we cook a delicious soup, which we have with the bread. Dessert is baked apples. Wonderful.

2 30))

Tuesday
Liz I don't feel ill – a good start – so we enjoy a freegan breakfast of avocados, which were a present from Ash and Ross, and we have the rest of yesterday's bread. We decide to visit the bins by the supermarket where we found the vegetables yesterday. Again, we find lots of vegetables and fruit – potatoes, peppers, a melon, and some salad. The salad is close to the sell-by date, but if it were in your fridge, you'd eat it. Other sell-by dates are not for another week. I don't understand why they were thrown away. After a lunch of yesterday's soup, we search at bakeries but find nothing. Luckily, we've found enough food this morning for dinner and tomorrow's breakfast.
We've decided that it's OK to use a few shop-bought ingredients such as pasta, so on the menu tonight is a spicy pasta soup with green peppers and the carrots from yesterday. For dessert we have another baked apple.

Wednesday
Liz Today, after a breakfast of melon, we head off to check out the bins in the market, which smell terrible compared with the supermarket rubbish. We find enough food to eat like kings: sausages,

cabbage, lemons, and some onions. Although three days is a short time to live as a freegan, I've already learned that a lot of food is thrown away for no good reason. Perhaps I should continue with my freegan lifestyle? After all, the food we found, after a good wash, was the same as the food you buy in a shop. Except, of course, it was free.

② 43))

Rosie In the fashion industry, it's almost impossible to get a job unless you do an internship first. Companies get so many applications for internships that they don't need to pay you. The most I got was about £15 a day for lunch and transport.

It's slave labour, but it teaches you a lot. I learned loads about making and designing clothes. I sometimes worked beyond 11 p.m., and that wasn't easy, but then you look in the newspapers and see a model who's wearing a hat that you helped to make. It's so exciting.

I'm in a lot of debt after doing three months' unpaid work in London. My parents were able to help me a bit, but I had to earn money by working in a bar as well.

Overall, I think internships are brilliant. I'd definitely advise someone to do an internship – despite the hard work and the debt, you learn so much that it's worth it.

Joe I had an internship in the music industry for a few months when I was in my early twenties. The positive side was having a job. An internship is a position in an organization like any other job, so you feel that you've taken a step in the right direction. And I enjoyed working in the music industry – I liked the office environment and my colleagues.

The downside was that I was paid very little – the minimum wage – and it all went on food and travel. And the job itself wasn't very interesting, to be honest. There were boring repetitive tasks like writing the company newsletter or managing their social media channels.

But all in all it was positive. I think the best experience was sometimes being in the same room as the boss and listening to his phone calls – that was first-hand experience of how to run a business. And of course the internship went straight onto my CV. Any experience is better than no experience from an employer's perspective.

Lauren I've done four internships in publicity. My last one was two months at a small PR agency. They paid for my travel expenses and lunch, and I learned a lot. That really helped me when I applied for jobs because I knew what I was talking about.

But in the other three I worked ten-hour days, six days a week, and I got no money at all, so I also had to work in a pub to support myself. Each time I was told, 'Do well and there'll be a job at the end of it.' But then you realize there is no job. It makes you angry.

During one of those internships, the manager went on holiday for a month and I had to manage everything. In another one, I worked from home, using my own phone, and wasn't paid a penny, not even to cover the phone bill. I only met the boss once – it was all done by email. She promised me a job after three months, but it never happened.

③ 8))

Interviewer Welcome back. My next guests are two sisters who write scripts for *Bob's Burgers*, an animated series which will be shown next month on Sunday evenings. Please welcome Wendy and Lizzie Molyneux! Lizzie, Wendy, thanks so much for joining us.

Wendy / Lizzie Thanks, it's great to be here, our pleasure.

Interviewer Now, tell us a bit about *Bob's Burgers*.

Wendy Well, like The Simpsons, it's meant for adults and older kids even though obviously it's a cartoon.

Lizzie It's a comedy – it's about a funny guy who owns a hamburger restaurant, and his weird kids and weird wife. They all work in the restaurant and live in the apartment above it, and they have lots of problems keeping the restaurant in business.

Interviewer So, how did you get the job as writers?

Wendy A few years ago we wrote a script for another animated series that the network decided not to make. But people read our script and they liked it.

Lizzie Yeah. So later we had an interview with the producers of *Bob's Burgers*. We loved the show and the producers, so we were sure we would never get the job.

Wendy But then we did!

Lizzie Happy ending!

Interviewer What's it like to be a TV writer? I mean, what's your daily routine?

Lizzie Er, we start work at about 10.00 in the morning. Most weekdays we are either working on a story or coming up with some new jokes for scripts that have already been written. Then in the afternoon it's more of the same.

Interviewer How long does it take to actually write and create an episode?

Wendy Actually, it takes a really long time – about six to eight months from the idea to recording. First, you come up with an idea for a story. Then, you work with a bunch of other writers to create an outline for the story.

Lizzie There are about ten full-time writers on the show.

Wendy Right. Then, you go write a full script. That script gets read aloud by the actors, then we record their voices in a studio. Once we have the recording, the artists create an animatic, which is like a rough draft of the cartoon, in black and white.

Lizzie And after that, the rough drawings are sent to a studio in Korea where the colour animation is created.

③ 9))

Interviewer Who do you think is most important to the show: the actors, the writers, or the director? Or someone else?

Lizzie Well, on our show it is definitely the creator of the show, Loren Bouchard. He's always at the office. He manages the writers, the directors, the actors, and pretty much everything else.

Wendy Yeah. He barely even has time to eat, but when he does he pretty much only eats baked potatoes.

Interviewer Sounds like a strange guy. Do you have guest stars on *Bob's Burgers*?

Wendy Actually yes, we've had a lot of amazing guest stars on our show, like Jon Hamm from *Mad Men*.

Interviewer What's it like being sisters and co-writers? Did you write things together when you were children?

Lizzie We probably collaborated on making fun of our other sisters, but we didn't actually write together until we were adults.

Interviewer Apart from *Bob's Burgers*, what TV programmes do you like?

Wendy Actually I love watching dramas like *Game Of Thrones* or *Homeland*. I don't always want to watch other comedies, because then I'd be thinking about work. I will watch anything with zombies as well!

Lizzie I also enjoy terrible reality shows like *The Real Housewives of Beverly Hills*.

Interviewer One last question. What are your future ambitions?

Wendy To write more TV!

Interviewer Wendy, Lizzie, thank you for coming on the programme.

Wendy / Lizzie Thank you. Our pleasure.

③ 15))

Melissa I live in Istanbul now, in Turkey, but I used to live in the country in the province of Sakarya. It was an amazing place to live – just so beautiful. There's a large lake nearby and the hills are covered with pine trees – people go to picnic there. The coast is also not far away. When I lived there it was as if time had stood still. There was no water or electricity – we had our own well and generator – and there was only one shop. We had to wait for a minibus from the nearest town to bring fresh bread and the newspapers every morning! I worked in a school in a nearby town – in fact the one that sent the bread and papers – and in my free time I played tennis, went for walks, and played the piano. I made my own entertainment. In the end I had to move to Istanbul for work, but I really miss the fresh food and fresh fish, the peace. I sometimes used to think when I was living there that there wasn't enough choice of things to do, things to buy, but now I think I have too much choice.

Eric A few years ago my wife and I retired and we moved to a little town in the mountains here in Colorado. It's gorgeous. We have a house on a hill, and we are surrounded by mountains, which we can see from our window, as well as the woods and a very pretty lake. There are lots of paths and we walk every morning with our dog, er, who loves chasing after sticks and things.

There's so much to do. In the summer we go hiking and we have a little canoe we take on the lake, and of course in the winter we go skiing. We have lots of friends here and we often have dinner parties or we have our book club meetings. There's a joke here that we only have three seasons: summer, winter, and 'mud season'. That's after the snow has melted and everything, I mean everything, is covered in mud. That's the only bad time to be here. And the other problem is that we don't have a supermarket. The nearest one's about 20 miles from here.

③ 19))

Interviewer How long have you been on *The Archers*?

Tim Well, I celebrated 30 years on *The Archers* this June.

Interviewer Which character do you play?

Tim I play a character called David Archer, who is a farmer, who's the son of Phil Archer, who in turn was the son of Dan Archer, who was the very first Mr Archer back in 1951, when the programme started.

Interviewer What kind of person is David Archer?

Tim Well, David is some…, some might say he's a bit thick, 'thick' meaning stupid. He's not. He's a simple soul. He's extremely honourable, he's extremely hard-working, he's honest, he's dependable. But he's a farmer, and that's the most important thing in his life, making the farm work and keeping his family together.

Interviewer How much did you know about life on a farm before you joined the cast?

Tim Well, unusually, I actually knew a bit because I'd worked on farms when I was a child. And I was in fact born on a sheep station in Tasmania. And so when I was a boy I used to go and work casually at the local farm. And then also my father in the 1970s gave up being an advertising executive and went off down to Devon to live off the land, and so he started this ten-acre organic smallholding in Devon. And my wife and I went down and helped him to get that going, so I've got quite a lot of practical experience on the farm.

Interviewer Is that an exception on *The Archers*?

Tim Yes, yes, most of the actors don't know one end of a cow from the other, to be honest.

Interviewer Do you think that country and city people react to *The Archers* in a different way?

Tim Yes, they do. City people look at Ambridge, which is the village that we live in, as a kind of an English ideal of the countryside. It's an old-fashioned England where everybody's nice to each other. There's not much crime. There aren't any yellow lines so that you can't park. And that's, I think, what they love about it. And from the country people, what they tend to like is the fact that they all say, 'That's exactly like the village that I live in.' There's the vicar, there's the doctor, there's the person who runs the pub – and there's the bossy woman who runs around trying to organize everybody, you know.

Interviewer Would you actually like to live on a farm yourself – or do you?

Tim We've got a cottage in Norfolk, so we're – I'm up in the country every weekend. And also I was brought up in the country. Until I was 21, we lived just north of London, in Hertfordshire. So I'm a country boy at heart and, er, you know…

Interviewer Have you ever lived in a city?

Tim Yeah, we do now. I mean, I've lived in London since – for 30 years. So I'm a country boy who's kind of ended up in the town because that's where the work is.

Interviewer Thank you very much.

Tim My great pleasure.

3 21))

Rob He was attacked?

Jenny That's right. The police found him at the airport.

Rob You're sure it's the same person?

Jenny Definitely. I saw his picture. His name's Andrew Page and he's a scientist.

Rob And you spoke to him?

Jenny He helped carry my bags! I mean, I could have been the last person to see him before it happened.

Rob I think you should go to the police.

Jenny I know. And Rob, there's something else.

Rob What is it?

Jenny Well, I don't want to worry you, but your dad hasn't come home. We were supposed to have dinner at seven.

Rob What time is it now?

Jenny It's a little after nine.

Rob What? That is worrying. Dad's usually really punctual.

Jenny Should I call the police?

Rob I think you should. It's really not like him.

Jenny OK, and Rob?

Rob Yeah?

Jenny Oh, it's nothing.

Rob What is it?

Jenny I know this seems odd but the house feels strange.

Rob What do you mean?

Jenny I don't know, but I don't like being alone here.

Rob Well, it's late and you're tired.

Jenny That's true. But I don't think I'll be able to sleep here.

Rob Why don't you ring Luke? You could stay with him, and you could go to the police together and tell them about Dad.

Jenny OK, I think I'll do that.

Rob I'll ring you later.

Jenny OK, Rob, I'll be fine. Don't worry. Bye.

3 24))

Jenny Good morning.

Luke Hi.

Jenny Thanks for letting me stay. I feel a lot safer here.

Luke What? Oh, no problem.

Jenny I tried Henry again. Still no answer. I wonder if…

Luke Yes! I've done it! I'm in.

Jenny What?

Luke I've cracked the security code on your computer.

Jenny That's great, Luke, but Henry…

Luke Wait a minute, that's not right. The username says A. Page… and all the files are encrypted.

Jenny A. Page? Are you sure?

Luke Let me just see if I can open the files. What the…? Jenny, take a look at this. It's a formula or something.

Jenny What does it mean?

Luke I have no idea.

Jenny It's a message from Henry!

Luke What? What does it say?

Jenny It's a video. Hang on.

Henry Hello, Jenny. As you can see, I'm all right. I can't tell you where I am. But listen carefully. These people want some documents on your computer. They want you to leave it at the house. To prove that I'm OK, here's a copy of this morning's paper.

Henry There's one last thing that they want me to tell you. Don't go to the police again. If you go to the police, you know what'll happen. Now, Jenny, please don't worry. Tell Rob his old man will be in his study again soon.

Jenny We need to call Rob.

1A

pronouns

pronouns and possessive adjectives

subject pronouns	object pronouns	possessive adjectives	possessive pronouns
I	me	my	mine
you	you	your	yours
he / she / it	him / her / it	his / her / its	his / hers
we	us	our	ours
you	you	your	yours
they	them	their	theirs

🔍 **each other**
We use *each other* to talk about an action between two people or groups of people, e.g.
We gave each other our email addresses.
They send texts to each other all the time.

direct / indirect object pronouns and word order

1 He gave **me** **some money**.   1 8 🔊
   I'm going to lend **her** **my camera**.
   They've shown **their friends** **their new flat**.
   I'll send **you** **an email**.
   We bought **our father** **some books**.
2 He gave **it** **to me**.
   I'm going to lend **it** **to her**.
   They've shown **it** **to them**.
   I'll send **it** **to you**.
   We bought **them** **for him**.

1 Some verbs can have two objects, usually a thing (the **direct object**) and a person (the **indirect object**). If the direct object is a noun (*some money, a digital camera,* etc.), we usually use verb + indirect object + direct object.

2 If the direct object is a pronoun (*it, them*), we usually use verb + direct object + indirect object, with either *for* or *to* before the indirect object – it depends on the verb. Some common verbs which can have two objects are:

bring (for / to), buy (for), cook (for), find (for), get (for), make (for)

give (to), lend (to), offer (to), read (to), sell (to), send (to), show (to), take (to), write (to)

- If the indirect object is a pronoun, remember to use the object pronoun, not the subject pronoun:
  I bought it for her. NOT ~~I bought it for she.~~
  I gave them my number. NOT ~~I gave they my number.~~

a ⓒircle the correct form.

   *Me | **My** middle name's Alexandra, but **I** | me never use it.*
1 My sister doesn't have a tablet. *He | She* prefers *his | her* laptop.
2 **A** Are these *your | yours* books here?
   B Yes, they're *my | mine*.
3 Most people are happy with *theirs | their* names, but Kim doesn't like *her | hers*.
4 **A** What are *hers | her* children called?
   B I don't know, she's never told *me | my*.
5 I gave *them | their* my phone number, but they didn't give me *theirs | their*.
6 **A** Is this *ours | our* car key?
   B No, *ours | our* says 'VW'.
7 This is *my | mine* pen, so that one must be *your | yours*.
8 She'll phone *us | we* when *her | hers* flight arrives.
9 You should send *he | him* some photos – this is *his | him* email address.
10 *It's | They're* a really good restaurant but I can never remember *his | its* name.

b Rewrite the **highlighted** phrases. Replace the **bold** words with a pronoun and use *to | for*.

   I gave you **that pen**. *I gave it to you.*
1 They sent me **a new password** yesterday.
2 I gave my girlfriend **some flowers**, but she's still angry with me.
3 She found me **some hotels** online.
4 My sister wrote me **these letters** when she was living in Japan.
5 Will you lend him **the money**?
6 My son made me **a birthday card** at school.
7 They didn't have the keys so they couldn't show us **their new flat**.
8 We didn't buy our daughter **a computer** because we think she's too young.
9 I read the children **the first Harry Potter book** last week.
10 A friend at university sold me **these CDs** for 50p each.

1B

adjectives

Revise the basics

1 It's a **poisonous snake**. NOT *snake poisonous*
2 They're very **powerful people**. NOT *powerfuls people*
3 I'm **older than** my brother. NOT *more old that*
4 Rome isn't **as expensive as** Paris. NOT *as expensive than*
5 It's **the most difficult** exercise in the book. NOT *the difficultest*

comparative and superlative adjectives

adjective	comparative	superlative
tall	taller	the tallest
hot	hotter	the hottest
modern	more modern	the most modern
busy	busier	the busiest
dangerous	more dangerous	the most dangerous
interesting	less interesting	the least interesting
good	better	the best
bad	worse	the worst
far	further	the furthest

adjective + *one* / *ones*

I've lost my suitcase. It's a **big, blue one**.   **1 16**))
Expensive laptops are usually more reliable than **cheap ones**.

- We use *one* / *ones* after an adjective instead of repeating a singular or plural noun.
- We don't use *one* / *ones* with uncountable nouns.
  I'm looking for full-time work, but I'd be happy with part-time. NOT *part-time one*

more rules for comparatives and superlatives

1 I feel **more tired** than I did yesterday.   **1 17**))
   She's **the most stressed** person in the office.
2 She's **the cleverest** girl in the class.
   The old road was much **narrower** than the new one.
   It would be **simpler** to go back to the beginning.

1 One-syllable adjectives which end in *-ed* always use *more* and *the most* for comparatives and superlatives, e.g. *bored, pleased, shocked, stressed, tired.*
2 Some two-syllable adjectives can make comparatives and superlatives with *-er* and *-est*. Common examples are *clever, narrow, polite, quiet, simple, stupid.*
   - A good dictionary will tell you the usual comparative and superlative form for a two-syllable adjective.

a bit and *much* + comparative adjective

1 It's **a bit cloudier** today than yesterday. **1 18**))
   This phone's **a bit more expensive** than that one.
2 Your job is **much more stressful** than mine.
   The business is **much busier** than it was last year.

1 We use *a bit* + comparative adjective to say that a difference is small.
2 We use *much* + comparative adjective to say that a difference is large.

a Are the highlighted forms right ✓ or wrong ✗? Correct the wrong ones.

   He's happier than he was yesterday. ✓
   She's a person very ambitious. ✗
   She's a very ambitious person.
1 That's the baddest film I've ever seen.
2 I'm not as sporty than my brother.
3 Cats are more selfish than dogs.
4 Mexico is further to travel, but the hotels are less expensive.
5 I always lose my phone, so I bought a cheap one.
6 My husband's a more good driver than I am.
7 These shoes are the more comfortable ones I have.
8 My brothers and sisters are all very successfuls.
9 This exercise is easyer than the other one.
10 It's the biggest room in the house.

b Complete the sentences to mean the same thing.

   Adam is friendlier than Chris.
   Chris isn't *as friendly* as Adam.
1 Tom isn't as lucky as his brother.
   Tom's brother is _____ than he is.
2 Their house is much bigger than ours.
   Our house is _____ than theirs.
3 My new password is easier to memorize than my old one.
   My old password was _____ to memorize than my new one.
4 This flat is nicer than the other two we've looked at.
   This flat is _____ of the three we've looked at.
5 My sister's children are more helpful than mine.
   My children aren't _____ as my sister's.
6 The weather wasn't as good as we'd expected.
   The weather was _____ than we'd expected.
7 The film was much less exciting than the book.
   The book was _____ than the film.
8 Yellow will look better than red for your kitchen.
   Red won't look _____ as yellow for your kitchen.

2A

present tenses

action and non-action verbs

1 A What **are** the children **doing** now? ① 33)))
   B Mark**'s playing** tennis and Anna**'s reading**.
   A Hi, Marta. **Are** you **waiting** for someone?
   B Yes, I**'m waiting** for Tim.
2 I **like** vegetables now, but I didn't use to.
   Oh, now I **remember** where I left my glasses.

1 Many verbs describe actions. These verbs are used in the present continuous to talk about actions happening now or in the future.
2 Some verbs describe states and feelings, not actions. Examples are *agree, be, believe, belong, depend, forget, hate, hear, know, like, look like, love, matter, mean, need, prefer, realize, recognize, remember, seem, suppose, want*. These verbs are normally used in the present simple, not the continuous, even if we are referring to now.

verbs which can have action and non-action meanings

Do you **have** any sunscreen? = possession (non-action) ① 34)))
He**'s having** a shower at the moment. = an action
Do you **think** we should have lunch in the hotel? = opinion (non-action)
They**'re thinking** about going on a cruise. = an action
I **see** what you mean. = understand (non-action)
I**'m seeing** the hotel manager tomorrow morning. = an action

- Some verbs have two meanings, an action meaning and a non-action meaning, e.g. *have, think, see*.
  If they describe a state or feeling, not an action, they are not usually used in the present continuous.
  If they describe an action, they can be used in the present continuous.

present continuous for future arrangements

I**'m leaving** tomorrow. ① 35)))
We**'re seeing** our grandparents this weekend.
When **are** they **coming** to see us?
She **isn't going out** tonight, she**'s staying in**.

- We often use the present continuous for future arrangements.

present simple for 'timetable' future

The train **leaves** at 6.30 in the morning. ① 36)))
Our flight **doesn't stop** in Hong Kong, it **stops** in Singapore.
When **do** you **arrive** in New York?

- We can use the present simple to talk about things which will happen according to a timetable, especially travel times and arrangements. The present continuous is usually possible as well.

a Complete the sentences with the present simple or present continuous form of the verbs in brackets.

Do you *know* how to waterski? (know)

1 _____ you _____ camping or staying in cheap hotels? (prefer)
2 We _____ of going on a safari next year. (think)
3 _____ we _____ to take insect repellent? (need)
4 She _____ to Frankfurt for a business meeting next week. (fly)
5 A This hotel _____ Wi-fi. (not have)
   B It _____, we can go to a café. (not matter)
6 A What _____ you _____? (do)
   B I _____ the spare memory card for my camera. (look for)
7 Tanya _____ a massage at the moment, and I _____ for souvenirs. (have, shop)
8 A Where _____ you _____ this weekend? (go)
   B We _____ at home. (stay)

b (Circle) the correct form of the verb. Tick ✓ if both are possible.

(We're going) / We go to New Zealand on Saturday. The flight [1] *leaves / is leaving* at 6.50 in the morning. [2] *We need / We're needing* to check in two hours ahead, so [3] *we go / we're going* to the airport the night before, and [4] *we stay / we're staying* in an airport hotel (£200 a night, but it's better than getting up at 2.00 a.m.!). The first part of the flight, to Singapore, [5] *takes / is taking* 14 hours, and [6] *we break / we're breaking* the journey there for a couple of days. Then it's on to Auckland. The flight [7] *gets in / is getting in* at nearly midnight, but our friends [8] *meet / are meeting* us at the airport, and [9] *they look after / they're looking after* us for a week or so. Then [10] *we travel / we're travelling* round North and South Island – [11] *we rent / we're renting* a camper van. [12] *We have / We're having* to be back in Auckland on February 22, but I don't think I'll want to come home!

2B

possessives

possessive 's

> 1 That's **Mark's** jacket. ⓵ **41**)))
> Have you seen **Andrew's** phone?
> He's my **sister's** boyfriend.
> 2 I asked **Chris'** advice. / I asked **Chris's** advice.
> 3 This is a photo of my **parents'** house.
> That's the **children's** bedroom.
> 4 We spent the weekend at **Paul's**.
> I went to **my grandmother's** yesterday.

1 We usually use possessive *'s* to show possession after the names of people, animals, organizations: *Have you seen the dog's lead? What do you think of the government's plans for education reform?*
2 If a name ends with *-s*, we make the possessive with *'* or *'s*. Both are pronounced /ɪz/.
3 Possessives are different for regular and irregular plurals.
   • After a plural noun ending in *-s*, we make the possessive with a final *'* (but no extra *s*).
   • After an irregular plural not ending in *-s*, we make the possessive with *'s*.
4 We can use *name / person + 's* to mean that person's house or flat.

> 🔍 **'s after two names**
> *We saw Tom and Mary's parents.* = Tom and Mary are brother and sister. We saw their parents.
> *We saw Gill's and David's parents.* = We saw Gill's parents and we saw David's parents.

of to show possession

> 1 What's **the name of the street** where you live? ⓵ **42**)))
> They sat at **the back of the bus**.
> I've found **the top of the shampoo bottle**.
> 2 That man over there is **a friend of mine**.
> This is **an interesting book of Sarah's**.
> Tell me about **this plan of theirs**.
> Where's **that husband of yours**?

1 With other nouns (not people or animals), we often use *of*.
2 We often use noun + *of* + possessive pronoun or name / noun + *'s* after *a / an* or *this / that*, not *'s*.

own

> I'd love to have **my own** business. ⓵ **43**)))
> That's my magazine – you can get **your own**.
> Our town is going to get **its own** shopping centre.
> Small bakers often sell **their own** bread and cakes.

We can use *own* after a possessive adjective for emphasis:

---

a Complete the sentences with apostrophes (') where necessary (possession or contraction).

> Mark's brother works in a chemist's.

1 There are lots of expensive womens clothes shops round here.
2 We went to James and Amandas party last night.
3 Thats the towns only bakers.
4 On Saturdays I often look round the shops.
5 Theres been a florists on that corner for years.
6 Two of my friends wives run small businesses from home.
7 Shes going to spend a few nights at her parents.
8 There are too many estate agents in this neighbourhood.
9 Charles sisters both live in flats in the centre.
10 The towns only greengrocers closed down last year.

b (Circle) the correct form.

> What's (the name of the street) / the street's name where you live?

1 That's *the car of my friend / my friend's car* over there.
2 He's 95 years old but he still does *all his own / all their own* shopping.
3 I live in the flat at *the building's top / the top of the building*.
4 I quite like supermarket pizza but I prefer to make *my own / mine own*.
5 I can't remember *the name of the book / the book's name*.
6 **A** Who's Sarah?
   B She's *my husband's sister / my sister's husband*.
7 Every Christmas we go to *my wife's parents' / my wife's parent's*.
8 I've known him for years – he's a very good *my friend / friend of mine*.
9 Not many people live in *the centre of London / London's centre*.
10 I'm always really tired at *the day's end / the end of the day*.

3A

past simple, past continuous, or *used to*?

Revise the basics

past simple

1 When I **was** young I **loved** playing outside.
2 We **didn't live** in a big city.
3 Where **did** you **go** to school?

past continuous

4 I **was watching** TV when you arrived.
5 She **wasn't studying** when I called her.
6 What **were** you **doing** at 9.00 this morning?

used to

7 He **used to have** long hair.
8 They **didn't use to live** in London.
9 What music **did** you **use to like** when you were young?

past simple and past continuous

1 I **saw** him two minutes ago. (2)(3)))
  Humans **didn't live** in cities until about 8,000 years ago.
  Where **did** you **grow up**?
2 What **were** you **doing** at 7.00 this morning?
  He **was texting** a friend when the accident **happened**.
  Sorry, what **did** you **say**? I **wasn't listening**.

---

1 We use the past simple for finished past actions or states (when we say, ask, or know when they happened). We can use the past simple for things which happened at any time in the past – very recently, or a long time ago. The important thing is that we see them as finished.

➤ *For irregular past simple verbs see **Irregular verbs** p.165.*

2 We use the past continuous:
- to talk about an action in progress at a specific time in the past.
- to describe a past action which was interrupted by another action (expressed in the past simple).

used to

1 We **used to live** in Rome. (2)(4)))
  I **used to have** very long hair.
2 I **often went** to the cinema **when I lived in London**.
  He **never wore** a suit and tie **when he was a student**.

1 We use *used to* (not the past continuous) to describe a habit or state that was true for a significant period in the past, and that has now finished.
- We <u>don't</u> say *We used to live in Rome* if:
  – we only lived in Rome for a short period of time, e.g. three weeks (= *We **lived** in Rome for three weeks*).
  – we still live in Rome. (= *We've lived | We've been living in Rome for the last three years*).
2 We can also often use the past simple with an adverb of frequency instead of *used to*.

---

a (Circle) the correct form of the verb. Tick ✓ if both are possible.

(I grew up) | I was growing up in a little village.

1 They *were having | used to have* dinner when I *phoned | was phoning* them.
2 When we were young our parents *took | used to take* us to the beach every weekend.
3 She *was still having | still had* breakfast when the taxi *arrived | used to arrive*.
4 *Did your brother teach | Was your brother teaching* you to play the guitar when you were young?
5 When I was younger I *used to love | was loving* helping my mum cook.
6 He *had | used to have* a beard when he *was | was being* at university.
7 We *used to spend | were spending* all day playing together when we were children.
8 He *was using | used* his mobile when the accident *happened | was happening*.
9 We *didn't go | didn't use to go* abroad last year.
10 They *didn't use to have | weren't having* a car when I *knew | was knowing* them.

b Are the highlighted forms right ✓ or wrong ✗? Correct the wrong ones.

Where did you use to go on holiday last year? ✗
Where did you go on holiday last year?

1 This time last week I was sitting on a beach.
2 When did they use to get married?
3 I used to find it very hard to get a job when I left university.
4 We used to love going to concerts when we were students.
5 Were you seeing anything good on TV last night?
6 My brother and I didn't use to get on very well when we were young.
7 He was never studying much at school.
8 Where did you grow up?
9 Sorry, I didn't hear what you said, I listened to the radio.
10 We were moving to Manchester when my father got a job there.

3B

prepositions

prepositions of place

> She sat **in** the square and watched the tourists.　　(2)(20)))
> There's a box **under** your bed.
> You'll find some cash **inside** my purse.
> The cups are **on** that shelf there.
> There's a man standing **in front of** the gate.

- Prepositions that describe place, like *in* and *on*, have an independent meaning. They can be used with different verbs and places and the meaning doesn't change.

prepositions of movement

> They flew **over** the city.　　(2)(21)))
> He ran **across** the road.
> He walked **through** the door.
> Go **along** the street, **past** the supermarket.
> Don't run **down** the steps. You'll fall.

- Prepositions that describe movement, like *over* and *through*, have an independent meaning. They can be used with different verbs of movement and the meaning doesn't change.

dependent prepositions after verbs and adjectives

> 1　We **waited for** the film to start.　　(2)(22)))
> 　　They all **laughed at** me.
> 2　I'm **worried about** my camera – the flash isn't working.
> 　　She's **interested in** astrology.
> 3　He's **good at spending** other people's money.
> 　　She **believes in taking** lots of pictures and then **choosing** the best.

1. Some verbs are always followed by the same preposition.
2. Some adjectives are always followed by the same preposition.
3. If there is a verb after the preposition, we use the *-ing* form, not the infinitive.

> 🔍 The verbs *ask, discuss, enter, marry,* and *tell* have no preposition, e.g.
> I **asked Jack** for directions. NOT ~~asked to~~
> We **discussed the situation**. NOT ~~discussed about~~
> The police officers **entered the building**. NOT ~~entered in~~
> She **married her personal trainer**. NOT ~~married with~~
> The photographer **told everyone** to smile. NOT ~~told to~~

➤ *For a list of prepositions after verbs and adjectives see p.164.*

---

a Complete the story with the correct prepositions.

| across | onto | under | into | ~~down~~ | off | towards |
| next to | round | on | between | in | along | |

The mouse ran *down* the stairs, [1]_____ the corridor, and [2]_____ the kitchen. It jumped [3]_____ the table, and ran [4]_____ the salt and pepper and [5]_____ the coffee pot. There was some cheese [6]_____ a plate. The mouse stole a piece, jumped [7]_____ the table, and disappeared [8]_____ the door. Then it ran [9]_____ the garden and stopped [10]_____ the gate. But unfortunately two cats were hiding [11]_____ the grass, and they started to creep [12]_____ the mouse…

b Complete the sentences with the correct preposition.

She paid *for* my flight home.

1. I'm tired _____ all this work – I'm ready _____ a holiday!
2. I'm not looking forward _____ apologizing _____ what happened.
3. He's very proud _____ his new camera.
4. Mum! Josh won't share his sweets _____ me!
5. You can't always rely _____ the trains here – they're often late.
6. What are you talking _____?
7. The pilot told us not to worry _____ the turbulence.
8. Who's responsible _____ updating the website?
9. There's no point arguing _____ it now – let's wait _____ the boss to get here.
10. I'm interested _____ photography, but I'm not very good _____ taking photographs!

4A

future forms: *will / shall* and *going to*

will / shall

1 Predictions   ② 38))
Who do you think **will win** tomorrow's game?
The climate probably **won't change** much in the next five or ten years.

2 Future facts
I'll be at work on Monday.
The election **will be** on 6 May.

3 Instant decisions
A Is that the phone ringing?
B Yes, I think so. **I'll get** it.

4 Promises
A Have you been using my laptop? You didn't switch it off.
B Oh sorry. **I'll remember** next time.
A The battery's almost run down!
B Sorry. I promise I **won't do** it again.

5 Offers and suggestions
I'll cook dinner tonight.
Shall I **throw away** this bread?
What **shall** I **do** with my old phone?
Where **shall** we **go** for lunch today?

We use *will | won't* + infinitive:

1 to ask for or make predictions about what we think or believe will happen.
2 for future facts.
3 for instant decisions.
4 to make promises.
5 to offer to do something. If the offer is a question, we use *Shall I | we…?*
We also use *shall* with *I* and *we* to ask for suggestions.

going to

1 Plans   ② 39))
I'm **going to buy** a new phone this weekend.
He's **going to make** pizza for dinner.

2 Predictions
England **aren't going to win** – they're 3–0 down and there are only ten minutes left.
It's getting cloudy – the weather forecast says it's **going to rain** this afternoon.

We use *going to* + infinitive:

1 when there is a plan to do something – a decision has been made.
2 to make predictions when we feel more sure of the future, for example if we can see what's going to happen.

We can often use either *will* or *going to* for predictions.

> 🔍 **Present continuous for future arrangements**
> We use the present continuous when there is an arrangement to do something – something has been organized.
> *We're having Liz and Nick round for dinner tonight.*
> *I'm meeting my bank manager tomorrow.*
> There is sometimes very little difference between a plan and an arrangement, and we can often use either *going to* or the present continuous.

---

a Are the highlighted forms right ✓ or wrong ✗? Correct the wrong ones.

> Shall I take the rubbish out? ✓
> That's the phone – I'm going to get it. ✗ *I'll get*

1 A What are your plans for the weekend?
   B I'm going to do lots of gardening, and we're going to see a film on Sunday.

2 A These cardboard boxes are all empty. Will I put them in the bin?
   B No, I spoke to David and he's going to use them.

3 A I've decided to buy a new camera. I'll get one with a good zoom.
   B Do I help you choose one? I know a bit about cameras.

4 A Is Katie going to be at the party?
   B I don't know. Pass me my phone and I'm going to text her.

5 A Did you finish all the biscuits?
   B Yes, I'm really sorry. I'm going to leave you some next time.

b Complete with the correct form of *will*, *shall*, or *going to* and the verbs in brackets.

> We've decided that we *'re going to stay* in the UK for our holiday this year. (stay)

1 A It's really hot in here!
   B I _____ the air conditioning. (turn on)

2 Can I borrow £10? I _____ you back tomorrow. (pay)

3 A What are you planning to do with these old clothes?
   B I _____ them to the charity shop. (take)

4 A _____ I _____ some more bread when I go out? (buy)
   B Yes, please. I've decided I _____ sandwiches for lunch. (make)

5 Are you going home by bus? I _____ you a lift if you like. (give)

6 A Let's go to the cinema.
   B OK. What film _____ we _____? (see)

7 A What _____ you _____ with all those old bottles and jars? (do)
   B I _____ them to the bottle bank for recycling. (take)

8 A I told you not to use my laptop without asking!
   B Sorry, I _____ it again. (not do)

first and second conditionals

first conditional

> 1 If I **have** time, **I'll write** my CV tonight. (2)(45))
>   If you **don't work** hard, you **won't get** promoted.
> 2 If he **does** well at school, he **can go** to a good university.
>   I **might (may) go back** to college if I **can't find** a job.
>   If you **apply** for that job, you **must prepare** an up-to-date CV.
>   If they **fail** their exams, they **should take** them again.
> 3 If you **get** an interview, **think** carefully about what to wear.

We use the first conditional to talk about a possible future situation and its consequence.

1 The first conditional normally uses *if* + present simple, *will* / *won't* + infinitive.
2 We can also use other modal verbs instead of *will*, e.g. *can*, *might*, *may*, *must*, or *should*.
3 We can also use an imperative instead of *will*.

> **Unless**
> We can use *unless* instead of *if... not* in conditional sentences.
> *I won't come unless you come too.* (= I won't come if you don't come too.)

second conditional

> 1 If I **had** more money, I **wouldn't need** evening work. (2)(46))
>   If they **offered** you a part-time job, **would** you **accept** it?
> 2 I **might meet** more people if I **lived** in a hall of residence.
>   You **could apply** for a scholarship if you **got** a place to study in the US.
> 3 If he **was (were)** here, he'**d know** what to do.
>   **I'd take** it back to the shop if I **were** you.

We use the second conditional to talk about a hypothetical or imaginary situation, or one that we *don't* think is a possibility.

1 The second conditional normally uses *if* + past simple, *would* / *wouldn't* + infinitive.
2 We can use *might* or *could* instead of *would*.
3 When we use *be* in the *if* clause, we can use *was* or *were* after *I* / *he* / *she* / *it*.
  However, in the phrase *if I were you*, which is often used to give advice, only *were* is used. NOT ~~If I was you.~~

> **First or second conditional**
> The conditional we use depends on how likely the condition is. Compare:
> *If I have more time, I'll do it.* (I think it's a real possibility that I'll have time.)
> *If I had more time, I'd do it.* (I think it's unlikely or impossible that I'll have more time.)

---

a (Circle) the correct form.

If I go to university, *I'd study* / (*I'll study*) engineering.

1 If she had her own car, she *doesn't* / *wouldn't* need to borrow yours.
2 If I *had* / *have* a good degree, I'll get a better job.
3 You wouldn't always be late for work if you *get* / *got* an earlier bus.
4 We can't help you unless you *tell* / *told* us what the problem is.
5 If you *find* / *found* your phone, you can send me a text later.
6 *You'd* / *You'll* save time if you did your shopping online.
7 I *won't* / *wouldn't* go there unless I really had to.
8 They'd enjoy life more if they *didn't* / *don't* study all the time.
9 If you *can't* / *couldn't* find the street, just give me a ring.
10 If I *earned* / *earn* more, I could afford to go on an exotic holiday.

b Complete the sentences with the verbs in brackets.

I *wouldn't want* to do research if I didn't enjoy working on my own. (not want)

1 If I _____ to stay at university, I'll probably do a PhD or a master's degree. (decide)
2 If you didn't spend so much on clothes, you _____ borrow money all the time. (not have to)
3 I think my sister and her boyfriend _____ soon, if they can afford to pay for the wedding. (get married)
4 If I have time over the summer, I _____ for an internship. (apply)
5 I think Andy might get a scholarship if he _____ on working hard. (keep)
6 If we _____ a bigger house, we could rent a couple of rooms to students. (buy)
7 I might enjoy my job more if I _____ such awful colleagues. (not have)
8 If I _____ get a job, I won't retake my exams. (can)
9 My tutor says I must attend all the seminars if I _____ to fail. (not want)
10 I'd get more job offers if I _____ better qualified. (be)

5A

present perfect simple

Revise the basics

+		-	past participle
I **have**	I**'ve**	I **haven't**	
You **have**	You**'ve**	You **haven't**	
He / She / It **has**	He / She / It**'s**	He / She / It **hasn't**	**seen** the news.
We **have**	We**'ve**	We **haven't**	
They **have**	They**'ve**	They **haven't**	
Have you **seen** the news?		Yes, I **have**. / No, I **haven't**.	
Has he **seen** the news?		Yes, he **has**. / No, he **hasn't**.	

1 I**'ve been** to Brazil but I **haven't been** to Argentina. ③ 10))
  Have you **ever lost** your suitcase?
  She**'s never liked** skiing.
2 I don't believe it! We**'ve won** £500 on the lottery!
  He**'s just sent** me a text – I'll tell you what it says.
3 **Have** / **Haven't** you **had** breakfast **yet**?
  I **haven't talked** to her **yet** – I'm calling her later.
4 **A** **Have** you **painted** the kitchen?
  B Yes, and I**'ve already done** the bathroom too.
5 She**'s known** him **for twenty years**.
  I**'ve** only **worked** here **since last week**.
  He**'s been** out **all morning**.

1 We use the present perfect for past experiences when we don't say when they happened. If we say when they happened (*five minutes ago, yesterday, last week*, etc.) we use the past simple, e.g. *I've been to Brazil a few times. I went to Rio in 2013.*
2 We use the present perfect to give news. If something has happened very recently, we often use *just*.
3 We use the present perfect with *yet* to ask if something has happened, or to say that it hasn't happened but that it will.
4 We use the present perfect with *already* to say that something has happened earlier than expected.
5 We can use the present perfect to talk about situations that started in the past and have continued to the present. We don't use the present simple or the present continuous, e.g.
  I've lived here for three months. NOT *I live here for three months | I'm living here for three months.*
  • To express a period of time we often use *for* or *since*.
    We use *for* + a period of time, e.g. *for two minutes | ten years | ages | a long time.*
    We use *since* + a time in the past, e.g. *since this morning | 5.00 | September | 2004 | I was a child.*
  • We can use phrases with *all* to express a period of time, e.g. *all my life, all day, all year*, etc. We don't use *for* with *all*, e.g. *I've been here all day.* NOT *I've been here for all day.*

➤ For irregular past participles see **Irregular Verbs** *p.165.*

a (Circle) the correct form.

  We're late – the film (*has already started*) | *hasn't started yet.*

1 This programme's been on for *an hour | 10.30.*
2 I'm not really hungry because *I've already had | I haven't had* breakfast.
3 I've been to Canada but *I never went | I've never been* to the US.
4 We've known them since *we were at university | five years.*
5 I've only been at work for an hour but I've *just | already* done a lot.
6 They got married in May so *they're | they've been* married for six months.
7 You'll love New York – *have you been | did you go* there before?
8 He's lived here *since all his life | all his life.*
9 We've never been to Sweden but *we went | we've been* to Norway last year.
10 I moved to Paris eleven months ago so *I've lived | I live* here for nearly a year.

b Complete the sentences with the present perfect or past simple form of the verbs in brackets.

  Have you *ever been* to the Edinburgh Festival? (ever / be)

1 **A** When _____ you _____ here? (get)
  B I arrived at the weekend, so I _____ here for a few days. (only / be)
2 **A** _____ you _____ the weather forecast yet? (hear)
  B No, I _____ the radio. (just / turn on)
3 **A** Bad news – Ben _____ a bike accident. (have)
  B Oh no! When _____ that _____? (happen)
4 **A** Where's Linda?
  B I think she _____ for lunch. (just / go)
5 **A** _____ you _____ him at tennis? (ever / beat)
  B No, but I _____ a set the last time we played. (win)
6 **A** _____ he _____ his new job? (already / start)
  B Yes, his first day _____ last Monday. (be)
7 **A** How long _____ you _____ a motorbike? (have)
  B I _____ my first one twenty years ago. (buy)
8 **A** _____ you _____ that amazing documentary last night? (see)
  B No, I _____ it. (miss)

5B

present perfect continuous

Revise the basics

+		–	
I **have**	I**'ve**	I **haven't**	
You **have**	You**'ve**	You **haven't**	
He / She / It **has**	He / She / It**'s**	He / She / It **hasn't**	**been living**
We **have**	We**'ve**	We **haven't**	here all year.
They **have**	They**'ve**	They **haven't**	
Have you **been playing** much tennis?		Yes, I **have**. / No, I **haven't**.	
Has he **been playing** much tennis?		Yes, he **has**. / No, he **hasn't**.	

1 A What **have** you **been doing** lately?　　　　　　(3 16))
  B I**'ve been playing** a lot of tennis.
  She**'s been going** for a walk every morning this week.
  My friends **have been coming round** a lot recently.
2 A You look tired.
  B I**'ve been working** in the garden.
  A You're covered in paint.
  B Yes, I**'ve been decorating** the kitchen all day.
3 How long **have** you **been looking for** a new house?
  We**'ve been living** here since last year.
  It**'s been raining** all day.

1 We use the present perfect continuous with 'action verbs' for repeated actions that started in the past and have continued till now. We often use time expressions like *recently | lately.*

2 We use the present perfect continuous for continuous actions which have present results.

3 We use the present perfect continuous to ask or talk about situations which started in the past and are still happening now. We often use *for | since* or time expressions like *all day | all morning | all week.* We don't use the present continuous or the present simple, e.g.
  I've been waiting since ten o'clock.
  NOT ~~I'm waiting since ten o'clock.~~
  ~~I wait since ten o'clock.~~

• If you say *when* something happened, use the past simple, not the present perfect continuous, e.g.
  *I've been watching a lot of TV lately. I **saw** a great programme **last night.** NOT ~~I've been seeing a great programme last night.~~*

a Match the questions and answers, and complete the answers with the present perfect continuous.

	Why are your clothes so wet?	E
1	Why are you so late?	
2	It's hot in here, isn't it?	
3	Do you want a coffee?	
4	Are you going to move to London?	
5	Are you hungry?	
6	Is her English good?	
7	How's your new camera?	
8	Why are your hands all red?	
9	Do you think it's safe to drive?	
10	Have you lost a bit of weight?	

A I _____ strawberries. (pick)
B No, thanks. I _____ too much lately. (drink)
C Yes, I _____ to fix the air-conditioning. (try)
D I don't think so. It _____ very heavily. (snow)
E I *'ve been cleaning* the car. (clean)
F Not really. I _____ biscuits all afternoon. (eat)
G I hope so. We _____ a flat we can afford.
   (look for)
H Yes, she _____ it for a long time. (learn)
I Brilliant – I _____ pictures all day. (take)
J Yes, I _____ a lot of exercise. (do)
K I _____ in a traffic jam for two hours. (sit)

b (Circle) the correct form.

(I've been working)/ I'm working too hard lately.
1 *I've been living | I'm living* in a small village for five years.
2 *She's travelling | She's been travelling* a lot for work at the moment.
3 *I haven't been sleeping | I'm not sleeping* well lately.
4 I arrived yesterday and *I've been staying | I'm staying* for two weeks.
5 He's not answering his phone – maybe *he's driving | he's been driving.*
6 At last! *I'm waiting | I've been waiting* for you for ages.

7 I can't stand this weather – *it's raining | it's been raining* all week.
8 Be quiet! *I've been trying | I'm trying* to concentrate.
9 *I've been seeing | I'm seeing* a lot of my family recently.
10 I need a rest. *I'm cooking | I've been cooking* all day.

Adjective suffixes

1 DESCRIBING PEOPLE

a Add an ending to the nouns and verbs below to form adjectives. Write them in the correct column.

act /ækt/   assert /əˈsɜːt/   attract /əˈtrækt/   boss /bɒs/   cheer /tʃɪə/
create /kriˈeɪt/   envy /ˈenvi/   glamour /ˈglæmə(r)/   help /help/
impulse /ˈɪmpʌls/   mood /muːd/   possess /pəˈzes/   power /paʊə/
rebel /rɪˈbel/   rely /rɪˈlaɪ/   self /self/   sense /sens/   style /staɪl/

> **Word endings for adjectives**
> Many adjectives are formed by adding suffixes (= endings) such as *-able / -ible*, *-y*, *-ive*, *-ous*, and *-ful* to a noun or verb. Sometimes another small spelling change is required, e.g. losing a final *e* (*fame – famous*). Check the spelling changes in your dictionary. Knowing typical suffixes will help you to recognise that a new word is an adjective.

-able / -ible	-y	-ive	-ous	-ful	-ish
sociable responsible	lucky	aggressive sensitive *active*	ambitious	beautiful	childish

b **1 10))** Listen and check.

2 DESCRIBING PLACES AND THINGS

a Add an ending to the nouns and verbs on the right to form adjectives. Write them in the correct column.

afford /əˈfɔːd/   comfort /ˈkʌmfət/   desire /dɪˈzaɪə/
dirt /dɜːt/   expense /ɪkˈspens/   health /helθ/
impress /ɪmˈpres/   luxury /ˈlʌkʃəri/   noise /nɔɪz/
profit /ˈprɒfɪt/   risk /rɪsk/   space /speɪs/   stress /stres/
success /səkˈses/   suit /suːt/   use /juːs/

-able / -ible	-y	-ive	-ous	-ful
recognizable incredible *affordable*	easy	addictive	delicious dangerous	colourful

b **1 11))** Listen and check.

3 *-FUL* AND *-LESS*

> **-ful and -less**
> *-ful* and *-less* are suffixes which add the meaning 'with' or 'without' to the base word, e.g. *careful* = with care, *careless* = without care, *hopeful* = with hope, *hopeless* = without hope. However, not all words which can form an adjective with *-ful* can also form one with *-less*, e.g. we can say *successful* but NOT ~~successless~~, and not all words which can form an adjective with *-less* can also form one with *-ful*, e.g. we can say *endless* but NOT ~~endful~~.

a Look at the *-ful* adjectives in the charts in 1 and 2. Tick the ones that *can* form an adjective with *-less*.

b **1 12))** Listen and check.

4 DESCRIBING COLOURS

a Match the phrases to the four shades of blue.

  dark blue (also navy blue)
  greyish blue
  light blue (also pale blue)
  bright blue

b **1 13))** Listen and check. What does the suffix *-ish* means when you add it to another adjective, e.g. a colour?

c With a partner, say exactly what colour the things you are wearing are.

◀ *p.8*

Holidays

1 THINGS TO PACK

a Match the words and pictures.

- adaptor /əˈdæptə/
- brush /brʌʃ/
- comb /kəʊm/
- flip flops /ˈflɪp flɒps/
- guidebook /ˈgaɪdbʊk/
- hairdryer /ˈheədraɪə/
- insect repellent /ˈɪnsekt rɪˈpelənt/
- make-up /ˈmeɪkʌp/
- memory card /ˈmeməri kɑːd/
- nail scissors /ˈneɪl sɪzəz/
- (phone) charger /ˈtʃɑːdʒə/

- pyjamas /pəˈdʒɑːməz/
- raincoat /ˈreɪnkəʊt/
- razor /ˈreɪzə(r)/
- *1* sunscreen /ˈsʌnskriːn/
- swimming trunks /ˈswɪmɪŋ trʌŋks/
- swimsuit /ˈswɪmsuːt/
- toothbrush /ˈtuːθbrʌʃ/
- toothpaste /ˈtuːθpeɪst/
- towel /ˈtaʊəl/
- wash bag /ˈwɒʃ bæg/ (also sponge bag) /ˈspʌndʒ bæg/

b **1 24)))** Listen and check.

c With a partner, say which things in **a** you always pack when you go on holiday. Are there any other things that you always pack?

2 VERB PHRASES WITH *GO*

a Match the phrases and pictures.

go + verb + ing
- camping
- hiking
- sailing
- *1* scuba diving
- sightseeing
- snorkelling
- waterskiing
- windsurfing

b Match the phrases.

go on + noun

1 go on a cruise	a of a city or a building
2 go on a (guided) tour	b with everything included
3 go on a safari	c on a lake
4 go on a boat trip	d round the Mediterranean
5 go on a package holiday	e to see wildlife

c **1 25)))** Listen and check your answers to **a** and **b**.

d With a partner, ask and answer about each phrase.

Have you ever been camping?

Yes, I have. I went camping last summer. Have you ever...?

3 MORE VERB PHRASES

a Complete the verb phrases.

climb do get have pack see ~~sunbathe~~ unpack watch

1 *sunbathe* on the beach
2 _____ sunburnt (bitten by insects)
3 _____ the sights (a show)
4 _____ the sunset (sunrise)
5 _____ voluntary work (a course)
6 _____ a mountain (a hill)
7 _____ and _____ your bags
8 _____ a massage (spa treatments)

b **1 26)))** Listen and check.

◀ p.14

Shops and services

1 PLACES

a Match the words and pictures.

baker's /'beɪkəz/

butcher's /'bʊtʃəz/

chain store /'tʃeɪn stɔː/

chemist's /'kemɪsts/

delicatessen /delɪkə'tesn/
(also deli /'deli/)

DIY store /diː aɪ 'waɪ stɔː/
(also hardware store
/'haːdweə stɔː/)

dry cleaner's /draɪ 'kliːnəz/

estate agent's /ɪs'teɪt eɪdʒənts/

fishmonger's /'fɪʃmʌŋgəz/

florist's /'flɒrɪsts/

greengrocer's /'griːngrəʊsəz/

health food store /'helθ fuːd stɔː/

hypermarket /'haɪpəmaːkɪt/

jeweller's /'dʒuːələz/

launderette /lɔːn'dret/

market stall /'maːkɪt stɔːl/

newsagent's /'njuːzeɪdʒənts/

off-licence /'ɒf laɪsns/

1 stationer's /'steɪʃənəz/

travel agent's /'trævl 'eɪdʒənts/

b (1 38)) Listen and check.

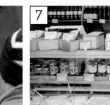

2 PHRASAL VERBS RELATED TO SHOPS AND SHOPPING

a Match the highlighted phrasal verbs and the definitions.

1 A lot of local shops and businesses have closed down because of the recession.

2 **A** Do you need any help?
   B No thanks, I just want to look round.

3 Did you know they're opening up a new Thai restaurant where that old French one used to be?

4 **A** Is there somewhere where I can try on this sweater?
   B Yes, the changing rooms are over there.

5 Excuse me, can you help me? I'm looking for a butcher's. Someone told me that there was one near here.

6 **A** Do you have these in a medium?
   B I'm sorry, we're out of mediums at the moment, but we should be getting some in soon.

a not have in stock

b put something on to see if it fits

c start trading or doing business

d stop trading or doing business

e try to find something

f walk round a place to see what there is

b (1 39)) Listen and check.

◀ *p.18*

🔍 Shop names with 's

- The names for many sorts of shops end in 's, which is short for 's shop, e.g. *baker's* = *baker's shop*, *chemist's* = *chemist's shop*.
- In the plural of these shops there is no apostrophe, e.g. *There are several bakers here.*
- Nowadays some shops sometimes use another word, e.g. *bakery* instead of *baker's*.

Other places to buy things in the UK

Charity shops sell second-hand items (especially clothes) which have been given to them by people to raise money for charity.

Pound shops sell a variety of cheap goods which cost one pound.

Craft fairs are events where you can buy handmade things, often made by local people.

Photography

1 DESCRIBING A PHOTO

a Look at the photos and complete the sentences with a word or phrase from the list. Use capital letters where necessary.

---
behind /bɪ'haɪnd/   in front of /ɪn 'frʌnt əv/   ~~in the background /'bækɡraʊnd/~~
in the <u>bottom</u> right-hand <u>corner</u> /'bɒtəm raɪt hænd 'kɔːnə/   in the <u>centre</u> /'sentə/
in the <u>distance</u> /'dɪstəns/   in the <u>foreground</u> /'fɔːɡraʊnd/
in the top right-hand <u>corner</u> /tɒp raɪt hænd 'kɔːnə/   on top of /ɒn 'tɒp əv/   <u>opposite</u> /'ɒpəzɪt/

---

b (2 14)) Listen and check.

Photo 1

1 *In the background* there's a mountain, and some low cloud.

2 _____ there's a grandmother and three children.

3 The boy in an orange T-shirt is standing _____ his grandmother.

4 _____ of the photo there's a building with lots of steps.

5 There's a small building that looks like a temple _____ a small hill.

Photo 2

6 _____ there's a woman standing on a terrace looking at the view.

7 The woman is standing _____ a low wall looking at the view.

8 _____ the woman there's a building with a tower that looks like a church.

9 _____ on the left you can just see an old building which looks like a ruin.

10 _____ there are two cypress trees.

🔍 **on top of** or **at the top of**

The bird is **on top of** the photo.

The bird is **at the top of** the photo.

---

2 TAKING PHOTOS

a Match the sentences halves.

1   *e*   You **use flash** when…
2   You **zoom in** when…
3   A photo can be **out of focus** if…
4   Many cameras have a **portrait setting** to use when…
5   A photo can be **blurred** if…
6   With good cameras you can use different **lenses**, e.g. a wide-angle lens, when…
7   You **enlarge** a photo when…

a   you are far away from something and you want to take a close-up of it.
b   you can't step far away from your subject, but you want to get all of it in the picture.
c   you move when you are taking it.
d   you want to take a photo of a person.
e   you want to take a photo somewhere dark, e.g. indoors or at night.
f   your camera isn't automatic and you haven't used the right settings.
g   you want to make it bigger.

b (2 15)) Listen and check.

◄ p.28

Rubbish and recycling

VOCABULARY BANK

1 RUBBISH: NOUNS AND PHRASAL VERBS

a Read the definitions for *rubbish* and *waste*. Then match the other nouns to their definitions.

nouns

bin /bɪn/   bin bag /'bɪn bæg/
dustman /'dʌstmən/
landfill site /'lændfɪl saɪt/
rubbish /'rʌbɪʃ/   waste /weɪst/
waste-paper basket /weɪst 'peɪpə bɑːskɪt/

1 *rubbish* — things that you throw away because you don't want them any more (AmE *garbage* or *trash*)
2 *waste* — materials that are not needed, and thrown away, e.g. *industrial ~, toxic ~*
3 _____ a container kept outside that you put rubbish in (also *dustbin*)
4 _____ a plastic bag which you put rubbish in and then throw away
5 _____ a small basket kept in a room where people throw away paper and small things
6 _____ the person whose job it is to take away the rubbish (also *refuse collector*, NAmE *garbage collector*)
7 _____ an area of land where large amounts of waste are covered with earth

b (2 32)) Listen and check.

c Complete the sentences with a phrasal verb from the list.

phrasal verbs

give away /gɪv ə'weɪ/   take away /teɪk ə'weɪ/
take out /teɪk 'aʊt/   throw away /θrəʊ ə'weɪ/

1 If that pen doesn't work, just _____ it _____. I hate having pens around that don't work.
2 Please could you _____ _____ the rubbish? I did it yesterday.
3 I'm moving house in a few weeks, and I've decided to _____ _____ a lot of books and clothes to a charity shop.
4 In many countries there are special containers for used glass and cardboard. People then come and _____ it _____ to be recycled.

d (2 33)) Listen and check.

2 PACKAGING

a Match the words and pictures.

▢	bottle /'bɒtl/
▢	can /kæn/
▢	cardboard box /'kɑːdbɔːd bɒks/
▢	carton /'kɑːtn/
1	jar /dʒɑː(r)/
▢	lid /lɪd/
▢	packet /'pækɪt/
▢	plastic bag /'plæstɪk bæg/
▢	polystyrene tray /pɒli'staɪriːn treɪ/
▢	pot /'pɒt/
▢	sell-by date /'sel baɪ deɪt/
▢	tin /tɪn/
▢	tub /tʌb/
▢	wrapper /'ræpə/

b (2 34)) Listen and check.

c What kind of packaging is normally used for…?

yoghurt   biscuits   olives   soft drinks
sardines   a washing machine
ice cream   milk

3 THE PREFIX RE-

a Complete the sentences with a verb from the list.

reapply /riːə'plaɪ/   recycle /riː'saɪkl/   reheat /riː'hiːt/
replay /riː'pleɪ/   rethink /riː'θɪŋk/   reuse /riː'juːz/

1 There's a bottle bank at the local supermarket where you can *recycle* all your glass bottles and jars.
2 Many supermarkets now charge extra for plastic bags. They prefer customers to have shopping bags which they can _____.
3 If you're not sure about the project, you should _____ the whole thing.
4 You can _____ your dinner in the microwave.
5 They'll have to _____ the match next Saturday.
6 You should _____ sunscreen every hour if you have fair skin.

b (2 35)) Listen and check.

◄ p.35

Study and work

1 HIGHER EDUCATION

a Read the text about University College London (UCL) and complete it with words from the list.

> campus /ˈkæmpəs/   dissertation /dɪsəˈteɪʃn/   faculties /ˈfækltiz/
> halls of residence /ˈhɔːlz əv ˈrezɪdəns/   lectures /ˈlektʃəz/
> postgraduates /pəʊstˈɡrædʒuəts/   professors /prəˈfesəz/
> seminars /ˈsemɪnɑːz/   thesis /ˈθiːsɪs/   tutor /ˈtjuːtə/
> undergraduates /ˌʌndəˈɡrædʒuəts/   webinars /ˈwebɪnɑːz/

UCL

Search UCL	GO

| DISCOVER UCL | STUDYING AT UCL | WORKING AT UCL | RESEARCH AT UCL |

University College London, also known as UCL, is one of London's most important universities. Founded in 1826, it is based in the Bloomsbury area of central London. The main ¹ _campus_ is located around Gower Street.

UCL currently has around 26,000 students, both ² _____ (students studying for their **first degree**) and ³ _____ (students studying for **further degrees**). Further degrees include a **master's degree**, usually a one-year course at the end of which students have to write a ⁴_____, or a **PhD** (doctorate), during which students have to write a doctoral ⁵_____.

UCL has around 4,000 **academic and research staff**, and 650 ⁶_____ (the highest ranked university teacher), which is more than any other British university. The research and teaching is divided into ten ⁷_____, e.g. Arts and Humanities, Engineering Sciences, Medical Sciences, etc.

Many students, particularly first year undergraduates and **overseas students**, live in ⁸_____. The majority of others find their own accommodation. Students are taught in **tutorials** (small groups of students with a ⁹_____), or through ¹⁰_____ (larger classes where students discuss or study with their teacher) or ¹¹_____ (where a large group of students listen to a talk but do not participate). Some teaching may also be in the form of ¹²_____ (seminars conducted over the internet).

Famous past students range from Alexander Graham Bell, the inventor of the telephone, and Mahatma Gandhi, to all the members of the pop group Coldplay, who met while at university there.

b (2 40)) Listen and check. What do the **bold** phrases mean?

c With a partner, say three things which are the same and three which are different about universities in your country.

2 APPLYING FOR A JOB OR COURSE

a Complete the gaps with a noun or verb from the list.

> apply   attend   experience   get   look
> qualifications   a referee   skills   work   write

What you may need to have

- ¹ _qualifications_ (e.g. a degree, a diploma)
- ² _____ (having done some work before)
- ³ _____ (e.g. languages, IT)
- ⁴ _____ (a person who would be prepared to recommend you) and their contact details

What you may need to do

- ⁵ _____ out for **job vacancies** or **courses**
- ⁶ _____ for a job (**a work permit**, a place on a course, **a grant / scholarship** = money that an organization gives sb to help pay for education)
- ⁷ _____ a **CV** and a **covering letter**
- ⁸ _____ an interview
- ⁹ _____ a **job offer** or an offer for a place on a course
- ¹⁰ _____ as an **intern** or a **trainee**

b (2 41)) Listen and check. What do the **bold** phrases mean?

🔍 **attend** or **assist**

attend = to be present at an event
Students must attend at least 95% of lectures to pass the course.
assist = to help sb to do sth
Jack was happy to assist Peter with gathering information for the report.

apprenticeship or **trial period**
apprenticeship = a period of time working for an employer to learn the particular skills needed for a job
The apprenticeship to be an electrician lasts three years and there is an exam you must pass at the end.
trial period = a fixed period of time which tests the ability or performance of sb before they are offered the job permanently
They agreed to employ me for a trial period of three months.

◀ p.38

Television

1 TV AND PHRASAL VERBS

a Label the picture with words from the list.

remote (control) /rɪ'məʊt (kən'trəʊl)/
screen /skriːn/   stand /stænd/
speakers /'spiːkəz/

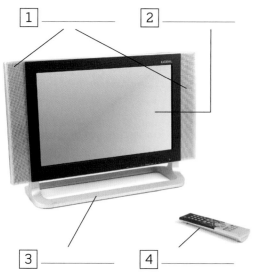

1 _____   2 _____
3 _____   4 _____

b Complete the sentences with a phrasal verb from the list.

be on /biː ɒn/
switch over /swɪtʃ 'əʊvə/
turn down /tɜːn 'daʊn/
turn off /tɜːn 'ɒf/
turn on /tɜːn 'ɒn/
turn up /tɜːn 'ʌp/

1 Please _____ the TV = press a button to start it working (also *switch on*)
2 Please _____ the TV = press a button to stop it working (also *switch off*)
3 Please _____ the TV = make the volume louder
4 Please _____ the TV = make the volume quieter
5 The programme _____ now = it is being shown on TV now
6 Let's _____ to another channel = press a button to move to another channel

c (3 3))) Listen and check your answers to **a** and **b**.

2 TYPES OF PROGRAMME

a Match the TV screens with the types of programmes.

cartoons /kɑː'tuːnz/ (or animation /ænɪ'meɪʃn/)
chat shows /'tʃæt ʃəʊz/
commercials /kə'mɜːʃlz/ (or adverts /'ædvɜːts/)
cookery programmes /'kʊkəri 'prəʊgræmz/
current affairs programmes /'kʌrənt ə'feəz 'prəʊgræmz/
documentaries /dɒkju'mentriz/

drama series /'drɑːmə 'sɪəriːz/
live sport /laɪv 'spɔːt/
period dramas /'pɪəriəd 'drɑːməz/
quiz shows /'kwɪz ʃəʊz/
reality shows /ri'æləti ʃəʊz/
sitcoms /'sɪtkɒmz/
1 soaps /səʊps/
the news /ðə njuːz/
the weather forecast /'weðə 'fɔːkɑːst/

b (3 4))) Listen and check.

c Answer the questions with a partner.

1 What kind of programmes do you usually watch?
2 What do you never watch?
3 What's your favourite television programme of all time? What kind of programme was / is it?
4 What's the worst programme you have ever seen?

◀ p.44

The country

1 NATURE

a Match the words and pictures.

	bush /bʊʃ/		mud /mʌd/
	cliff /klɪf/		path /pɑːθ/
	fence /fens/		pond /pɒnd/
	field /fiːld/		rocks /rɒks/
	gate /geɪt/		sticks /stɪks/
	grass /grɑːs/		stones /stəʊnz/
	hedge /hedʒ/		stream /striːm/
	hill /hɪl/		valley /ˈvæli/
1	leaf (plural *leaves*) /liːf/ /liːvz/		wood /wʊd/

1

2

3

4

5

6

7

8

9

10

11

12

13

14

15

b ③11)) Listen and check.

> 🔍 **the country and the countryside**
> We normally use *the country* to talk about any area that is not a town or city, e.g. *I live in the country.* We use *the countryside* when we are talking about the scenery in the country, e.g. fields, woods, etc., usually in a positive way, e.g. *We stayed in a little village surrounded by beautiful countryside.*

2 ON A FARM

a Match the words and pictures.

1
2
3
4
5
6
7

	barn /bɑːn/
	cockerel /ˈkɒkərəl/
	cow /kaʊ/
	farmhouse /ˈfɑːmhaʊs/
	hens /henz/
	lambs /læmz/
	sheep /ʃiːp/

b ③12)) Listen and check.

c Complete the text with a verb or past participle from the list.

grow   harvested (x2)   pick   planted

In the UK, especially in the east of England, a lot of farmers ¹_____ cereals (for example, **wheat**), vegetables, and fruit. Most **crops** are ²_____ in the early spring and are ³_____ in the summer. For example wheat is ⁴_____ in August, and most potatoes from June onwards. Soft fruits like strawberries are usually **ripe** in June and July, and many farms invite people to come and ⁵_____ their own fruit.

d ③13)) Listen and check. What do you think the bold words mean?

◀ p.48

Appendix

Dependent prepositions

prepositions after verbs

I **agree with** my boss **about** the problem.
He **apologized for** being late.
She **applied for** the job.
We always **argue about** money.
I used to **argue with** my sister a lot.
We **arrived at** the airport at 6.00 a.m.
We **arrived in** Paris in the evening.
I don't **believe in** ghosts.
That bag **belongs to** me.
I can't **choose between** these two shirts.
Our weekend plans **depend on** the weather.
I **dreamt about** my grandfather last night.
They all **laughed at** me when I fell over.

I'm **looking forward to** my holiday.
I'll **pay for** your coffee.
We all **posed for** a photograph.
I **prefer** taking the train **to** flying.
You can always **rely on** your parents.
He **reminds** me **of** an old school friend.
She **shared** her sweets **with** my son.
They **smiled at** me.
I love **spending** money **on** clothes.
They **succeeded in** climbing the mountain.
I **talked to** the hotel manager **about** my room.
Are you **waiting for** someone?
Don't **worry about** it, it's not a problem.

prepositions after adjectives

She's **angry about** her salary.
She's **angry with** her boss.
He's very **close to** his father.
The film is **different from** the book.
I'm really **disappointed with** these photos.
She's **excited about** her new job.
Oxford is **famous for** its university.
I'm **fed up with** waiting. Let's go!
He's very **fond of** his teacher.
I'm **frightened** / **afraid** / **scared of** snakes.
He's **good** / **bad at** remembering names.
Vegetables are **good for** you.
She's **interested in** French literature.
I'm not very **keen on** fast food.
They were very **kind to** me.
He's **married to** my best friend.
I'm very **pleased with** my progress.
I'm **proud of** my children.
I'm **ready for** a holiday.
He's **responsible for** the sales team.
Don't be **rude to** him.
We're **sorry about** what happened.
They're **tired of** working every day.
She's **worried about** her car.

Verb patterns

verb + infinitive with *to*

be able (*to swim*)
afford (*to buy a flat*)
agree (*to help someone*)
arrange (*to meet*)
choose (*to do something*)
decide (*to buy a new computer*)
expect (*to fail an exam*)
forget (*to lock the door*)
help (*to cook dinner*)
hope (*to go to university*)
learn (*to swim*)
manage (*to escape*)
need (*to leave early*)
offer (*to do the washing-up*)
plan (*to start a family*)
pretend (*to be someone else*)
promise (*to pay someone back*)
refuse (*to cooperate*)
remember (*to buy a present*)
seem (*to be broken*)
try (*to repair the car*)
want (*to go on holiday*)
would like (*to travel abroad*)

verb + gerund (*-ing*)

admit (*stealing the money*)
avoid (*driving in the city centre*)
can't stand (*queueing*)
deny (*being involved*)
dislike (*going shopping*)
enjoy (*playing tennis*)
feel like (*going home early*)
finish (*having breakfast*)
hate (*being late*)
imagine (*living without the Internet*)
keep (*forgetting his name*)
like (*cooking for friends*)
love (*reading*)
mind (*working in the evenings*)
miss (*living in Spain*)
practise (*playing a difficult piece*)
prefer (*running to swimming*)
recommend (*opening a bank account*)
spend (*a long time practising*)
stop (*raining*)
suggest (*seeing a doctor*)

verb + object + infinitive with *to*

advise (*me to pay cash*)
allow (*us to leave early*)
ask (*her to help*)
invite (*us to go away for the weekend*)
need (*you to fill in a form*)
order (*him to sit down*)
persuade (*me to come to the party*)
teach (*me to play the piano*)
tell (*them to be quiet*)
want (*you to explain*)

verb + object + infinitive without *to*

let (*me stay up late*)
make (*me tidy my room*)

Irregular verbs

Infinitive	Past simple	Past participle
be /biː/	was /wɒz/	been /biːn/
beat /biːt/	beat	beaten /ˈbiːtn/
become /bɪˈkʌm/	became /bɪˈkeɪm/	become
begin /bɪˈɡɪn/	began /bɪˈɡæn/	begun /bɪˈɡʌn/
bite /baɪt/	bit /bɪt/	bitten /ˈbɪtn/
break /breɪk/	broke /brəʊk/	broken /ˈbrəʊkən/
bring /brɪŋ/	brought /brɔːt/	brought
build /bɪld/	built /bɪlt/	built
buy /baɪ/	bought /bɔːt/	bought
can /kæn/	could /kʊd/	–
catch /kætʃ/	caught /kɔːt/	caught
choose /tʃuːz/	chose /tʃəʊz/	chosen /ˈtʃəʊzn/
come /kʌm/	came /keɪm/	come
cost /kɒst/	cost	cost
cut /kʌt/	cut	cut
do /duː/	did /dɪd/	done /dʌn/
draw /drɔː/	drew /druː/	drawn /drɔːn/
dream /driːm/	dreamt /dremt/ / dreamed /driːmd/	dreamt / dreamed
drink /drɪŋk/	drank /dræŋk/	drunk /drʌŋk/
drive /draɪv/	drove /drəʊv/	driven /ˈdrɪvn/
eat /iːt/	ate /eɪt/	eaten /ˈiːtn/
fall /fɔːl/	fell /fel/	fallen /ˈfɔːlən/
feel /fiːl/	felt /felt/	felt
find /faɪnd/	found /faʊnd/	found
fly /flaɪ/	flew /fluː/	flown /fləʊn/
forget /fəˈget/	forgot /fəˈɡɒt/	forgotten /fəˈɡɒtn/
get /get/	got /ɡɒt/	got
give /ɡɪv/	gave /ɡeɪv/	given /ˈɡɪvn/
go /ɡəʊ/	went /went/	gone /ɡɒn/
grow /ɡrəʊ/	grew /ɡruː/	grown /ɡrəʊn/
hang /hæŋ/	hung /hʌŋ/	hung
have /hæv/	had /hæd/	had
hear /hɪə/	heard /hɜːd/	heard
hide /haɪd/	hid /hɪd/	hidden /hɪdn/
hit /hɪt/	hit	hit
hurt /hɜːt/	hurt	hurt
keep /kiːp/	kept /kept/	kept
know /nəʊ/	knew /njuː/	known /nəʊn/

Infinitive	Past simple	Past participle
lay /leɪ/	laid /leɪd/	laid
learn /lɜːn/	learnt /lɜːnt/	learnt
leave /liːv/	left /left/	left
lend /lend/	lent /lent/	lent
let /let/	let	let
lie /laɪ/	lay /leɪ/	lain /leɪn/
lose /luːz/	lost /lɒst/	lost
make /meɪk/	made /meɪd/	made
mean /miːn/	meant /ment/	meant
meet /miːt/	met /met/	met
pay /peɪ/	paid /peɪd/	paid
put /pʊt/	put	put
read /riːd/	read /red/	read /red/
ride /raɪd/	rode /rəʊd/	ridden /ˈrɪdn/
ring /rɪŋ/	rang /ræŋ/	rung /rʌŋ/
run /rʌn/	ran /ræn/	run
say /seɪ/	said /sed/	said
see /siː/	saw /sɔː/	seen /siːn/
sell /sel/	sold /səʊld/	sold
send /send/	sent /sent/	sent
set /set/	set	set
sew /səʊ/	sewed /səʊd/	sewn /səʊn/
shine /ʃaɪn/	shone /ʃɒn/	shone
shut /ʃʌt/	shut	shut
sing /sɪŋ/	sang /sæŋ/	sung /sʌŋ/
sit /sɪt/	sat /sæt/	sat
sleep /sliːp/	slept /slept/	slept
speak /spiːk/	spoke /spəʊk/	spoken /ˈspəʊkən/
spend /spend/	spent /spent/	spent
stand /stænd/	stood /stʊd/	stood
steal /stiːl/	stole /stəʊl/	stolen /ˈstəʊlən/
swim /swɪm/	swam /swæm/	swum /swʌm/
take /teɪk/	took /tʊk/	taken /ˈteɪkən/
teach /tiːtʃ/	taught /tɔːt/	taught
tell /tel/	told /təʊld/	told
think /θɪŋk/	thought /θɔːt/	thought
throw /θrəʊ/	threw /θruː/	thrown /θrəʊn/
understand /ʌndəˈstænd/	understood /ʌndəˈstʊd/	understood
wake /weɪk/	woke /wəʊk/	woken /ˈwəʊkən/
wear /weə/	wore /wɔː/	worn /wɔːn/
win /wɪn/	won /wʌn/	won
write /raɪt/	wrote /rəʊt/	written /ˈrɪtn/

Vowel sounds

	usual spelling		! but also
fish	**i**	risky bin lid tin sitcom since	pretty women busy decided village physics
tree	**ee** **ea** **e**	sheep screen stream leaf recycle thesis	people machine key field receipt
cat	**a**	pack campus active cash packet stand	plaits
car	**ar** **a**	carton charger starter jar craft drama grass	aunt laugh heart
clock	**o**	bossy rock top bottom off on	watch want wash sausage because
horse	**(o)or** **al** **aw**	torch corkscrew stall fall awful saw	war quarter pour fought saucer caught audience board
bull	**u** **oo**	bush butcher's wood cookery look good	could should would woman
boot	**oo** **u*** **ew**	spoon zoom glue true screw crew	suitcase cruise shoe move soup through queue
computer	Many different spellings. /ə/ is always unstressed. <u>speaker</u> <u>spa</u>cious <u>a</u>round con<u>tain</u> prof<u>e</u>ssor		
bird	**er** **ir** **ur**	serve prefer dirty circle turn blurred	research work world worse journey
egg	**e**	pet hen lens sell fence selfish	friendly already healthy jealous many said

	usual spelling		! but also
up	**u**	brush dustman mug mud bucket jug	money front someone enough touch couple
train	**a*** **ai** **ay**	gate baker's nail waiter replay tray	break great weight straighten they grey
phone	**o*** **oa**	remote stone tone rope boat soap	grow show bowl although sew
bike	**i*** **y** **igh**	tie wire dry recycle light bright	buy eyes height
owl	**ou** **ow**	round out found foreground towel crowd	
boy	**oi** **oy**	noisy avoid oil join enjoy employ	
ear	**eer** **ere** **ear**	cheerful volunteer here we're clear hear	really idea period theatre series
chair	**air** **are**	airport repair fair hairdresser careful square	their there wear area
tourist	A very unusual sound. euro tour sure manicure luxurious		
/i/	A sound between /ɪ/ and /iː/. Consonant + *y* at the end of words is pronounced /i/. happy angry thirsty		
/u/	An unusual sound between /ʊ/ and /uː/. education usually situation		

* especially before consonant + *e*

○ short vowels　● **long** vowels　○ diphthongs

166

Consonant sounds

		usual spelling	! but also
parrot	**p** **pp**	plate packet adaptor trip opposite apply	
bag	**b** **bb**	bulb bin bag probably tub rubbish robbed	
key	**c** **k** **ck**	comb score keep trekking brick padlock	chemist's scholarship qualifications account
girl	**g** **gg**	greengrocer's guidebook forgetful vinegar aggressive luggage	
flower	**f** **ph** **ff**	florist's safari pharmacy photography cliff affairs	enough laugh
vase	**v**	valley vacancy travel envious CV shave	of
tie	**t** **tt**	tutor teapot stick start batteries bottle	asked passed
dog	**d** **dd**	drill handle comedy hairdryer addictive middle	planted bored
snake	**s** **ss** **ce/ci**	swimsuit likes bossy dissertation fence cinema	science scene cycle
zebra	**z** **s**	quiz razor easy newsagent's loves reuse	
shower	**sh** **ti (+ vowel)** **ci (+ vowel)**	shop toothbrush childish cash ambitious stationer's delicious facial	sugar sure machine chef
television	An unusual sound. revision decision massage usually		

		usual spelling	! but also
thumb	**th**	throw rethink thread path tablecloth maths toothpaste	
mother	**th**	the that with weather sunbathe together	
chess	**ch** **tch** **t (+ure)**	chat chicken stretch match lecture future	
jazz	**j** **g** **dge**	jeweller's pyjamas dangerous package hedge bridge	
leg	**l** **ll**	lay lucky until reliable skill rebellious	
right	**r** **rr**	result referee profitable story current carry	written wrong
witch	**w** **wh**	war waste webinar switch whistle which	one once DIY
yacht	**y** before **u**	yet yellow yoga yourself university argue	
monkey	**m** **mm**	memory stream mountain moody hammer swimming	lamb climb
nose	**n** **nn**	needle pond intern barn spinning thinner	knife know
singer	**ng** before **k**	unpacking flying string bring thanks pink	
house	**h**	hill hiking behind farmhouse unhappy perhaps	who whose whole

⬤ voiced ⬤ unvoiced

ACKNOWLEDGEMENTS FOR WORKBOOK

The authors and publisher are grateful to those who have given permission to reproduce the following extracts and adaptations of copyright material: p.9 Adapted extract from "Colour therapy", The Observer, 6 July 2008. Copyright Guardian News & Media Ltd 2008. Reproduced by permission. p10 Extracts from "Rights and Responsibilities" and "Visiting the UK", www.ukba.homeoffice.gov.uk, accessed 20 November 2013. Contains public sector information licensed under the Open Government Licence v2.0. p.19 Adapted extract from "Women FINALLY appreciate their mothers at the age of 23… and only after 183 rows" by Martha De Lacey, Daily Mail online 14 May 2013. Reproduced by permission of Solo Syndication. p.23 Extract from "Top 10 UK and Ireland Driving Tips" by Ferne Arfin. © 2013 Ferne Arfin (http://gouk.about.com/). Used with permission of About Inc., which can be found online at www. about.com. All rights reserved. p.28 Adapted extract from "Top 25 Young Entrepreneur Success Stories" by Nicholas Tart, http://juniorbiz. com, 3 September 2010. Reproduced by kind permission of Nick Tart. p.34 Information taken from http://www.parksidefarmpyo.co.uk, 14th October 2013. Reproduced by kind permission of FJ Whitman & Sons Ltd, Parkside Farm.

Although every effort has been made to trace and contact copyright holders before publication, this has not been possible in some cases. We apologise for any apparent infringement of copyright and if notified, the publisher will be pleased to rectify any errors or omissions at the earliest opportunity.

Sources: www.bbc.co.uk; www.dailymail.co.uk; www.telegraph.co.uk; www.edibleapple.com; www.thisblogrules.com; www.wikihow.com; www.wikipedia.com

The publisher would like to thank the following for their kind permission to reproduce photographs: Farrhad Acidwalla p.28; Alamy pp.6 (PSL/CAT logo, Ingvar Björk/Twitter logo, TK/construction vehicle), 7 (Ruslan Kudrin), 13 (Stockpicz/phone), 30 (Lightroom Photos/man on moon), 33 (Paul White-Real Yorkshire), 35 (Bildagenturonline/Klein); Catherine Blackie p.13 (passport); Savannah Britt p.28; Corbis p.13 (Andre Davies/Robert Harding Specialist Stock/crab); Future Publishing p.6 (Gizmodo logo); Getty Images pp.4 (Elle Macpherson, Michael Ochs Archives/John Wayne) 6 (George Grall/caterpillar), 11 (Ian Woolcock), 17 (Blend Images/Mike Kemp), 19 (JGI/Jamie Grill), 20 (AFP), 22 (Craig Ferguson/photographers, Thomas Kokta/fishermen, Amos Chapple/ children playing in fountain), 25 (MCT), 26 (Alistair Berg), 30 (Prince William wedding, Queen Elizabeth 11 coronation, AFP/Barak Obama); Alonso Herranz Hudson p.21, Istockphoto p.31; North News and Pictures p.13; Rex Features pp.4 (Elton John), 13 (Steve Meddle/knife, Martin Lee/houmous), 15 (Alex Segre), 30 (Daily Mail / Bruce Adams/Olympics, Red Bull Content Pool/ Felix Baumgartner); Adorra Svitak p.28.

Illustrations by: Christina Hart Davies p.34, Dutch Uncle Agency/Atsushi Hara pp.5, 29, 32, Roger Penwill pp.8, 21.

Christina Latham-Koenig
Clive Oxenden

with Jane Hudson

ENGLISH FILE

Intermediate Plus Workbook **A** with key

OXFORD

Paul Seligson and Clive Oxenden are the original co-authors of
English File 1 and *English File 2*

OXFORD

UNIVERSITY PRESS

Contents

2

STUDY **LINK** iChecker

Audio: When you see this symbol **iChecker**, go to the iTutor disc in the back of your Student's Book. Load the disc in your computer.

1

Choose the 'iChecker' tab at the top left of the screen.

2

Choose the File. Then select the audio track from lesson A or B.

You can transfer audio to a mobile device, e.g. your iPod, from the '**MOBILE LEARNING**' folder on the disc.

File test: At the end of every File, there is a test. To do the test, select '**TEST**' from the '**FILE**' menu.

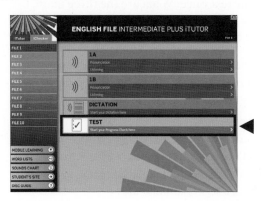

Dictation: At the end of every File, there is a dictation exercise. To do the dictation, select '**DICTATIONS**' from the '**FILE**' menu.

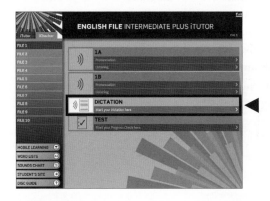

There is also more practice available on the English File website: www.oup.com/elt/englishfile

No copying or file sharing

> **I call everyone 'Darling' because I can't remember their names.**
> *Zsa Zsa Gabor, American actress*

1 READING & VOCABULARY

a Read the text once. What are the three main reasons the article gives for why people want to change their names?

b Read the text again and mark the sentences **T** (true) or **F** (false).

1 More people change their names today than in the past. _T_
2 Elton John changed his name because it wasn't very masculine. ___
3 Elle Macpherson changed her name because it wasn't very fashionable. ___
4 Some ordinary people change their names to the name of a celebrity. ___
5 The name 'Amy Winehouse' is more popular than the name 'Wayne Rooney'. ___
6 Shaun McCormack is happy with his new name. ___
7 Not everybody changes their name in search of fame. ___
8 Wafah Dufour changed her name because she separated from her husband. ___
9 A deed poll is an official document that says you have changed your name. ___
10 British people have to pay a lot of money to change their names. ___

ELLE MACPHERSON

JOHN WAYNE

ELTON JOHN

DON'T LIKE YOUR NAME?
THEN CHANGE IT!

These days, more and more people are changing their names. Last year in the UK, around 58,000 people decided that they wanted a different one. So why do people make this choice, and how easy is it to do so?

Celebrities change their names because they need to create a new image for themselves. In the past, male actors needed to have a masculine name, which is why Marion Robert Morrison chose to call himself John Wayne. Singers look for a name that their fans will remember, which explains why Reginald Kenneth Dwight decided to become Elton John. In the world of fashion, Eleanor Nancy Gow did not become successful until she changed her name to something more stylish: Elle Macpherson.

However, it is not only the famous who seek to change their name. Today, ordinary people do it too, and some of them do it for fun. They often find inspiration in their favourite singers or sporting heroes. In the past few years, 30 men have changed their names to Michael Jackson, 15 more to Wayne Rooney, and five women have become Amy Winehouse. But you have to feel sorry for Liverpool fan Shaun McCormack who changed his name to Fernando Torres six months before the Spanish footballer moved to a different club.

Other people have more serious reasons for changing their names. In many cases, they want to have more privacy, so they choose a name that will not stand out. John Smith is the most popular of these names, and recently, over 300 people have chosen it. Women who separate from their husbands often want to change their children's surnames to their own. Others want to escape the past or unwanted connection. After the events of 11 September 2001, US-born model Wafah Dufour took her mother's maiden name because she did not want to be associated with her uncle. His name was Osama bin Laden.

So how do you go about changing your name? In the UK, it is easy because no one is legally obliged to use the name on their birth certificate. However, if you want to change your name on your bank account or on official documents, you need proof. The proof can be a letter from a responsible person, such as a doctor, a public announcement in a local newspaper, or an official document called a deed poll. Deed polls are available free of charge on the internet, although some people prefer to pay a solicitor to help them with the papers.

The fixation with changing one's name shows no sign of slowing down, and there will probably be more Wayne Rooneys by this time next year. But whichever celebrity is popular at the time, their name will never be a match for the latest group of John Smiths.

c Match the highlighted words and expressions in the text to the definitions below:

1 change the general impression of yourself that you give to other people *create a new image*
2 start trying to do something _____
3 information that shows that something is true _____
4 try to do something _____
5 be easily seen or noticed _____
6 a lawyer who prepares legal documents _____
7 not seriously _____
8 the official document that states the date and place where you were born _____
9 feel sadness or pity for someone _____
10 a woman's family name before she gets married _____

2 PRONUNCIATION vowel sounds

a Write the names in the chart.

~~Adele~~ Alex Bill Chris Emily Eve James Joe
Kate Leo Mike Paula Ryan Sam Sean Sophie

1 æ	2 eɪ	3 e	4 iː
		Adele	

5 ɪ	6 aɪ	7 ɔː	8 əʊ

b **iChecker** Listen and check. Then listen again and repeat the names.

3 GRAMMAR pronouns

a Right (✓) or wrong (✗)? Correct the mistakes in the highlighted phrases.

1 My wife and I are having a baby girl. We're going to call her Eloise. ✓
2 I'd like you to meet my new boyfriend. Her name's Tom. ✗
  His name's Tom.
3 Do you know where my keys are? I can't find their. ☐
  _____
4 I'm staying at my sister's house when I'm in the UK. I always stay with her. ☐
  _____
5 We aren't going to Emma and Ian's wedding. They haven't invited ours. ☐
  _____
6 Can I borrow your book, please? I can't find the mine. ☐
  _____
7 We go everywhere by public transport. The bus stops right outside our house. ☐
  _____
8 I've got two nieces. Her names are Sarah and Laura. ☐
  _____
9 My car hasn't got any petrol. Let's take your. ☐
  _____
10 It's my dad's birthday tomorrow. I mustn't forget to call him. ☐

b Order the words to make sentences.

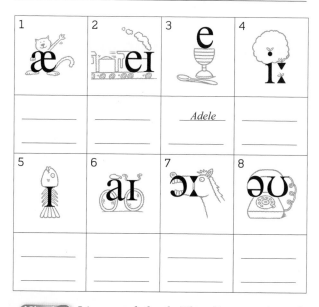

1 has / present / bought / His / him / a / girlfriend / surprise
  His girlfriend has bought him a surprise present.
2 parents / us / names / gave / very / My / unusual
  _____
3 friend / tonight / me / is / A / dinner / cooking / for
  _____
4 is / weekend / the / going / us / apartment / Our / to / neighbour / lend / his / for
  _____
5 is / dress / making / Becky's / a / her / party / mum / for
  _____
6 to / sell / car / to / I'm / my / neighbour / old / going / a
  _____
7 lot / writes / letters / of / friends / My / a / to / dad / old / his
  _____
8 box / gave / a / of / the / chocolates / We / hosts
  _____

5

c Complete the dialogues. Change the word order in the answer and use pronouns for the direct and indirect objects.

1 A Who cooks your grandfather his lunch?
   B My aunt _cooks it for him._
2 A Who sent Sophie those flowers?
   B Her husband _____.
3 A Who is reading the children the story?
   B Their grandmother _____.
4 A Who lent your brother the money?
   B My parents _____.
5 A Who found you your flat?
   B A colleague _____.
6 A Who brought you and your brothers and sisters those presents?
   B Our grandparents _____.
7 A Who is going to buy your girlfriend a car?
   B Her father _____.
8 A Who showed you the email?
   B My best friend _____.

4 LISTENING

a Match the logos with the company's description.

GIZMODO   manufacturer of construction vehicles

social networking site

design and technology blog

b **iChecker** Listen to a radio programme where a guest is giving advice on how to name a company. Answer the questions with the company names in **a**.

Which company's name?
1 is the right length _____
2 is a word you can't find in the dictionary _____
3 has a story behind it _____

c Listen again and complete the sentences. Use one word in each space.

1 Good company names often have _____ syllables.
2 To choose a name, you first have to _____ ideas.
3 Then you should wait for at least a _____.
4 The best names are the names you _____.
5 Another idea is to _____ a new word.
6 You can also change the _____ of a word in the dictionary.
7 A caterpillar is a small _____.
8 Somebody thought that the new tractor _____ like a caterpillar.
9 The name 'Caterpillar' shows that you can find _____ anywhere.

d Listen again with the audio script on *p.69* and try to guess the meaning of any words you don't know. Then check in your dictionary.

Man needs colour to live. It's just as necessary an element as fire or water.

Fernand Léger, French painter, sculptor, and film maker

1B True colours

1 VOCABULARY adjective suffixes

a Make adjectives from the nouns and verbs in the list, and complete the sentences.

> ~~ambition~~ boss cheer create glamour
> possess power rely self social

1 Jack is extremely ___ambitious___. He'd like to be the company director.
2 My colleague is really _____. She's always telling me what to do.
3 Dave's girlfriend is very _____. She doesn't let him talk to other girls.
4 My sister is always _____. She looks happy all the time.
5 Jane's husband is really _____. He only ever thinks of himself.
6 My best friend is very _____. She's always there when I need her.
7 Mike is really _____. He enjoys being with other people.
8 My brother's wife is very _____. She looks like an actress!
9 He's a very _____ businessman. He has a lot of influence over other people.
10 Anna is really _____. She's made some wonderful sculptures.

b Complete the text with the adjective form of the words in brackets. In some cases, you may need to add a negative prefix (*un-*) as well as a suffix to the word.

> In the past, very few people ate at the restaurant on the corner of my road because it was dark and ¹___dirty___ (dirt) inside. It was also very ²_____ (noise) because the owner liked loud music. In the end, it closed down because it was ³_____ (profit). Last year, the restaurant changed hands and now it is ⁴_____ (recognize). The new owner has painted the walls yellow, so it looks cleaner and much more ⁵_____ (space). He has bought new tables and chairs, which are more ⁶_____ (comfort) than the old ones, and he has also changed the menu. The old menu was full of ⁷_____ (health) fast food like burgers and chips, but now they serve ⁸_____ (impress) three-course meals. We often go there for Sunday lunch, because the food is quite ⁹_____ (afford).

2 PRONUNCIATION word stress

a <u>Underline</u> the stress on the words. Then write them in the correct column in the table.

> ~~active~~ ad|dic|tive ag|gres|sive de|sir|able
> en|vi|ous in|ex|pen|sive ir|re|spon|sible re|bel|li|ous
> sens|ible styl|ish un|at|trac|tive un|suc|cess|ful

Stress on first syllable	Stress on second syllable	Stress on third syllable
active	_____	_____
_____	_____	_____
_____	_____	_____
_____	_____	_____

b (iChecker) Listen and check. Then listen and repeat the adjectives.

3 GRAMMAR adjectives

a Right (✓) or wrong (✗)? Correct the incorrect phrases.

1 Blue eyes are less common than brown eyes. ✓
2 I like the hat purple best. ___the purple hat best___ ✗
3 Your glasses are more stylish that mine. ☐
   _____
4 She bought two differents jackets in the sale. ☐
   _____
5 Silver isn't as expensive than gold. ☐
   _____
6 My best friend is the more reliable person I know. ☐
   _____
7 Your hair is more dark than mine. ☐
   _____
8 My aunt wears clothes very colourful. ☐
   _____
9 These are the most comfortable jeans I've ever bought. ☐
   _____
10 Yellow is popularer than red this season. ☐
   _____

7

b Complete the dialogue with *one* or *ones* where neccessary.

1 A Which is your coat?
  B The red __one__ .

2 A Which biscuits shall I get?
  B The chocolate _____ . They are my favourite.

3 A Shall I use brown or white bread for the sandwiches?
  B Brown _____ . There isn't any white left.

4 A Where's your car?
  B Over there. It's the green _____ .

5 A Do you prefer Chinese or Indian food?
  B Indian _____ . I love really spicy food.

6 A Which earrings do you like best?
  B The gold _____ . They look great.

c Complete the sentences with the correct comparative or superlative form of the adjectives. In some cases, more than one answer may be possible.

1 Michelle is the __quietest__ person in our office. (quiet)

2 I was _____ than my husband by our daughter's new haircut. (shocked)

3 My friend's new boyfriend is the _____ person I know. (stupid)

4 The person who is _____ about the birth is the baby's grandmother. (thrilled)

5 My sister is _____ than me. (clever)

6 I'm _____ in class this year than I was last year. (bored)

7 I've never been _____ than when I bought my first flat. (stressed)

d Complete the sentences with *much* or *a bit* + the comparative form of an adjective from the list.

~~assertive~~ good polite short spacious

1 His girlfriend is __much more assertive__ than he is. She really says what she thinks.

2 I'm _____ than my brother. He's 1.82m and I'm 1.80m.

3 My children are _____ than my sister's. Hers never even say 'please' or 'thank you'.

4 I'm feeling _____ than yesterday, but I don't think I'll be able to go back to work till next week at the earliest.

5 My flat is _____ than the old one. It's 80m², and the old one was 70m².

4 READING

a Read the text and complete it with the missing headings.

A **WHAT RESULTS CAN YOU EXPECT?**
B **WHO CAN BENEFIT FROM IT?**
C **IS THERE ANY EVIDENCE THAT IT WORKS?**
D ~~**WHAT IS IT?**~~
E **WHERE DID IT ORIGINATE?**

b Read the text again and choose a, b, or c.

1 Experts think that colour therapy …
  a is good for patients' minds and bodies.
  b helps people who are under a lot of pressure.
  c should only be done in one way.

2 According to Ingrid Collins, colour therapy can make people feel …
  a hungrier.
  b less moody.
  c more active.

3 Dr Max Lüscher used colour therapy to treat his patients' …
  a medical problems.
  b psychological problems.
  c family problems.

4 June McLeod thinks that colour therapy …
  a should only be used by certain people.
  b can be used by people of all ages.
  c shouldn't be used by very ill people.

5 In general, colour therapy makes people feel …
  a more assertive.
  b less aggressive.
  c more ambitious.

c Match the highlighted words in the text to the definitions below.

1 small electric lamps that you hold in your hand __torches__
2 showed _____
3 working at the same time or speed _____
4 a meeting with somebody to get advice _____
5 sad, depressed _____
6 helps something to develop _____
7 ill people _____
8 something that is done to make somebody look good or feel better _____
9 the smallest units of living matter that can exist on it's own _____
10 long rolls of a kind of paper with writing on them _____

COLOUR THERAPY

Colour therapists believe that the seven colours of the rainbow relate to the body's seven main energy centres. So, if you're feeling blue, a multi-coloured treatment could be just what you need.

1 _D_

According to the experts, the different colours in the spectrum affect the body's inner vibrations. If your vibrations are not synchronized, colour therapy can help to restore the balance. This will improve your mood and your physical health. There are different types of colour therapy. Many therapists shine coloured lights on the body, and some give their patients coloured silks to wear. Others use different coloured liquids in bottles, or small torches to shine coloured light at the relevant pressure points on the body.

2 ____

Several studies have been done on the effects of colour. In 1958, an American scientist called Robert Gerard did some research which showed that the colour red can make us feel anxious, while the colour blue promotes calm. The results also revealed that colour can affect appetite, blood pressure, and aggression. Consultant psychologist Ingrid Collins believes that colour therapy can affect our energy levels. The atoms in all the cells of the human body consist of particles of energy that are always moving. When colour is applied to the body, the cells receive more energy.

3 ____

Papyrus scrolls dating back to 1550BC suggest that the ancient Egyptians used colour to treat the sick. Colour therapy also appears in Ancient Chinese texts. The treatment became more common during the 20th century, when Swiss psychologist Dr Max Lüscher developed the Lüscher-Colour-Diagnostic test. During the test, a person is asked to rank eight colours in order of preference. The results are said to show your worries and their solutions.

4 ____

According to therapist June McLeod, colour therapy is suitable for everyone from the young to the old. She suggests that it can help people suffering from all sorts of problems, including stress, insomnia and even serious illnesses.

5 ____

After a session of colour therapy, people usually feel more positive and more in control of their lives. In addition to your strengths, it may also show you your weaknesses, so that you can do something about them. According to the experts, when people leave a consultation, they have a feeling of freshness and a sense of power that they have never experienced before.

5 LISTENING

a   iChecker Listen to an interior designer giving advice on which colours to paint each of the rooms of a house. Which colours doesn't he mention?

beige	black	blue	brown	cream	green
grey	orange	pink	purple	red	yellow

b   Listen again and complete the notes.

DINING ROOM
Use browns, reds, and oranges – they stimulate the
1 _appetite_ .
Avoid 2_____ – it stops people feeling hungry.

KITCHEN
Use colours that match the 3_____.
Mix strong colours with 4_____ colours.
Avoid 5_____ _____ and green.

LIVING ROOM
Consider the size and the 6_____.
Use warm colours to make the room look 7_____.
Use 8_____ to make the room more formal.

BEDROOM
Use 9_____ _____, green, or pink for a relaxing atmosphere.
Avoid red and 10_____ _____ – too intense and stimulating.

BATHROOM
Use light blue and 11_____ _____ for a spa effect.
Avoid 12_____ _____ – they make the room seem smaller.

---

c   Listen again with the audio script on *p.69* and try to guess the meaning of any words that you don't know. Then check in your dictionary.

USEFUL WORDS AND PHRASES

Learn the words and phrases.

reveal /rɪˈviːl/	bizarre /bɪˈzɑː/
analysis /əˈnæləsɪs/	a wide range
exchange /ɪksˈtʃeɪndʒ/	/ə waɪd reɪndʒ/
rarely /ˈreəli/	pleasant /ˈpleznt/
dye your hair	subtle /ˈsʌtl/
/daɪ jɔː heə/	shade (of a colour) /ʃeɪd/

---

1 REPORTING LOST LUGGAGE

Complete the dialogue between a passenger (P) and an attendant (A).

P Hello. I'm afraid my luggage hasn't ¹ **a**_rrived yet_ .
A Right. Where have you come from?
P From Madrid. The ²**f**_____ number is EZY3065.
A How many bags are missing?
P ³**J**_____ one – a rucksack.
A Can you describe it for me? What size is it?
P Oh, it's a bright blue ⁴**m**_____ **s**_____ rucksack.
A And what was in it?
P Clothes, toiletries, all my personal ⁵**b**_____ .
A Can I have your ⁶**c**_____ number in the UK?
P Yes, my number is 001 303 298 836.

2 SOCIAL ENGLISH

Complete the dialogues with the phrases in the box.

Allow me	isn't it	let me
miss you	~~That's awful~~	your day

1 A There was an accident on the road this morning so I was sitting in a queue for 2 hours.
   B Oh no! _That's awful_ .
   A Then I ran out of petrol just 4 miles before the service station.
   B It's not _____, is it?
2 A I'll put my bag in the boot.
   B No, no, _____ take that.
   A I'm afraid it's rather heavy.
   B You've carried it all the way here. _____.
3 A I can't believe you're so far away.
   B Yes, I know. It's strange, _____?
   A I really _____.
   B Me, too.

3 READING

a Read the text and answer the questions.

1 Which documents does a European national need to enter the UK?
2 Can the daughter of a European national come and live with him or her in the UK?
3 How long can you stay in the UK on a visitor visa?
4 Can a general visitor get married in the UK?
5 When can a student visitor stay in the UK for longer than six months?

Coming to the UK
European nationals

As an EEA or Swiss national, you have the right of residence in the UK if:
• you are working here, or
• you can support yourself and your family in the UK.

Entering the UK
When you enter the UK, you must show your passport or national identity card. You should use the separate channel marked 'EEA/EU', where it is available.

Your family
If you have the right to live in the UK, your family may join you here. Your family is defined as:
• your spouse (husband or wife) or civil partner;
• any children or grandchildren of you, your spouse or your civil partner who are dependent on you; and
• the parents or grandparents of you, your spouse or your civil partner.

For more information, see Residence documents for European citizens.

Non-European nationals

If you come to the UK as a visitor, you are normally allowed to stay here for a maximum of six months. If you want to stay here for longer than six months, check in the Visas section to see if you qualify for another type of visa.

Tourism and visiting friends
If you want to visit the UK as a tourist or to stay with friends in the UK, you should apply to come here as a general visitor. There are restrictions on what you can do in the UK in this category. For example, you cannot get married.

Visiting to study
If you want to study in the UK for up to 6 months (or up to 11 months if you will be studying an English Language course), and you will not work while you are here, you can come here as a student visitor.

For further information on visas, go to our Visiting the UK page.

b Look at the highlighted words and expressions. What do you think they mean? Check your ideas in your dictionary.

Holidays are about experiences and people, and tuning into what you feel like doing at the moment. Enjoy not having a watch.

Evelyn Glennie, British musician

2A Pack and go!

1 VOCABULARY holidays

a Complete the sentences.

1 I'll have to wear a T-shirt in bed because I've forgotten my p_yjamas_ .

2 There are a lot of mosquitoes in our apartment. Let's buy some i_____ r_____.

3 I can't plug in my charger. I didn't bring an a_____.

4 I need to transfer some photos to my computer. The m_____ c_____ is full.

5 Please shave before we go out. Did you remember your r_____?

6 Put on some s_____ before we go to the beach. You don't want to burn.

7 Do you prefer to wear a bikini or a sw_____ on the beach?

8 My hair is a mess. Can I borrow a b_____?

9 I think you should put on some other shoes. Fl_____-fl_____ are fine for the pool, but not for hiking.

10 If you need to borrow some toothpaste, there's some in my w_____ b_____.

b Complete the sentences with the correct form of verb + - *ing* or *on* + noun. Use the words below.

~~a boat trip~~ camp a cruise hike package holidays
a safari sail sightsee surf a tour

1 They went _on a boat trip_ along the Seine while they were in Paris.

2 I need to buy some strong boots. I'm going _____ at the weekend.

3 My parents have got a boat, so they go _____ every summer.

4 Have you ever been _____ around the Mediterranean?

5 He kept on falling off the board when he went _____ yesterday.

6 I hate going _____. I don't like tents.

7 Did you go _____ of the Colosseum when you were in Rome?

8 We bought a guidebook so that we could go _____ on our own.

9 One day, I'd like to go _____. I'd love to see lions in the wild.

10 I don't like going _____. Everything is much too organized.

c Complete the postcard with the past simple form of a suitable verb.

Dear Debbie

Sorry I haven't called. When I ¹ _unpacked_ my bag I realized that I'd forgotten my phone charger! We're having a great time here in Greece. We spent the first three days in Athens, where we ²s_____ all the sights. The best day was when we ³cl_____ the hill to see the Acropolis. It was amazing! While we were in the capital, we went to a spa and I ⁴h_____ a massage. I loved it! Now we're here in Santorini, and it's beautiful. On our first day, we ⁵d_____ a diving course, which was exhausting. In the evening, we were so tired that we just sat in a café and ⁶w_____ the sunset. Yesterday, we ⁷s_____ on the beach all day and we ⁸g_____ very sunburnt. My back really hurts!

See you when we get back on Friday.

Love

Anna & Thomas

2 PRONUNCIATION /s/ and /z/

a Circle the word with a different sound.

1 S	2 Z	3 S	4 Z	5 S
flip-flops	clothes	cruise	razors	books
(shoes)	pyjamas	massage	phones	bottles
socks	shorts	passport	liquids	laptops
sights	towels	sunset	belts	jackets

b iChecker Listen and check. Then listen and repeat the words.

11

3 GRAMMAR present tenses

a Circle the correct form.

1 Be quiet! *I try* | *I'm trying* to read.

2 Ben *uses* | *is using* sunscreen all year round, not just in the summer.

3 His wife *always packs* | *packs always* his suitcase for him.

4 Pay attention! You *don't listen* | *aren't listening* to me.

5 Elizabeth *doesn't usually wear* | *don't usually wear* make-up on the beach.

6 My boyfriend *never is* | *is never* in a hurry.

7 Sam and Richard *go* | *are going* hiking every weekend.

8 Who *your girlfriend is talking to* | *is your girlfriend talking to*?

9 My brother *speaks* | *is speaking* good French because he has lived in France.

10 *You go* | *Do you go* to the same place on holiday every year?

b Complete the dialogue with the present simple or present continuous form of the verbs in brackets.

A What ¹ _are_ you _doing_ next weekend? (do)

B I ² _____ to a concert. (go)

A Where?

B In Glasgow.

A That's a long way to go for a concert! How ³ _____ you _____ there? (get)

B I ⁴ _____ on Friday morning. (fly) My flight ⁵ _____ at 14.25. (leave)

A What time ⁶ _____ the plane _____ in Glasgow? (arrive)

B We ⁷ _____ at 15.15 and then my sister ⁸ _____. (land / pick me up)

A When is the concert?

B On Friday evening. It ⁹ _____ at 8.30. (start) We ¹⁰ _____ some friends at 7 o'clock because we ¹¹ _____ to be late. (meet / not want)

A Well, I hope you have a great time.

B Thanks. I ¹² _____ really _____ to it! (look forward)

c Complete the sentences with the present simple or present continuous form of a verb from the list.

not agree	belong	~~depend~~	have	not matter
recognize	not see	taste	think	not want

1 We might go camping, but it _depends_ on the weather.

2 I _____ that man. I've seen him before.

3 Josh isn't sure about the summer. He _____ about doing voluntary work.

4 Whose bag is this? _____ to you?

5 I _____ to buy anything. I'm just looking.

6 Can you call back later? We _____ dinner.

7 That isn't right. I _____ with you at all.

8 I _____ why we have to get up early. We're on holiday!

9 This soup _____ horrible. I'm not going to eat it.

10 She needs a holiday. It _____ where.

4 READING

a Read the text quickly and answer the questions.

1 What was Paul Smith's destination?

2 Did he manage to get there?

b Read the text again and choose the correct answers.

1 Paul Smith is known as 'The Twitchhiker' because …
   a he tweeted about his hitchhiking adventures when he got back.
   b he has accepted help from Twitter users to travel.
   c he always tweets when he goes hiking in the country.

2 Paul thought up his plan while …
   a he was walking around the supermarket.
   b he was paying for his shopping.
   c he was driving home to his wife.

3 Thousands of Twitter users knew about Paul's plan because …
   a he sent a message to everyone he knew.
   b he gave an interview to a national newspaper.
   c he had the support of a famous person.

4 Paul completed the first part of his journey …
   a by sea.
   b by rail.
   c by road.

5 After Paul had been travelling for a week, he was …
   a in Europe.
   b in the USA.
   c in New Zealand.

6 When he reached the end of his trip, Paul felt …
   a disappointed that he couldn't get to Campbell Island.
   b worried about how he was going to get home.
   c grateful to the people who had helped him.

c Look at the highlighted words and phrases and try to work out their meaning. Then check the meaning and pronunciation in your dictionary.

Have Twitter, Will Travel

No matter what you think of Twitter, you have to admit that connecting over 200 million people worldwide is a pretty big achievement. One of the site's greatest fans is ex-radio DJ Paul Smith, also known as 'The Twitchhiker'. Thanks to Twitter, Paul succeeded in going on a 30-day free journey, which took him half-way around the world. He didn't actually hitchhike as such, but he did rely on the kindness of other people to get him there.

The idea came to him in his local supermarket in Gateshead, northern England. The crowded store and inconsiderate customers made him wish he was in another country. By the time he reached the checkout, he had made a plan. He would use Twitter to help him travel to the point in the world that was furthest from his own home: a remote place called Campbell Island to the south of New Zealand. But first he had to convince Jane, his wife of only four days, to let him go.

Once Jane agreed (as he knew she would) Paul announced his plan online. Twitter users sent messages to British actor and journalist Stephen Fry, an enthusiastic supporter of the site, to tell him about Paul's journey. He in turn asked his tens of thousands of followers to help Paul on his travels. Five days later, Paul was ready to go. He tweeted his first message and waited for a response. It came from a local Twitter user called Leanne, who offered him an overnight ferry trip to Amsterdam. He was off!

After Amsterdam, two Parisian Twitter users paid for Paul to travel by rail to Paris. While he was there, a middle-aged German businesswoman sent him a high-speed train ticket from Paris to Saarbrücken and then drove him to Frankfurt. Shortly after that, a company director bought Paul a one-way flight from Frankfurt to New York. Within five days of leaving home, Paul had crossed the Atlantic! From New York, he was offered various lifts and bus rides – and even a flight on one occasion – until he reached Los Angeles. There, he received a message from a New Zealand airline offering to fly him to the capital. During his final week, he travelled the length of the country by plane, ferry, car, and camper van, before arriving at Stewart Island, just off the south coast. All he had to do now was to find the captain of a boat that would take him on the final leg of his journey – a six-day trip to Campbell Island, 900 km to the south.

But this was where Paul's luck ran out. Or did it? Paul never actually made it to Campbell Island, because he didn't get a ride. But he did receive another message from the airline offering to fly him home. Paul was delighted to have travelled so far, and decided that it was time to go home. When he got home, 30 hours later, Jane was waiting for him with an enormous smile and a big hug. Although Paul didn't actually reach his destination, he succeeded in travelling over 18,325 km around the world absolutely free. Eighteen months on, he is still in touch with the people who helped him on his journey; and through him, they have become friends with one another. Which just goes to show the power of Twitter.

5 LISTENING

a **iChecker** Listen to five speakers talking about their experiences at airport security. Match Speakers 1–5 with photos A–E.

A

B  C

D  E

b Listen again and match the speakers to the sentences.

- A I was very annoyed because I was going to have it for dinner.
- B As you can imagine, he wasn't at all amused.
- C It's a good job I found it and not the security scanner!
- D I was lucky to have found such a kind man.
- E Honestly, I don't know what I'd do without her!

c Listen again with the audio script on *p.69* and try to guess the meaning of any words you don't know. Then check in your dictionary.

USEFUL WORDS AND PHRASES

Learn these words and phrases.

item /ˈaɪtəm/
security screener /sɪˈkjʊərəti ˈskriːnə/
undisputed /ˌʌndɪˈspjuːtɪd/
keen on /ˈkiːn ɒn/
upmarket (restaurants) /ʌpˈmɑːkɪt/
eager /ˈiːgə/
soak up /ˌsəʊk ˈʌp/
hotelier /həʊˈteliə/
frugal /ˈfruːgl/
at the bottom /æt ðə ˈbɒtəm/

If I won the lottery, I'd start a charity that helped little family hardware shops and fruit shops to open in city centres.

Alexei Sayle, British comedian

1 VOCABULARY shops and services

a Read the clues. Complete the puzzle to find the hidden kind of shop. What does it sell?

| 1 | L | A | U | N | D | E | R | E | T | T | E | | |

1 A type of shop where you pay to wash and dry your clothes in machines is a *launderette*.
2 A very large shop outside a town that sells a variety of goods is a h_____.
3 A shop that sells flowers is a fl_____.
4 A shop that sells paper, pens, and pencils is a st_____.
5 A shop that sells medicine and toiletries is a ch_____.
6 The place where you go to look when you want to buy a house is an e_____ a_____.
7 A shop that sells meat is a b_____.
8 A shop that sells bread is a b_____.
9 A shop that sells fish is a f_____.
10 A shop that sells newspapers and magazines is a n_____.
11 A shop where jewellery and watches are sold and repaired is a j_____.
12 A shop that sells fruit and vegetables is a gr_____.

b Join a word from **A** with a word from **B** to form places on the high street. Then complete the sentences.

A chain craft DIY dry health food ~~market~~ off-travel

B agent's cleaner's fair licence ~~stall~~ store (x3)

1 My cousin has a ___*market stall*___ selling leather bags in Covent Garden.
2 Can you pick up my suit from the _____, please?
3 Tanya went to the _____ to buy some vitamins.
4 Did you book your flights online or at the _____?
5 We bought a beautiful hand-made wooden bowl at the _____.
6 *Zara* is a _____ that you find in many shopping centres all over the world.
7 They stopped at the _____ to buy a bottle of wine for dinner.
8 Our local _____ has a very good selection of gardening and carpentry tools.

c Rewrite the sentences, replacing the **bold** words with the correct form of the phrasal verbs in the list.

~~be out of~~ close down look for look round open up try on

1 I didn't buy any black trousers because they **didn't have my size in stock**.
   I didn't buy any black trousers because they ___*were out of*___ my size.
2 **I've walked round to see what there is**, but I haven't seen anything I want to buy.
   I _____ but I haven't seen anything I want.
3 A lot of new phone shops **are starting to do business** in the city centre.
   A lot of new phone shops _____ in the city centre.
4 Excuse me, where can I **put on** these jeans **to see if they fit**?
   Excuse me, where can I _____ these jeans?
5 The restaurant **stopped trading** after the health inspector's visit.
   The restaurant _____ after the health inspector's visit.
6 Hannah **was trying to find** a bikini, but she ended up with a swimsuit.
   Hannah _____ a bikini, but she ended up with a swimsuit.

2 READING

a Read the text and complete it with the missing headings. There is one extra heading you do not need to use.

A Customer service   D Online shopping
B The building   E The shopping experience
C Prices   F The location

b Read the text again and mark the sentences **T** (true) or **F** (false).

1 *Daunt's* is making a profit despite competition from the internet.   *T*
2 The Marylebone High Street branch is the newest store in the chain. ___
3 The building was originally built to be a bookshop. ___
4 *Daunt's* in Marylebone has been completely renovated. ___
5 There are only two floors in the store. ___
6 In the beginning, *Daunt's* only sold books about travel. ___
7 Books by French authors will be found in the same section as travel books on France. ___
8 People of all ages are welcome in the store. ___
9 *Daunt's* places a lot of importance on customer service. ___
10 Customers can buy books cheaper on the website. ___

c Look at the highlighted words and phrases and try to work out their meaning. Then check the meaning and pronunciation in your dictionary.

LONDON'S FINEST BOOKSHOP

Book stores have suffered a lot on the high street recently, due to the massive growth of online book sellers, such as Amazon. One of the few book stores to survive and, indeed, prosper over the last decade is *Daunt Books* in London, more commonly known as *Daunt's*. Read on to find out the secrets of its success.

1 _F_

There are six stores in the chain, but the original and most famous of them is the main store in Marylebone High Street. Marylebone is an affluent area of inner-city London which is very popular with shoppers. *Daunt's* is a favourite because of its reputation as 'the most beautiful bookshop in London'.

2 ___

The shop itself is housed in an old antique bookshop, which was built for the purpose in 1912. The shop front is full of character because of its large, historic windows. Inside the store itself, *Daunt's* maintains its original appearance. The walls are lined with wooden bookshelves, which extend right to the back of the long, narrow shop. There is a second level upstairs reached by a wooden staircase, and another staircase leads downstairs to the basement. The shop has a stained-glass window and a number of beautiful skylights in the ceiling which bathe both books and customers in natural light.

3 ___

Daunt's started life over 20 years ago when the shop was purchased by former banker James Daunt. At first, the store specialized in travel writing and the books were arranged by country. Later, the owner decided to expand without changing the organization of the store. Today you can still find travel guides and maps of Moscow in the section dedicated to Russia, but you can also find novels and poetry by Russian authors there, too. There are also sections dedicated to more unusual places, such as Ethiopia, Tibet, and the polar regions. At the front of the shop, there is a fantastic selection of newly published fiction and non-fiction, and a superb children's section full of weird and wonderful picture books.

4 ___

The staff at *Daunt's* have a reputation for being friendly, helpful, and knowledgeable, which makes it difficult for booklovers to stay away. Each customer is greeted when they enter the shop because they have to walk past the service desk. The assistants allow visitors to take their time looking round, yet they are always on hand to give advice when necessary.

5 ___

Unlike its competitors, *Daunt's* hasn't invested heavily in technology, because it hasn't needed to. Its website is basic, but charming. It contains a virtual tour of the Marylebone store, which is well worth exploring, and there are also reading lists and 'books of the week'. *Daunt's* competes on specialism and quality of selection rather than price, offering customers a breath of fresh air when they are looking for a particular book.

3 GRAMMAR possessives

a Reorder the words to make sentences.

1 boyfriend's / with / doesn't / her / on / Beth / get / parents
   Beth doesn't get on with her boyfriend's parents .

2 saw / car / James's / yesterday / new / We
   _____ .

3 a / at / barbecue / Saturday / John's / There's / on
   _____ .

4 is / of / very / mine / good / a / Karen / friend
   _____ .

5 a / a / of / beautiful / That's / painting / sunset
   _____ .

b Circle the correct answer. Tick (✓) if both are correct.

1 This is _Debbie's book_ | the Debbie's book.
2 That girl is _James' new girlfriend_ | _James's new girlfriend._ ✓
3 _The boy's bikes_ | _The boys' bikes_ need cleaning before they put them away.
4 _The house's door_ | _The door of the house_ is locked.
5 One day, we'd like to have _ours own shop_ | _our own shop._
6 I thought Alice was _a friend of you_ | _a friend of yours._
7 Where's _my old shirt_ | _that old shirt of mine?_

c Complete the sentences. Use the words in brackets with _'s_ or _of_.

1 Charlotte is wearing _her mother's earrings_ .
   (earrings / her mother)
2 We climbed to _the top of the mountain_ .
   (top / the mountain)
3 It's _____ next week.
   (wedding anniversary / my parents)
4 _____ has broken down.
   (car / Linda and Dave)
5 He's never been in _____ before.
   (office / his boss)
6 Can you see the _____? (lid / my pen)

4 PRONUNCIATION 's; linking

a Right or wrong? Tick (✓) if the pronunciation of _'s_ is right and cross (✗) if it is wrong.

1 Ella's phone	/z/	✓
2 my friend's daughter	/s/	✗
3 their aunt's house	/s/	__
4 Louise's flat	/z/	__
5 my boss's desk	/s/	__
6 Rory's laptop	/z/	__
7 my niece's wedding	/ɪz/	__
8 Mike's girlfriend	/ɪz/	__
9 Beth's children	/s/	__
10 my nephew's car	/ɪz/	__

b iChecker Listen and check. Then listen and repeat the phrases.

5 LISTENING

a iChecker Listen to a representative from a British newspaper giving a talk about a new campaign. What is the main aim of the campaign?

A To promote a new kind of store.
B To choose the most successful high street.
C To make residents want to shop in their high street.

b Listen again and answer the questions.

1 How many high streets are there in the UK today?
   About _____ .
2 How often do British people use the high street?
   They _____ _____ use it.
3 What is the name of the _Daily Telegraph_ campaign?
   It's called _____ the _____
   _____ .
4 Who do the campaigners hope will be able to use the high street in the future?
   They hope their _____ _____
   will be able to use it.
5 Apart from politicians, who will be involved in the discussions?
   _____ and _____ will be involved.
6 Which kind of store is new on the high street?
   The _____-and-_____ store is new.
7 What kind of people will be interviewed during the campaign?
   _____ will be interviewed.
8 Which title will the best high street receive?
   It will be called _____ _____ of
   the _____ .
9 According to the speaker, who has conflicting opinions about the high street?
   The _____ have conflicting opinions.

c Listen again with the audio script on _p.70_ and try to guess the meaning of any words that you don't know. Then check in your dictionary.

USEFUL WORDS AND PHRASES

Learn the words and phrases.

high street /ˈhaɪ striːt/	personalized
struggle (verb)	/ˈpɜːsənəlaɪzd/
/ˈstrʌɡl/	pottery /ˈpɒtəri/
crafts /krɑːfts/	(photo) frame /freɪm/
set up a business	workshop /ˈwɜːkʃɒp/
/set ʌp ə ˈbɪznəs/	hand-painted
wooden /ˈwʊdn/	/hænd ˈpeɪntɪd/

A diplomat is a man who always remembers a woman's birthday, but never remembers her age.

Robert Frost, American poet

3A The generation gap

1 GRAMMAR past simple, past continuous, or *used to*?

a Correct the mistakes in the highlighted phrases.

1 I didn't went out much when I was a teenager.
   I didn't go out
2 We taked my parents out for dinner last night.
   _____
3 My brother used to had a beard, but now he's shaved it off. _____
4 We were sit in the garden when my grandparents arrived. _____
5 Where you stayed when you went to Greece?
   _____
6 I didn't used to eat many vegetables when I was a child. _____
7 What was you doing when I saw you in town yesterday? _____
8 I gave up trying to explain when I realized that you didn't listening. _____
9 You use to play in the street when you were young?
   _____
10 My girlfriend stoped eating meat when she was a student. _____

b Complete the sentences with the correct form of the verbs. Use past simple, past continuous, or *used to*. Sometimes more than one answer may be possible.

1 My parents _didn't own_ a car until they _got married_. (not own, get married)
2 I _____ late this morning, so I _____ time for breakfast. (wake up, not have)
3 When our guest arrived, I _____ to the children and my husband _____ the dinner. (read, finished)
4 Emily _____ glasses until she _____ working at the computer all day. (not need, start)
5 Ben _____ the doorbell because he _____ to music with his headphones on. (not hear, listen)
6 Luckily, they _____ very fast when they _____ the lamppost. (not drive, hit)
7 I _____ in Germany for a year when I _____ a student. (live, be)
8 We _____ in the high street, but then they _____ a new hypermarket near our house. (go shopping, build)
9 My son _____ his boarding pass while we _____ at the airport for our flight. (lose, wait)
10 We always _____ our holidays in the same village when we _____ children. (spend, be)

c Complete the text with the correct form of the verbs. Use past simple, past continuous, or *used to*. Sometimes more than one answer may be possible.

I only ever ¹ _met_ (meet) one of my grandparents, and that was my dad's mother. We ² _____ (see) her every Sunday afternoon when I was little. One day, my Granny ³ _____ (look after) me because my parents ⁴ _____ (visit) a friend in hospital. In the morning, I ⁵ _____ (play) in the garden, while my gran ⁶ _____ (cook) lunch. She ⁷ _____ (call) me when the meal was ready. Unfortunately, while I ⁸ _____ (run) into the kitchen I ⁹ _____ (catch) my little finger in the door and pulled off the nail. It ¹⁰ _____ (hurt) a lot, but I was more upset because I ¹¹ _____ (not think) the nail would grow again. However, my gran patiently ¹² _____ (explain) that I would soon have a new fingernail. After that, I ¹³ _____ (look forward to) seeing her every Sunday, so that I ¹⁴ _____ (can) show her how my nail ¹⁵ _____ (progress).

2 PRONUNCIATION -ed endings

a Write the past simple forms of these regular verbs in the chart according to the pronunciation of the *-ed* ending.

~~ask~~ change decide end hate hope live miss
play start study travel want wash watch

1	2	3 /ɪd/
asked	_____	_____
_____	_____	_____
_____	_____	_____
_____	_____	_____

b **iChecker** Listen and check. Then listen again and repeat the past simple forms.

3 VOCABULARY stages of life

Complete the sentences with the singular or plural form of a word or phrase for a stage of life.

1 Their b_aby_ is only two weeks old, so he spends most of his time sleeping.
2 T_____ usually take more notice of their friends than they do of their parents.
3 I'm sure Jim isn't 40 yet, but he's definitely i_____ h_____ l_____ th_____.
4 One of the most important events for a p_____-_____ is starting secondary school.
5 Jake's dad is i_____ h_____ m_____ s_____, so he'll probably retire soon.
6 T_____ are exhausting when they've just learnt to walk.
7 Laura is in her third year of university, so she must be i_____ h_____ e_____ tw_____.
8 My mum is now officially a p_____. She was 65 last Friday.
9 My boyfriend says that he wants to have lots of ch_____, but I'm not so sure.

4 READING

a Read the article once and choose the best title.

A How to cope with a teenage daughter
B Mums and teenage girls: a love-hate relationship
C Why women eventually turn into their mothers

b Read the text again and mark the sentences **T** (true) or **F** (false).

1 Teenage girls often get angry because of their hormones.   _T_
2 They argue most with their fathers.   __
3 The most common cause of arguments between a teenage girl and her mother is the way the girl treats her brothers and sisters.   __
4 Mothers and daughters have more arguments about going out at night than about having relationships.   __
5 They usually don't stop arguing until the daughter is in their late twenties.   __
6 Less than half of the women said that they discussed their problems with their mothers when they were teenagers.   __
7 75% of the women in the study think that their mothers did a good job.   __
8 The ideal age for the mother of a 19-year-old girl is 40.   __
9 Nearly all of the women think that daughters should tell their mothers everything.   __
10 In general, mothers can give essential advice to teenage girls.   __

c Match the highlighted words and expressions in the text to the definitions.

1 brothers or sisters _____
2 noisy arguments _____
3 in the end _____
4 argue and stop being friends with somebody _____
5 replying rudely to somebody _____
6 a sudden explosion of anger _____
7 words that are considered offensive by most people _____
8 looked after and taught how to behave _____
9 near each other emotionally _____
10 in spite of _____
11 of very great value _____
12 conversations in which you say exactly what you feel _____

If you are part of a family with a teenage girl, you are no doubt aware of the chaos that their hormones can cause. A recent study has shown that, on average, teenage girls fall out with their brothers and sisters 257 times each year. The rows are not only reserved for siblings, however, as they also have 157 arguments with their fathers. But the person who is most frequently on the receiving end of a tantrum is their mother. The results of the study showed that a typical teenage girl has 183 rows with her mother each year.

According to the study, the third most common cause of rows between mother and daughter is the relationship the girl has with the rest of the family. Top of the list of causes is bedroom tidiness, followed by answering back. In fourth and fifth place come relationships with boys and staying out late. Other causes include appearance, attitude to school work, money, manners, and the use of bad language. This testing period can go on for several years, but the good news is that, in most cases, it eventually comes to an end.

It seems that women finally start to appreciate their mothers in their early twenties – by the age of 23, to be exact. But despite the frequent arguments, most mothers and daughters have moments when they are close. Four in ten of the women in the study said that they sometimes had heart-to-hearts with their mothers about things that were worrying them. They regard these conversations as crucial in helping them get through their difficult teenage years. At the same time, the study shows that three quarters of women are grateful to their mum for the way they were brought up, even if they didn't realize it at the time. And 67 per cent recognize that their mum made them the person they are today.

When the 2,000 women in the study were asked about the ideal age gap for the perfect mother-daughter relationship, they recommended a difference of around 25 years. But few of the women think it is necessary for daughters to discuss personal matters with their mothers. Only one in five feel that mums and their daughters should be best friends who tell each other everything. Instead, three quarters feel that the relationship is best if some things remain private.

In summing up the situation, a representative from the organization that carried out the study said, 'Being a teenager is hard, but having a mum to turn to and talk things through or ask questions is priceless in helping young women to manage.'

5 LISTENING

a **iChecker** Listen to a radio programme about a new TV series. Which word describes how the two groups of people feel about each other at the end of the first episode? Circle the correct answer/s.

1 hostile
2 neutral
3 sympathetic

b Listen again and correct the mistakes.

1 There are **four** participants in each group.
   five
2 The *juniors* are all in their **thirties**.
   _____
3 The *seniors* are all over **80**.
   _____
4 The *juniors* thought that they were going to be in **a documentary**.
   _____
5 Both groups were **pleased** to be sharing the same house.
   _____
6 Each group received **six hundred pounds** to go shopping with.
   _____
7 The *juniors* bought a lot of **healthy food**.
   _____
8 The *seniors*' questions were about **literature**.
   _____
9 Sam doesn't know much about **geography**.
   _____
10 The next episode of *Forever Young* is on **Friday**.
   _____

c Listen again with the audio script on *p.70* and try to guess the meaning of any words you don't know. Then check in your dictionary.

USEFUL WORDS AND PHRASES

Learn the words and phrases.

tomboy	/ˈtɒmbɔɪ/	ban	/bæn/
bookworm	/ˈbʊkwɜːm/	curfew	/ˈkɜːfjuː/
quarrel	/ˈkwɒrəl/	buggy	/ˈbʌgi/
well-behaved		scooter	/ˈskuːtə/
	/wel bɪˈheɪvd/	scream	/skriːm/
naughty	/ˈnɔːti/		

> When I say I want to photograph someone, what it really means is that I'd like to know them.
>
> *Annie Leibovitz, American photographer*

3B In the picture

1 READING

a Read the text quickly. Which information is not revealed about the *Afghan Girl*?

1 what she is called
2 how old she was when the photo was taken
3 whether she has a family
4 where she lives now

b Read the text again and choose a, b, or c.

1 The most remarkable thing about the photo is …
   a her hair.
   b her clothes.
   c her eyes.

2 The photographer did not take the girl's picture immediately because …
   a he wanted to give her time to get used to him.
   b he didn't notice her at first.
   c she refused to be photographed.

3 It was hard for the photographer to find the girl again because …
   a he wasn't allowed to talk to the refugees.
   b a lot of Afghan women looked like her.
   c he didn't know anything about her.

4 When the photographer found Sharbat Gula, she was living …
   a in a different refugee camp.
   b in an isolated part of Afghanistan.
   c in a different country.

5 What is the photographer's attitude towards Sharbat Gula today?
   a He is concerned about her and her family's future.
   b He is keen to take more photographs of her.
   c He is grateful to her for making him famous.

c Match the highlighted words and phrases in the text to the definitions below.

1 remembered   _____
2 said that something is true   _____
3 very noticeable   _____
4 the state of being alone and not disturbed by other people   _____
5 make somebody want to know something   _____
6 a job that you are given to do   _____
7 go near to somebody   _____
8 questions   _____

Who is the *Afghan Girl*?

In June 1985, a photograph of a young woman appeared on the front cover of the *National Geographic* magazine. The image showed a face with a pair of striking green eyes staring directly into the camera. A red scarf hung loosely over her hair. The title of the picture was *Afghan Girl,* and today it is regarded as one of the most viewed photographs in the world. So, who took it and what is the story behind it?

The photograph was taken by American photojournalist Steve McCurry. In 1984, he was sent to Afghanistan to take a series of photos reflecting the conflict in the area. McCurry spent most of his time on the border between Afghanistan and Pakistan, where there were a number of refugee camps. It was in one of these camps that he met the girl in the photograph. Realizing that she was very shy, he did not approach her at first. Instead he started photographing her classmates, hoping to arouse her curiosity. Eventually, she came up to him and agreed to have her photo taken.

Almost as soon as the photograph was published, the magazine received hundreds of enquiries about the girl's identity. But McCurry had not asked her name and so he could not answer. That is, until 2002, when *National Geographic* sent him to Afghanistan on an assignment to try and find her. With no name, no address, and no information about what tribe she came from, this was not an easy task. All McCurry and his team could do was to visit the refugee camps and show her photo to the remaining inhabitants. Many women claimed that they were the girl in the picture, but McCurry was not convinced. Then one day, he spoke to a man who said that he knew her brother. A message was sent to her hometown, and some time later, a much older version of the girl in the picture walked through McCurry's door.

The photographer discovered that the woman's name was Sharbat Gula. She had only been 12 years old when he had taken her photograph, but now she was 30 and had three daughters of her own. She had returned to Afghanistan from the refugee camp in 1992 and she was living in a remote region of the country with her husband, a baker. Sharbat recalled being photographed by McCurry, but she had never seen her famous portrait before.

Since their meeting, McCurry and his team are continually in contact with Sharbat. *National Geographic* has paid her for the photograph, so she has been able to send her daughters to school. However, the magazine is keeping the location of her hometown a secret to protect her privacy.

2 VOCABULARY photography

a Complete the description of the photo.

This photo was taken in a garden. ¹In the <u>foreground</u>, there's a woman and the trunk of a tree that has been cut down. The trunk is ²i_____ th_____ b_____ r_____-h_____ c_____ of the photo and the woman is standing ³b_____ it. She's leaning on the tree trunk with her left hand ⁴o_____ t_____ o_____ it. She's holding out her other hand. ⁵I_____ th_____ c_____ of the photo is an older man. He looks much smaller than the woman because he's ⁶i_____ th_____ d_____. It looks as if he is standing on the woman's hand. There's a bush ⁷i_____ fr_____ o_____ the man, and ⁸o_____ the woman there's a wall with a lot of flowers planted in it. ⁹I_____ th_____ b_____, there are a lot of trees and ¹⁰i_____ th_____ t_____ l_____-h_____ c_____, there's a large white house.

b Complete the sentences with the words in the list.

~~blurred~~ enlarge flash lenses out of focus
portrait setting zoom in

1 I moved when I was taking the photo, so the image is _*blurred*_ .
2 I use different _____, depending on the shot I want.
3 I wanted to take a close-up of my boyfriend, so I used the _____.
4 I'm going to _____ this photo and frame it for my parents as a present.
5 The people are too far away because I didn't _____ on them.
6 The photo is very dark because I didn't use the _____.
7 I didn't use the right setting, so the building is _____.

3 PRONUNCIATION word stress

a <u>Underline</u> the stressed syllable in the words. Then write them in the correct column in the table.

~~au|to|mat|ic~~ back|ground be|hind fore|ground
pho|to|co|py pho|to|ge|nic pho|to|gra|pher
pho|to|gra|phic pho|to|graph pho|to|gra|phy

Stress on first syllable	Stress on second syllable	Stress on third syllable
_____	_____	_*automatic*_
_____	_____	_____
_____	_____	_____
_____		

b [iChecker] Listen and check. Then listen and repeat the words.

4 GRAMMAR prepositions

a Look at the pictures. Complete the sentences with the past simple of the verbs and the correct prepositions.

~~climb~~ cycle dance fall run sit stand
swim walk across along down in front of
next to over past round ~~up~~

1 The cat _*climbed up*_ the tree.
2 We _____ the bridge.
3 The dog _____ the river.
4 Mark _____ Sophie in the café.
5 They _____ the pavement.
6 The band _____ us.
7 He _____ a parked car.
8 They _____ the fire.
9 She _____ the stairs.

b Complete the sentences with a word from the list, and a preposition if necessary.

arrived asked ~~belong~~ ~~entered~~ married
paid proud spend told worried

1 Who does this camera __*belong to?*__
2 Everybody stopped talking when we __*entered*__ the room.
3 They're very _____ their son because he has been very successful.
4 We _____ our meal by credit card.
5 The police officer _____ everyone to go home.
6 That actress is _____ a famous singer.
7 I'm very _____ my final exams.
8 When the taxi driver stopped we _____ a receipt.
9 How much money do you _____ food each month?
10 I _____ the hotel too late to call my parents.

c Complete the second sentence so that it means the same as the first. Use the word(s) in brackets.

1 Holly wants to do a photography course. (interested)
   Holly __*is interested in doing*__ a photography course.
2 I can't wait to go on holiday. (looking forward)
   I'm _____ on holiday.
3 My boyfriend can't draw very well. (good)
   My boyfriend isn't _____.
4 My friend said that I had broken her camera. (blamed)
   My friend _____ her camera.
5 I think it's important to have a healthy diet. (believe)
   I _____ a healthy diet.
6 He said sorry because he had forgotten my name. (apologized)
   He _____ my name.

5 LISTENING

a **iChecker** Listen to two people talking about a photography exhibition. Number the photos 1–3 in the order they are mentioned.

b Listen again and complete the sentences.

1 Next year's Photography Exhibition in the village hall will be in _____.
2 The tall building in Photo 1 is _____ building in the world.
3 Jack thinks Photo 1 will not look good if you _____.
4 Photo 2 _____ at sunset.
5 The hills in _____ make Photo 2 wild and mysterious.
6 Jane thinks the fountain in Photo 3 is not _____ enough for the theme of the exhibition.
7 Jack is worried that the _____ will be too big when they enlarge the photo.
8 They finally choose the photo with the _____.

c Listen again with the audio script on *p.71* and try to guess the meaning of any words that you don't know. Then check in your dictionary.

USEFUL WORDS AND PHRASES

Learn the words and phrases.

tower /ˈtaʊə/
hard drive /ˈhɑːd draɪv/
file format /faɪl ˈfɔːmæt/
resave /riːˈseɪv/
erase /ɪˈreɪz/

flash drive /ˈflæʃ draɪv/
data centre /ˈdeɪtə sentə/
offline (opp online) /ˌɒfˈlaɪn/
upload /ʌpˈləʊd/
back up /ˌbækˈʌp/

1 RENTING A CAR

a Complete the questions with two words.

Assistant

1 _Have you_ hired from us before?
2 _____ of car are you looking for?
3 _____ like an automatic?
4 _____ be any additional drivers?

Customer

5 _____ include insurance?
6 _____ leave the car at the airport?

b Match the questions with the responses a–f.

a No, this is the first time. ☐ 1
b Yes, it's included in the price. ☐
c Yes, it's an extra £50. ☐
d Yes, my wife. ☐
e A three-door would be fine. ☐
f No, I'd like a manual, please. ☐

2 SOCIAL ENGLISH

Complete the sentences with the correct word.

1 What's u_____? You sound upset.
2 I'm a_____ I can't take your call at the moment.
3 It's time for me to go. See you l_____.
4 Please leave your message after the t_____.
5 H_____ on. I'll be back in a moment.

3 READING

a Read the text once and correct the sentences.

1 A first time driver in the UK should rent a car at the airport. _____
2 There's usually a speed camera 200 meters after the speed limit sign. _____
3 In towns you can drive at 40mph. _____
4 You should only overtake a tractor if you are feeling confident. _____

b Look at the highlighted words and phrases. What do you think they mean? Use your dictionary to look up their meaning and pronunciation.

Driving in the UK

If you are planning to see more of the UK than just the major cities, you should consider renting a car to make it easier to travel around. Thousands of visitors enjoy driving in the UK, happily and safely, every year although driving on the 'wrong' side of the road for the first time can make some drivers nervous. Here are some tips for driving in the British Isles.

① START SLOW

If you've never driven in the UK before, don't plan to pick up a car at the airport and go straight onto a motorway heading for a major city. Use public transport to get to your holiday destination and try driving on the left on quieter roads first. Build up your confidence on smaller, less busy roads, before trying high speed motorways and big city centers.

② WATCH YOUR SPEED

On motorways, the speed limit is 70 mph (112 kph), but on other roads it goes down to 60-40 mph (96-64 kph). And once you enter a town or a village the speed limit is never more than 30 mph (48 kph). Always look out for the speed limit signs and remember that there are more speed cameras in the UK than in other European countries. If you see a white sign with a picture of a camera on it, there will be a speed camera within about 200 meters.

③ PARK SAFELY

Parking in the UK can be complicated and if you leave your car in the wrong place, the fines can be quite heavy, so it is best to find a car park. Most towns now have Pay and Display parking which makes life easier for visitors. Check the tariff board to see how much you have to pay and if there is a maximum parking time. Insert coins for the correct amount and the parking meter will give you a ticket to display in your window. Note that in some towns parking charges apply in the evenings and weekends.

④ STAY COOL

The most interesting and scenic roads in Britain are often the smallest. It's possible to get stuck behind a tractor with a load of hay moving at 24 kph. Even if you are feeling more confident, be very careful overtaking on these roads. It's safer to be patient and wait until you have a clear, long view of the road ahead.

In California they don't throw their garbage away – they make it into TV shows.

Woody Allen, American film director and actor

4A That's rubbish!

1 VOCABULARY rubbish and recycling

a Complete the text with the words in the list.

bins   dustmen   landfill site   packaging   ~~rubbish~~
take away   take out   throw away   waste   waste-paper basket

In my family, we do our best to recycle as much of our
¹ _rubbish_ as possible. We have two ² _____ in the
kitchen, one for household ³ _____ and the other for
plastic ⁴ _____ and cans. The children each have a
⁵ _____ in their room where they can ⁶ _____
their used paper. We ⁷ _____ the rubbish as soon
as the bins are full. Outside on the street, there are four
larger bins, which are all different colours. The green one
is emptied every evening by the ⁸ _____, but the
others are emptied less frequently. There's a yellow bin for
recycling plastic and cans, a green one for glass, and a blue
one for paper. A lorry comes to ⁹ _____ the contents
of these bins about once a month. I suppose that the things
that aren't recycled are taken to a ¹⁰ _____.

b How are the following products usually sold?

1 a chocolate bar   in a __*wrapper*__
2 crisps   in a p_____
3 jam   in a j_____
4 margarine   in a t_____
5 mineral water   in a b_____
6 orange juice   in a c_____
7 peeled tomatoes   in a t_____
8 soft drinks   in a c_____

c Rewrite the phrases in **bold** using the correct form of a
verb from the list and the object where appropriate.

reapply   recycle   ~~reheat~~   replay   rethink   reuse

1 Experts say that you should **warm up food again** only
   once.   __*reheat food*__
2 In the past, mothers washed their baby's nappies and **put
   them on again** because they were made of cloth. _____
3 This lipstick lasts for 24 hours, so you don't need to **put it
   on again** during the day. _____
4 Is it possible to **put polystyrene trays through a process
   so that they can be used again**? _____
5 The referee made a mistake, so they **repeated the last five
   minutes** of the match. _____
6 Dan is currently **considering his future again** because he
   failed his final exams. _____

2 PRONUNCIATION /ɪ/, /aɪ/, and /eɪ/

a Circle the different sound.

1 /ɪ/	2 /aɪ/	3 /eɪ/
biscuit	decide	container
(environment)	diet	garbage
lid	rubbish	paper
packet	wine	waste

4 /ɪ/	5 /aɪ/	6 /eɪ/
bin	away	danger
guilty	lifestyle	date
packaging	polystyrene	plastic
recycle	reapply	tray

b **iChecker** Listen and check. Then listen and
repeat the words.

3 READING

a Read the article once and complete it with the
missing sentences.

A The produce considered too ugly to sell is often
   left on the trees or in the fields.
B This is because they no longer invest time and
   money in buying food on the high street.
C This amounts to two billion tons of food.
D The researchers say that the waste costs the
   average household £480 per year.
E These discounts result in consumers buying far
   more food than they actually need.

WHAT A **WASTE!**

Up to half of the food bought in British supermarkets ends up in the bin, according to a new report. This amounts to a staggering seven million tons of food per year, worth around £10 billion. The report, entitled *Global food: waste not, want not*, was compiled by the Institution of Mechanical Engineers. ¹_____ That means that many families will throw away up to £24,000 worth of food during their lifetime, despite much of it being perfectly edible. Of the food that is binned, £1 billion worth is still within its sell-by date and good enough to eat.

The author of the report, Dr Tim Fox, places some of the blame for the waste on the consumer culture that exists in the UK. He believes that people have lost the sense of the value of food. ²_____ Instead, they prefer to do a weekly shop at one of the many huge supermarkets that have opened in the last decade. Today, the average British family spends only 11 per cent of its budget on food, the report found. Dr Fox explains that because people undervalue the food they buy, they do not think twice about throwing it away.

According to Dr Fox, the supermarkets themselves are also partly responsible for the waste. This is because they often have special offers, such as 'Buy One, Get One Free'. ³_____ The products are taken home, put away in a cupboard or in the fridge, and then forgotten about. Many of these items are near their sell-by date, and it isn't unusual for them to go off before they are eaten. The report suggests that it is often these cheaper products that people throw away.

It is not only food from the supermarket that goes to waste. About 30 per cent of the fruit and vegetables grown in the UK never even make it to the supermarket shelves. This is because of the strict marketing rules in the country, which require fruit and veg to be a certain shape, size, and weight. ⁴_____ Dr Fox estimates that between this agricultural waste and the fresh products thrown away by consumers, up to three quarters of the fruit and vegetables grown in Britain are never actually eaten.

Unfortunately, this colossal waste does not only occur in the UK. The situation remains the same across the globe, with around half of all food produced lost to waste. ⁵_____ That would be more than enough to feed all of the people in the world who are starving.

b Read the complete text again. Choose the right answer.

1 Every year, the average British family throws away food worth …
   a hundreds of pounds.
   b thousands of pounds.
   c billions of pounds.
2 People throw away so much food because …
   a they don't eat as much as they used to.
   b they go shopping more often than before.
   c they don't consider food to be important.
3 Discounted products often end up in the bin because …
   a customers buy more of them than they need.
   b customers don't really want them.
   c customers prefer better quality goods.
4 A lot of fruit and vegetables are wasted because …
   a consumers don't like the taste.
   b farmers don't have time to collect all the products.
   c shops aren't allowed to sell them.
5 Compared to the UK, other countries throw away …
   a less food.
   b the same amount of food.
   c more food.

c Match the highlighted words and phrases in the text to the definitions below.

1 thrown away _____
2 deals that sell goods at a lower price than usual _____
3 extremely large _____
4 good or safe to eat _____
5 become too old to eat _____
6 extremely hungry _____
7 the form of something _____
8 plan of how to spend money over a period of time _____
9 give something too little importance _____

4 GRAMMAR future forms: will / shall and going to

a Circle the correct future form. Tick (✓) if both forms are possible.

1 Could you take the rubbish out now? I think *it's raining* / *it'll rain* this evening. ___

2 *We're flying* / *We're going to fly* home on Saturday. Our flight leaves at 9 p.m. ✓

3 It's too late to call them now. *I'll call* / *I call* them in the morning. ___

4 What *shall we do* / *will we do* with our old sofa? ___

5 Why don't you give away your riding boots? *You're never going to wear* / *You'll never wear* them again. ___

6 Trust me. *I won't tell* / *I'm not telling* anyone. ___

7 Sit down. *I'm making* / *I'll make* you a cup of tea. ___

8 My sister *is getting married* / *is going to get married* in the spring. ___

9 Don't leave the butter out in this heat. *It'll melt* / *It's melting*. ___

10 Thanks for the lovely meal. *Will I clear* / *Shall I clear* the table? ___

b Complete the dialogue with the correct form of *will* / *shall* or *going to*. Sometimes more than one answer is possible.

A Hi Clare. Thanks for coming round to help.

B No problem. When ¹ _are you going to move_ (you move) to your new house?

A Next Saturday. I've got a week to pack everything up.

B Right. So, where ² _____ (we start)?

A I thought we could do the garage today. Wait there and ³ _____ (I move) the car.

B Have you got any boxes?

A Yes, they're in the kitchen.

B ⁴ _____ (I go) and get them for you.

B Right. Let's start. ⁵ _____ (you take) that ladder with you?

A No, ⁶ _____ (I not have) room for it. I'm moving to a flat. ⁷ _____ (I give) the ladder to one of my neighbours. ⁸ _____ (he come round) on Tuesday or Wednesday to pick it up.

B What about those old chairs. ⁹ _____ (you not have) room for those, either?

A Good point. What ¹⁰ _____ (I do) with them?

B Why don't you take them to the charity shop? Come on. ¹¹ _____ (I help) you put them in the car.

A Be careful. They're heavy.

B Don't worry. ¹² _____ (I not drop) them!

5 LISTENING

a (iChecker) You are going to listen to a radio programme about recycling around the world. Look at the list of countries. Which one do you think is the best at recycling? Which one is the worst? Listen and check your answers.

Australia   India   South Africa   Sweden

b Listen again and complete the notes.

	Amount of waste	Amount recycled	Recycled products
Australia	¹ ___ kg per person per year	a third of the total	paper and cardboard, plastic bottles, glass, ² _____
Sweden	³ ___ kg per person per year	96%	⁴ _____ clothes, drinks containers
India	⁵ ___ kg per person per year	a quarter of the total	⁶ _____ newspapers, electrical goods
South Africa	⁷ ___ kg per person per year	⁸ ___ %	cans, paper, glass, plastic

c Listen again with the audio script on *p.71* and try to guess the meaning of any words you don't know. Then check in your dictionary.

USEFUL WORDS AND PHRASES

Learn the words and phrases.

scavenge /ˈskævɪndʒ/	worthless /ˈwɜːθləs/
frozen /ˈfrəʊzn/	melt down /ˌmelt'daʊn/
feel guilty /fiːl ˈɡɪlti/	second-hand
local council	/sekənd ˈhænd/
/ˌləʊkl ˈkaʊnsl/	chemicals /ˈkemɪklz/
the environment	
/ði ɪnˈvaɪrənmənt/	

I'm going to college. I don't care if it ruins my career. I'd rather be smart than a movie star.

Natalie Portman, American/Israeli actress

4B Degrees and careers

1 VOCABULARY study and work

a Complete the crossword.

³U N D E R G R A D U A T E			

Clues across →

3 A university student who is studying for their first degree.
5 One department in a university, e.g. for Arts or Law.
6 A class in which a small group of students discuss a subject with a teacher.
7 A teacher who is responsible for a small group of students at university.
10 A long piece of writing you do as part of a master's degree.

Clues down ↓

1 A presentation that takes place on the internet.
2 A talk that is given to a group of students to teach them about a particular subject.
4 A university student who is studying for their second degree.
7 A long piece of writing you do as part of a PhD.
8 A university teacher of the highest level.
9 The area of land where the main buildings of a university are.

b Complete the text.

When Mary finished her degree, she started looking out for ¹job vacancies. She found that she had the right ²qu_____ for many of them, but she had no ³ex_____ because she had never worked before. One day, she saw an advert for an internship, and so she decided to ⁴a_____ f_____ it because she thought she might learn some useful ⁵sk_____. She quickly wrote out her CV and included the name of her university tutor as a ⁶r_____. Then she wrote a ⁷c_____ l_____ and sent everything off to the company. A week later, she received an email inviting her to ⁸a_____ an interview. The day after the interview, she ⁹g_____ an offer of a three-month placement, but she decided not to accept it. She hadn't realized that she wouldn't get paid if she ¹⁰w_____ as an intern!

2 PRONUNCIATION word stress

a <u>Underline</u> the stressed syllable in the words in the list. Then write them in the correct column in the table.

at|tend de|gree di|sser|ta|tion post|gra|du|ate
pro|fess|or re|fe|ree re|si|dence scho|lar|ship
se|mi|nar tu|to|ri|al un|der|gra|du|ate va|can|cy

Stress on first syllable	Stress on second syllable	Stress on third syllable
_____	*attend*	_____
_____	_____	_____
_____	_____	_____
_____	_____	_____

b **iChecker** Listen and check. Then listen and repeat the words.

3 READING

a Read the text once. Match headings 1–3 to paragraphs A–C.

1 A little money goes a long way
2 New career after an early disappointment
3 Sharing a talent for others to learn

b Read the text again and answer the questions. Write the letter of the paragraph.

Which entrepreneur …

1 made a large profit from his / her first business? ___
2 has broken a record? ___
3 has carried out a successful project together with a family member? ___
4 was employed by an organization at a very young age? ___
5 was given a present which developed his / her skill? ___
6 has colleagues in other countries? ___

c Match the highlighted words to the definitions below.

1 the unique name that identifies a website
   _____
2 a person who writes about new books, films, etc. _____
3 collected _____
4 the act of reporting an event _____
5 projects which you cannot be sure will succeed _____
6 good at expressing your ideas clearly
   _____

Young entrepreneurs

You don't have to wait until you leave school to make a lot of money, as the three young people below have shown. Read on to find out more about them.

A _____

Adora Svitak started writing when she was four years old, and she hasn't stopped since. At six, she received a laptop computer from her mother on which she quickly amassed hundreds of short stories. When she was seven, Adora published her first book: *Flying Fingers: Master the Tools of Learning Through the Joy of Writing*. It featured several of her stories, along with her tips on writing and typing. She published a second book, *Dancing Fingers*, with her older sister Adrianna four years later. Since then, she has turned her writing success into speaking and teaching success. At the age of 12, Adora is an articulate public speaker who has given talks at over 400 schools. She is now planning a conference for other kids like her.

B _____

When Farrhad Acidwalla was twelve, he borrowed $10 from his parents to buy his first domain name on the internet. He built a successful website related to aviation and model aircraft, which he later sold for far more than his initial $10 investment. Since then, Farrhad has tried out several different ventures. He is currently the CEO of Rockstah Media, a company devoted to web development, marketing, advertising, and branding. The company is just over a year old but it has clients and a team of developers, designers, and marketing experts all over the world. Farrhad is now 16 years old and he plans to continue running Rockstah Media, while he is studying finance at the College of Commerce & Economics in India.

C _____

Savannah Britt was a published poet by the age of eight. When she was nine, she started working for a newspaper called *The Kitchen Table News* as a reviewer of children's books. Two years later, however, the newspaper closed, and so Savannah found herself unemployed. But that didn't stop her. She started her own publication which was a magazine called *Girlpez*. She was only 11 at the time, so that made her the youngest magazine publisher in the world. The magazine features coverage of events, like concerts and fashion shows, along with interviews with singers, actors, and celebrities. Now aged 15, Savannah has guided her magazine as it has developed into an online-only format at Girlpez.com.

4 GRAMMAR first and second conditionals

a Right (✓) or wrong (✗)? Correct the wrong phrases.

1 If he's late again, he might lose his job. ✓

2 If I won't answer the phone, leave me a message. ✗
   If I don't answer

3 If they paid us more, we didn't complain. ☐
   _____

4 You'd miss the traffic if you left a bit earlier. ☐
   _____

5 We'll never finish everything if we won't work late. ☐
   _____

6 If Sally lived in the city centre, she could walk to her office. ☐
   _____

7 Max won't accept the job unless they don't agree to his conditions. ☐
   _____

8 He does a postgraduate course if he can't find a job. ☐
   _____

9 I wouldn't live at home if I will be a student. ☐
   _____

10 If you didn't have a part-time job, you'd have more time to study. ☐
   _____

b Write first and second conditional sentences.

1 I don't earn enough money so I can't buy my own flat.
   I could buy my own flat if _I earned more money_.

2 My sister has a boyfriend so she doesn't spend enough time studying.
   My sister would spend more time studying if _____.

3 If Becky gets a scholarship, she'll go to an American university.
   _____ unless she gets a scholarship.

4 Matt doesn't live in a hall of residence because it's too expensive.
   If it wasn't so expensive, _____.

5 If you don't have enough experience, they won't offer you the job.
   You won't get the job unless _____.

6 If you wear the right clothes, the interviewer will be impressed.
   _____, the interviewer will get a bad impression.

7 You miss your lectures because you get up late.
   If you got up earlier, _____.

8 Teachers always notice when students cheat in the exam.
   If you cheat in the exam, _____.

5 LISTENING

a (iChecker) Listen to a radio programme about unpaid internships. What is the expert's recommendation?

A Unpaid internships should be banned.
B All three-month internships should be paid.
C The length of internships should be reduced.
D Companies that don't pay interns should be punished.

b Listen again and complete the sentences.

1 Companies currently give jobs to about a _____ of all interns.

2 Olga Britten says that some graduates don't apply for internships because they wouldn't be able to pay their _____ expenses.

3 According to Olga, _____% of young people couldn't live in London without a salary.

4 Olga suggests that companies are employing the richest graduates instead of the most _____ ones.

5 Olga states that it is _____ to employ a person in a company for a long time without paying them.

6 Companies that break the law are punished with a heavy _____.

7 Olga agrees there will be _____ places for interns if companies have to pay them.

8 Olga thinks that young people should do work _____ instead of internships.

c Listen again with the audio script on p.72 and try to guess the meaning of any words that you don't know. Then check in your dictionary.

USEFUL WORDS AND PHRASES

Learn the words and phrases.

advert /ˈædvɜːt/
internship /ˈɪntɜːnʃɪp/
be exploited /bi ɪkˈsplɔɪtɪd/
stack shelves /ˌstæk ˈʃelvz/
sell (sth) door to door /sel dɔː tə ˈdɔː/
delivery service /dɪˈlɪvəri sɜːvɪs/
do a round /ˌdə ə ˈraʊnd/
minimum wage /mɪnɪməm ˈweɪdʒ/
the checkout /ðə ˈtʃekaʊt/

I find television very educational. Every time someone turns it on, I go into another room and read a book.

Groucho Marx, American comedian

1 READING

a Match photos 1–6 with the dates below. Then read the text once and check your answers.

2 June 1953   20 July 1969   4 November 2008   29 April 2011   27 July 2012   14 October 2012

TELEVISION: PAST AND PRESENT

Nothing illustrates the meaning of the word 'progress' more than the way television has developed over the last 90 years. In less than a century, the system for transmitting visual images and sound has gone from being non-existent to becoming an important mass media the world over.

The first televised moving images were made during the 1920s by Scottish engineer John Logie Baird. But it was after the coronation of Queen Elizabeth II on 2 June 1953 that television really took off in the UK. Over 20 million viewers followed the event, which was broadcast around the world in 44 languages. Few could afford to have a TV set in those days, so those who had the money to buy one invited their neighbours – which sometimes meant the whole street – to watch the ceremony on their small black and white screen.

Since then, many more historic moments have been witnessed on TV. The first moon landing on 20 July 1969 was watched by around 14% of the total world population. Although it was the middle of the night in some parts of the world, an estimated 530 million watched in amazement as Neil Armstrong took his first step. More recently, numerous people around the globe saw Barack Obama's 'Yes, we can'

speech on 4 November 2008 when he became the first black American President. Sporting events and royal weddings have also had extremely high ratings lately. Nearly a billion people all over the world watched the opening ceremony of the 2012 London Olympics on 27 July of that year, and nearly two billion are reported to have seen Prince William marry Kate Middleton on 29 April 2011.

Of course these days, the transmission of momentous occasions is not limited to television. Today, streaming allows viewers to watch internet videos and webcasts of live events in real time. On 14 October 2012, Felix Baumgartner's record-breaking skydive from the stratosphere was seen live by viewers all over the world on their computers, tablets, and smartphones. The event was streamed as it happened by more than 140 digital companies, as well as being transmitted in 50 countries by 40 television networks.

Technology has been advancing at an incredible rate since the 1920s. In the UK today, there are 480 different television channels. Every year, 27,000 hours of content is produced. Although Logie Baird also developed high-definition and 3D pictures in the 1940s, this is surely something that even the father of television could not have imagined.

b Read the text again and choose the right answer.

1 The writer thinks TV is a great example of progress …
   a because it can transmit pictures and sounds.
   b because people can watch it all over the world.
   c because it has developed so fast.

2 Before the Queen's coronation …
   a very few people had a television.
   b people weren't interested in the royal family.
   c television sets were not very expensive.

3 The most popular programme on TV in the last 60 years was …
   a the London Olympics.
   b Prince William and Kate Middleton's wedding.
   c Neil Armstrong's moon walk.

4 More people were able to watch Felix Baumgartner's skydive because …
   a it was televised in many different countries.
   b it was very well publicized by social networks.
   c it was shown live on different media.

5 If John Logie Baird were alive today, he would be surprised by …
   a the size of the television industry.
   b the quality of the images transmitted.
   c the appearance of 3D television.

c Look at the highlighted words and phrases and try to work out their meaning. Then check the meaning and pronunciation in your dictionary.

2 VOCABULARY television

a Complete the text with the words in the list.

remote control screen speakers stand switched over
turn down turned off turned on turned up was on

My friend's brother gave him a 3D TV with a 60-inch
¹ _screen_ for his birthday. The TV was so big that it
didn't fit on the ² _____ he had, so he decided to
buy a new one. Once he had the TV where he wanted
it, he ³ _____ it _____ and set up the
channels with the ⁴ _____. When it was ready,
he sat down to watch a film that ⁵ _____, but the
sound wasn't very good. He ⁶ _____ the volume,
but he still couldn't hear the actors very clearly. He had
the same problem when he ⁷ _____ to another
channel. So he decided to go and buy a pair of
⁸ _____ to attach to the set. He ⁹ _____
the TV, drove into town, and found what he wanted.
But he had a shock when he tried out the new sound
system, because he had forgotten to ¹⁰ _____
the volume. The noise was so loud that it made
everybody jump!

b Match the descriptions to the types of programmes below.

cartoon chat show cookery programme documentary
live sport period drama quiz show reality show soap

1 It's Abi's birthday, and Tanya is determined to give her a good time. __soap__

2 When a 'cool' couple moves in next door, Homer tries to be just like them, but Marge and Bart have problems fitting in. _____

3 Coverage of stage two of the prestigious cycling race. _____

4 Daily round-up of highlights, revealing how the housemates are getting on. _____

5 Today, Jamie prepares more quick meals, including an interesting pork recipe. _____

6 On a journey taking him from Luxor to Istanbul, Neil Oliver explores the story behind the last Pharaoh of Egypt. _____

7 Another episode in the life of the aristocratic Crawley family and their servants in the post-Edwardian era. _____

8 Two more contestants compete against each other to see who will go through to the next round. _____

9 Tonight's guests are former Bond girl Britt Ekland and politician John Prescott. _____

3 PRONUNCIATION /w/, /v/, and /b/

a iChecker Listen and complete the sentences.

1 What's the _____ _____ for the _____?

2 The viewers _____ for the _____ _____.

3 Have you ever _____ _____ or Cambodia?

4 Did you _____ the _____ show on _____?

5 The _____ team won a _____ _____.

6 We've been _____ _____ since we set up our new _____.

b Listen and check. Then listen and repeat the sentences.

4 GRAMMAR present perfect simple

a Right (✓) or wrong (✗)? Correct the mistakes in the highlighted sentences.

1 Have you heard tomorrow's weather forecast? ✓

2 The reporter haven't switched on her microphone. ✗
   hasn't switched on

3 The documentary has finished just . ☐
   _____

4 They've had the same TV set since 20 years . ☐
   _____

5 I've already seen this film. ☐
   _____

6 Have you ever be on TV? ☐
   _____

7 I haven't watched that programme since they
   changed the presenter . ☐
   _____

8 We know each other for ages. ☐
   _____

9 I haven't never liked watching live sport. ☐
   _____

10 Has the news started yet ? ☐
   _____

b (Circle) the correct answers.

1 Let's switch over. (We've seen) | We saw this
  documentary before.

2 Have you heard the news? The President _has just
  resigned_ | _just resigned_!

3 I went to sleep on the sofa last night and _haven't turned
  off_ | _didn't turn off_ the TV.

4 Don't tell me what happens – _I haven't watched_ | _I didn't
  watch_ the last episode yet.

5 That programme _is on_ | _has been on_ since I was a child.

6 I don't need to see the film because _I've already read_ | _I
  already read_ the book.

7 The children have had the TV on _all day_ | _for all day_.

8 They've only known each other _for a month_ | _since a
  month_ and they're getting married.

c Complete the second sentence so that it means the same as the first. Use the word in brackets.

1 Is this your first time in Spain? (been)
  Have you been to Spain before?

2 My friend bought his speakers a week ago. (had)
  My friend _____ a week.

3 I got home two minutes ago. (just)
  I _____ home.

4 Jodie Foster became and actress when she was a child.
  (since) Jodie Foster _____ she was
  a child.

5 We moved house in 2005, 2008, and 2012. (times)
  We _____.

6 I didn't like cartoons in the past and I don't like them
  now. (never) I _____ cartoons.

7 They have been married for ten years. (get)
  They _____.

8 I don't want a coffee, I had one at home. (already)
  I don't want a coffee, I _____.

5 LISTENING

a [iChecker] Listen to five speakers comparing their use
of television and the internet. Answer the questions.

1 Which speakers spend more time watching TV? __ __

2 Which speakers spend more time online? __ __ __

b Listen again and match speakers 1–5 to sentences A–F.
There is one extra sentence that you do not need to use.

☐ A He / She gets easily distracted in front of the TV.

☐ B He / She doesn't often watch TV.

☐ C He / She values TV as time to spend with the
     family.

☐ D He / She uses social media to chat about TV
     programmes.

☐ E He / She is usually too busy to watch TV.

☐ F He / She is very selective about which TV
     programmes to watch.

c Listen again with the audio script on _p.72_ and try
to guess the meaning of any words you don't know.
Then check in your dictionary.

USEFUL WORDS AND PHRASES

Learn the words and phrases.

release (a film or TV series)	review /rɪˈvjuː/
/rɪˈliːs/	cable TV /keɪbl ˌtiː ˈviː/
season /ˈsiːzn/	binge watch
viewer /ˈvjuːə/	/ˈbɪndʒ wɒtʃ/
flashback /ˈflæʃbæk/	a hit /ə hɪt/
cliffhanger /ˈklɪfhæŋə/	streaming /ˈstriːmɪŋ/

When I go out into the countryside and see the sun and the green and everything flowering, I say to myself 'Yes indeed, all that belongs to me!'

Henri Rousseau, French painter

5B The country in other countries

1 VOCABULARY the country

a Order the letters to make words that match the definitions.

1 an area of land that is covered with trees (ODOW)
   wood

2 a high area of land that is not as high as a mountain (LIHL) _____

3 the low land between two mountains that often has a river flowing through it (LAYVEL) _____

4 put seeds in the ground to grow (TLNAP) _____

5 a cereal crop which can be made into flour (THAWE) _____

6 ready to be picked and eaten (PERI) _____

7 a small river (MASTER) _____

8 a plant like a small, thick tree with many low branches (HUBS) _____

9 collect a crop on a farm (STRAVEH) _____

10 the part of a fence that can be opened to let people through (TEGA) _____

11 a high, very steep area of rock, especially next to the sea (FLICF) _____

12 an area of water that is smaller than a lake (NOPD) _____

b Complete the text.

One of the best ways to see the English countryside is from the air. Green ¹ _fields_ separated by ²h_____ or ³f_____ stretch out below you as far as the eye can see. ⁴Cr_____ are growing in some of them, while in others there are animals peacefully eating the ⁵gr_____. As the plane nears the ground, you can see black-and-white ⁶c_____ standing in groups, and in the spring you can see ⁷sh_____ with their ⁸l_____. Every so often, there is a ⁹f_____ with a tractor parked outside the door. Usually, there is an enormous ¹⁰b_____ nearby where the grain is stored. Outside, there are sometimes ¹¹h_____ walking around the farmyard looking for something to eat. There's usually a ¹²c_____ in a high place above the female birds looking out for them.

2 PRONUNCIATION vowel sounds

a (Circle) the different sound.

1	2	3
ʊ	ɑː	iː
bush	farm	hedge
(mud)	grass	field
look	path	leaf
wood	valley	sheep

4	5
aʊ	ɒ
cow	stones
mountain	crops
grow	pond
town	cockerel

b **iChecker** Listen and check. Then listen and repeat the words.

33

3 READING

a Read the leaflet once and answer the questions. What time does the farm open on Wednesdays? What else can you buy on the farm apart from fresh fruit and vegetables?

Parkside Pick Your Own

Fancy some fresh fruit and vegetables? At Parkside Farm we grow a wide variety of delicious summer fruits and high-quality vegetables for you to come and pick your own. Why not pay us a visit?

About us

Our family has been farming at Parkside Farm since 1938. Although we no longer keep cows, we still have some grassland and some fields of wheat and other crops. ¹_____ Since then, we have extended the Pick Your Own area and we now grow about 20 different crops.

Opening times

The season starts in late June, but opening hours are variable the first week. Please ring our message line to check. From July onwards, we are open Tues to Sat from 9 a.m. to 5.30 p.m. (last entry 5 p.m.) ²_____ Mondays CLOSED.

Crop calendar

Some crops may be in limited supply at certain times, so always ring the message line for daily updates before setting out.

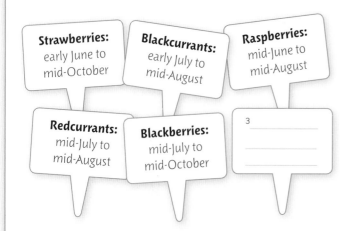

Strawberries: early June to mid-October

Blackcurrants: early July to mid-August

Raspberries: mid-June to mid-August

Redcurrants: mid-July to mid-August

Blackberries: mid-July to mid-October

3 _____

Please check our website for crop dates of vegetables.

Prices

⁴_____ This means that every person has to spend at least £3 on Pick-Your-Own fruit or they will be charged this amount when they leave. It is NOT an additional charge to the cost of your produce, because you only have to pay it if you pick less than £3 each.

Strawberries: £4.49/kg
Raspberries: £6.39/kg
Blackcurrants: £4.79/kg
Redcurrants: £4.79/kg
Blackberries: £5.39/kg
Plums: £2.99/kg

Please check our website for prices of vegetables.

Facilities

- large car park
- toilets (including disabled)
- containers available for picking
- ⁵_____
- debit cards accepted
- **Shop:** sells ice cream, cold drinks, meringues, Parkside honey, sugar for jam-making

Find us

Parkside Farm is in the London borough of Enfield, north of the city centre.

By car: Take the A1005 north and turn off at Hadely Road. Follow the signs to Parkside Farm.

By train: ⁶_____

By tube: Cockfoster's tube station is about 4.5 km away, but mini cabs are available.

For more information, please call our message line on **020 8367 2035** or check our website: **www.parksidefarmpyo.co.uk**

b Read the text again and complete it with the missing information.

A Plums: mid-July to early September

B The nearest railway station is Gordon Hill, about 1.5 km away.

C picnic area

D We started growing strawberries for Pick Your Own back in 1979.

E There is a minimum charge of £3 for each adult or child who enters the Pick Your Own area.

F Opening hours are variable on Sundays.

c Look at the highlighted words and phrases and try to work out their meaning. Then check the meaning and pronunciation in your dictionary.

4 GRAMMAR present perfect continuous

a Complete the text with the present perfect continuous form of a verb from the list.

not add	drink	not eat	go	make
play	swim	~~try~~	use	walk

My husband and I ¹ _have been trying_ to lead a healthier lifestyle recently. We ² _____ jogging together every day before we go to work. He ³ _____ to work instead of driving, and I ⁴ _____ the stairs in my office instead of taking the lift. We ⁵ _____ a lot of water during the day, and we ⁶ _____ any snacks. After work, I ⁷ _____ every evening and my husband ⁸ _____ tennis twice a week. Instead of cooking a big meal when we get home, my husband ⁹ _____ us some lovely salads. He ¹⁰ _____ a lot of oil to the salads, but they still taste delicious!

b Write present perfect continuous sentences with *for* or *since*. Use contractions where possible.

1 I'm looking after my neighbour's dog. They went on holiday last Saturday. (since)

   I_'ve been looking after my neighbour's dog since last Saturday._

2 My brother lives in Paris. He went there two years ago. (for)   My brother _____.

3 Emma is my girlfriend. We started going out a year ago. (for)   Emma and I _____.

4 Rosie is studying. She started when she came home. (since)   Rosie _____.

5 They're training for the new season. Their first session was three weeks ago. (for)

   They _____.

6 It's raining. It started at about 8 o'clock. (since)

   It _____.

5 LISTENING

a iChecker Listen to an interview with Susan, a woman who moved to the country from the city. Where would she like to live in the future?

b Listen again and correct the sentences.

1 Susan lives in southern Germany.

   _____

2 The village school has around 90 pupils.

   _____

3 Their organic food company buys fruit from other organic farms.

   _____

4 The company sells its products in Germany.

   _____

5 Susan likes going running through the fields behind her house.

   _____

6 She plays in an orchestra.

   _____

7 She doesn't like going out at night because it's too quiet.

   _____

8 She would like to live nearer the hospital.

   _____

c Listen again with the audio script on *p.72* and try to guess the meaning of any words that you don't know. Then check in your dictionary.

USEFUL WORDS AND PHRASES

Learn the words and phrases.

move to (a place/house) /ˈmuːv tə/	theme tune /ˈθiːm tjuːn/
move in (to a place/house) /muːv ˈɪn/	increase productivity /ɪnˈkriːs prɒdʌkˈtɪvəti/
move back /muːv ˈbæk/	shortage /ˈʃɔːtɪdʒ/
fit in /fɪt ˈɪn/	rationing /ˈræʃənɪŋ/

1 MAKING A POLICE REPORT

Order the words to make questions and match the questions with the answers.

1 help I you can? _Can I help you?_
2 unusual notice this did anything you evening?
_____
3 anything there else is?
_____
4 her you describe can?
_____
5 her see you when last did?
_____
6 do know you her were what plans?
_____

[1] a Yes, my grandmother is missing.
[ ] b Well, she's 85 years old. She's quite short and quite thin with grey hair and glasses.
[ ] c Last night. I always go round on my way home from work.
[ ] d She didn't mention anything.
[ ] e Yes, the front door was open, which was strange.
[ ] f Yes, she hadn't put the shopping away.

2 SOCIAL ENGLISH

Complete the dialogues.

1 A Where is everyone else?
  B I have no_ idea_ .
2 A Can you tell me again what the homework is?
  B Yes, but l_____ c_____ this time, because I won't tell you again.
3 A I texted John and this is his reply.
  B I don't understand. What does i_____ m_____?
4 A Are you sure you don't want me to come round?
  B No, don't worry. I'm a_____ r_____.
5 A Was that your phone?
  B Yes. It's a m_____ fr_____ my boyfriend.

3 READING

Missing Persons

When a person is identified as missing, and it is an emergency, always dial 999. For all non-emergency cases, contact us on 101.

How can you report someone missing to the Police?
First hand reporting from a relative or friend is the most common way that Police are notified of a missing person.

We will take reports of missing persons in any of the following ways:
• Dial 101 to speak to your local police
• By a visit to a police station
• Contact with a Police Officer/Police Staff away from a police station

What happens when you report someone missing to Police?
Once a Police Officer has taken a report from you about the missing person, he/she enters all the information onto a computer at the police station and circulates the person as 'missing' on the Police National Computer. Immediate enquiries are undertaken by the Initial Investigating Officer to try to find the missing person as soon as possible.

If they are not found then the investigation is passed on to a nominated officer within the police station who will now deal with all further enquiries.

What can they do
The officer will firstly make sure that we have all the necessary details so that an efficient investigation can be conducted, these will include:
• Details of friends or relatives
• Places that the missing person is known to frequent
• Health or medical conditions that they may suffer from
• Financial account details
Officers will also need to search with your consent the home address.

What can you do?
Police realise that this is a very traumatic time for you, but this is also a time where you can help them by making many enquiries yourself.

a Read the text. Number the sentences in the correct order.

1 You believe that a person is missing.
__ A police officer completes a computer report.
__ The police encourage you to continue asking questions.
__ The report is uploaded onto the Police National Computer.
__ Police officers look for evidence at the missing person's house.
__ You contact the police.
__ The police contact the press.
8 The missing person is found.

b Look at the highlighted words and expressions. What do you think they mean? Check your ideas in your dictionary.

Listening

1 A))

Presenter Hello and welcome to the show. Giving a company the right name can mean the difference between success and failure. Our business expert Julia is in the studio with us today and she's going to give us some tips on naming a company. Good morning, Julia.

Julia Hello.

Presenter What advice would you give to someone who is looking for a name for their company?

Julia First of all, you want your customers to be able to remember the name. This means that it has to be quite short. Two syllables seems to be about right – think of eBay, Twitter, and Nike, and you'll see what I mean.

Presenter That makes sense. What else do you recommend, Julia?

Julia Well, there's no magic formula for finding the right name, so you need to take your time over it. First have a brainstorming session, and write down all the ideas that come into your head. Then, take a week or so to think about the names on the list – you might be surprised by the ones that you remember! And this is the point, really. If a name stays in your mind, your customers will probably remember it, too.

Presenter Are there any kinds of words that make a good company name?

Julia Not really. The name can be absolutely anything. You can even invent your own word, if you like. Try joining two words together to form a completely new one, or spell an existing word incorrectly – anything to make your company sound different. Gizmodo is a good example of this – the word isn't in a dictionary; the founders just made it up.

Presenter Have all company names come from brainstorming sessions?

Julia No, not at all. Some companies got their names by chance. Somebody saw or heard something which gave them the idea for a name.

Presenter Can you give us an example?

Julia Yes, of course. Um, have you heard of a company called Caterpillar?

Presenter Yes, I have.

Julia You know how a caterpillar moves, don't you?

Presenter What do you mean?

Julia They have a lot of legs and they move slowly sort of pulling themselves up and down. Well, this company, which makes tractors used to be called the Holt Tractor Company. But one day, the founder, Benjamin Holt, heard someone talking about the company's new tractor. The person said that the vehicle moved 'like a caterpillar'. Mr Holt liked this image so much that he changed the company name to Caterpillar. The lesson here is that inspiration can come at any time, so you have to keep your eyes and ears open.

Presenter What an interesting story! Julia, thank you so much for joining us.

Julia My pleasure.

1 B))

Presenter Hi, my name's Paul Coombs and I'm an interior designer. Today I'm going to give you some tips on choosing the right colours for each of the rooms of your house.

Let's start with the dining room. Most people choose warm colours like browns, reds, and oranges for this room. If you believe in colour psychology, red and orange are said to be stimulants, so they increase a person's appetite. Colours on the other side of the spectrum, like blue for example, have the opposite effect and stop people from feeling hungry. That's why blue is a poor colour choice for a dining room.

Moving onto the kitchen: now, the colour you paint this room depends on the colour of your kitchen cupboards – you probably won't want to change the ones you've got because they're quite expensive. Popular colours to use in the kitchen are brown, peach, and yellow. Strong colours like brick red or dark green can also look nice when they are used with more neutral colours. Colours I wouldn't recommend for a kitchen are lighter shades of green and blue, for the same reason as why they aren't suitable for the dining room.

As for the living room, you have to take the size of the room and the lighting into account here, and you also have to think of the effect you want to create. Light colours will make a room seem larger, whereas darker colours will make it feel more comfortable, more cosy. Warm colours like beige, cream, or some shades of yellow can make a room look inviting, while cooler colours like grey can add a touch of formality. Intense colours such as bright red are generally not good choices for a living room as they are too stimulating.

Now let's take a look at the bedroom. You really want to choose relaxing colours for a bedroom – colours like pale blue, green, or pink usually work well. Red, bright yellow, and other intense colours are too stimulating for a restful room like this, so you shouldn't really use them.

And finally, the bathroom. Again, the colours you use depend on what effect you want to create. Light colours and natural shades such as light blue and sea green have always been popular for bathrooms because they can create a relaxing spa feeling. In the bathroom, you need to avoid dark colours because it will just make the room seem smaller.

Don't forget to take your own colour preferences into consideration when you're deciding which colours to use – you're the one who will have to use the room once it's painted. But if you take my advice, you're sure to be pleased with the result. Good luck with your decorating!

2 A))

Speaker 1 This happened a long time ago when my youngest son, Mati, was about 5. We had been visiting friends in England, and they had given him a plastic knife as a present. When we got to airport security, the knife showed up on the screen, and a customs official took it out of our bag. While I was talking to the customs official and explaining about the knife, I heard my son shout: 'Hands up!' I turned around and saw him pointing his plastic water pistol at the customs official.

Speaker 2 Recently, I went to visit a friend in Spain. When I got to the airport to fly home, I realized that I'd left my phone at her house. I needed to contact her urgently so that she could bring the phone to the airport, but I had absolutely no idea of her number. Then I remembered that she had sent it to me in a message on Facebook. I explained my problem to one of the men at security, and he let me use his smartphone to access the site and find the number. When I found it, I called my friend and she brought my phone to the airport.

Speaker 3 I live abroad and I miss certain things from home, especially hummus. In case you don't know, hummus is a Middle Eastern dish which is a kind of thick paste you can put on bread. In England, you can buy it in a jar from a supermarket. Anyway, on my last trip home to London, I had bought some hummus to take home with me. Unfortunately, the security screener saw the jar in my bag and told me that hummus counts as a liquid. She said that I couldn't take it with me and then threw it away.

Speaker 4 It was summer, and my children were quite young at the time. The day before our flight, we had been to the beach. We had spent most of the day on the rocks with a net and a bucket catching crabs. We put the crabs back before we left the beach and then we went home. The next day, at the airport, I noticed that my daughter's bag was extremely wet. When I opened it, I discovered that she had put one of the crabs in an old coffee jar filled with water. Apparently, she wanted to show it to her friends back home.

Speaker 5 You won't believe what I did at the airport once! When we got to the security gate, I suddenly remembered that I had a small bottle of mineral water in my backpack, so I took it out to throw it away in the containers they have there. Unfortunately, I had my wallet with my passport and my boarding pass in the same hand, so when I threw the bottle in, everything else fell in, too. I was hysterical when I realized what I had done, but fortunately my girlfriend was there to help me. She put her arm in the container and felt around until she found my wallet.

2 B))

Journalist Hello everyone and thank you for turning up here today. Let me start with a question: How often do you go shopping in the high street of your town or village? The answer is probably 'not very often.' But if I asked you if you wanted your high street to survive, it's quite likely that you would say 'yes'. And this is the problem facing the nation's estimated 5,000 high streets today: we want them to be there, but we hardly ever use them. Sadly, they won't survive on this mixture of kind thoughts and nostalgia.

Which is why we are starting a new campaign. We've called it *Reinventing the High Street*, and that is exactly what we aim to do. We want to make sure that our historic shopping communities will exist in the future so that our children's children will be able to use them. We hope that our campaign will help to identify the changes needed to adapt the high street to life in the 21st century.

In the weeks and months ahead, we will bring together experts, consumers, and representatives from local and national government to discuss the problem. We want to draw up an action plan to inject new life into the country's high streets. We will highlight ideas that some areas have already adopted which have made them more popular. One example is the click-and-collect store, where consumers go to collect the products they have ordered online. This kind of store provides a much needed modern service for customers, and at the same time attracts people to the store, and so it is good for both sides.

We will also invite well-known faces to share the secrets of their favourite shopping destinations with us. A long list of celebrities has already agreed to be interviewed. And we would also like you, the readers, to nominate the high streets that you feel have found the answer to survival. These will be shopping communities where there is a balance between large and small stores, and where both consumers and store owners meet each other's needs. At the end of the year, a panel of experts will choose a High Street of the Year, which will serve as a model for all of the others in the country.

Most of all through our campaign, we aim to unite the two conflicting opinions that residents have about their high streets. Somehow, it must be possible both to want your high street to be there and to want to use it. Only when these two desires are brought together as one will our high streets be safe in the future.

3 A))

Presenter And now for television. A new reality show called *Forever Young* premiered on TV Land last night. Like most reality shows, it puts a group of people in a house to see how they get along – nothing new you may think. But in this particular show, there are two different groups: juniors and seniors. The juniors are three men and two women in their twenties, while the seniors, with the same mix of men and women, have all passed their 70th birthdays. The idea is to see if the two groups can bridge the generation gap and learn something from people who are so much older – or younger – than they are.

In the first episode last night, we met the participants. The seniors, Arthur, Emileen, Eugene, Lou, and Shirley were the first to arrive at the house. They knew that they were going to be in a reality show, but expected the other housemates to be of a similar age. Enter the juniors - that's Andree, Angelina, Christian, Mike, and Sam. They had been told that they were going to star in a fun new TV series, so you can imagine their reaction when they came face-to-face with the seniors. When both groups realized that they were going to share the same house, they were shocked!

Once the participants had calmed down, it was time for the first task. The producers gave each group $500 to buy everything the whole house would need for the next week. At the supermarket, the differences between the two generations soon became apparent. While the seniors were discussing which cleaning products to buy, the juniors were busy filling their trolley with junk food. Of course, both groups were horrified when they saw what the other had bought.

In the next task, called 'Bridging the gap', the seniors team had to answer quiz questions about pop culture, while the juniors were asked about recent history. 78-year-old Arthur managed to identify the Jonas Brothers from a photo for the seniors, but 24-year-old Sam got no points for saying that the American Civil War happened after the Second World War. Despite Sam's ignorance, the juniors went on to win the quiz.

So, the question is, will the two groups manage to bridge the generation gap? Right now, it seems that neither group wants to make contact with the other, but will that change during the show? The only way to find out is to watch the second episode of *Forever Young* next Wednesday. I know that I'm going to!

3 B))

Jack Jane, do you have a minute? I was asked to choose a photograph for the poster of next year's Photo Exhibition in the village hall in March. I'm struggling to choose the best one, can you help?

Jane Sure, would be happy to. Is there a theme for the photo exhibition?

Jack Yes, we're asking people to send their best travel and holiday pictures, so I'm trying to find something for the poster to inspire people. What I want to do is to choose one photo, enlarge it, and then put the text on top of the photo, with the details of the Exhibition.

Jane OK, so let's see what you have here.

Jack Well, I managed to narrow down the list to these three photos.

Jane Wow, they all look very professional. I like this one with tourists in the foreground looking at the scenery.

Jack Yes, it's one of my favourites because I took a similar photo from exactly the same spot when I was travelling in Asia. A lot of people go up there just before sunset; it's the best view in Taipei. You can see the whole city below with all the modern tower blocks and skyscrapers, but they all look tiny next to this incredibly tall building. I think it's the third tallest building in the world!

Jane These men on the left-hand side of the picture really give you a perspective, don't they? They make you realize how enormous the tower is. But what I really like about this picture is the way the setting sun is shining on the rock – giving it a lovely, warm brown colour.

Jack Yeah, I quite like the colours of this picture; the brown rock against the green tree and green tower. But I'm not sure it will look that good if you enlarge it to poster-size: these rocks will look too big and I think you won't be able to see the text clearly on the poster.

Jane Ok, how about this one, then? It looks like it was also taken at sunset.

Those hills in the distance look so wild and mysterious, and I love the way the sun reflects on the water.

Jack I quite like this one, too. The ducks sitting on the boats drinking and cleaning themselves – they make me smile every time I look at this photo. I think people will really like this picture because it's very peaceful and warm, but at the same time the ducks make it fun.

Jane OK, so this one is a possibility. How about the third photo? Everybody likes pictures of children playing, and this one just makes you want to jump on the fountain and run around with the kids.

Jack I agree, it's a very happy picture; even though you can't see the faces of the children, you can tell they are enjoying themselves. I also like the bright background against the dark foreground. Do you think it would look good on the poster?

Jane I'm not sure. I really like this photo, but you said the theme of the exhibition is travelling and holidays, so I think you want to show something a bit more exotic than a fountain on the poster.

Jack You're right, I'm also worried that the boy in the foreground might look too big when you enlarge it and you won't be able to read the text on the poster.

Jane OK, so it's the three men in the boat with the ducks, then.

Jack Yes, it looks like the best choice. Thanks for your help, Jane.

Jane No problem, I'd love to see the poster when it's finished.

4 A))

Presenter Welcome back. Now we're going to take a look at recycling around the world. So, Abby, where shall we start?

Abby Let's start with one of the countries that produces the most waste in the world: Australia. According to the OECD Factbook, that's the Organisation for Economic Co-operation and Development, every Australian creates about 600 kg of waste each year, which is nearly as much as the USA. The good news is that recycling in Australia has grown in popularity in recent years and now about a third of the waste is recycled. Now, nearly all households recycle or reuse paper and cardboard, plastic bottles, glass,

and plastic bags. In fact, Australia is the number one recycler of old newspapers – every year, more than two billion copies are recycled.

Presenter That certainly is good news! What have you got next for us?

Abby We're going to Scandinavia next, to Sweden. In Sweden, recycling is a way of life. Everything from electrical goods to clothes to drinks containers is recycled, and Sweden is the leader in recycling plastic bottles and aluminium cans in Europe. Although the country produces quite a lot of waste – in 2009, the amount was about 480 kg per person per year – only 4% of that ends up in landfill sites. The rest is used in a special programme called the Waste-to-energy Programme. Waste is burnt to provide heat and energy for hundreds of thousands of homes. In fact, recently Sweden ran out of waste for the scheme and it had to be imported from abroad.

Presenter What about countries that aren't so good at recycling?

Abby The main problem with recycling in many countries of the world is that there is no official garbage collection. That means that the State does nothing about recycling, either. Take India, for example. Local newspapers report that each person on average only produces half a kilo of waste per year, but with a population of well over a thousand million, that's still a lot of rubbish!

Presenter So in countries like India, nothing is recycled?

Abby Actually, lots of things are recycled in India, but it's often in a very unofficial way. People call on houses to buy old clothes, out-of-date newspapers, and broken electrical goods cheaply. Then they sell these items at a higher price to companies who make something different out of them. In the end, about a quarter of the waste is recycled.

Presenter Abby, tell us about another country like India.

Abby Well, South Africa has the same kind of problem, although most households do have access to a garbage collection. The problem is there aren't many places to take recyclables, and at the moment all of the waste ends up at a landfill site. In 2011, a waste management report said that the average South African currently produces about 0.7 kg of waste per year and only about 3.3% of this is recycled. This is mostly done by people who collect cans, paper, glass, and plastic from dustbins and landfill sites. But the government has recently introduced a new law to try to improve the situation. The aim of the new Waste Act is that all households separate their rubbish within the next four years.

Presenter Let's hope it works! Abby, thank you for joining us.

Abby You're very welcome.

🔊 **4 B**

Presenter Hello and welcome to the programme. Now, you may have noticed how important internships are today if you want to get a job. Around a fifth of young people are being taken on by companies after working as interns. Now, is it fair that companies are employing, often very well-qualified, young people without paying them? Today, we have Olga with us. Olga, you worked as an intern, and now, I'm pleased to say, you are in full-term employment. What's your view?

Olga Well, I'd like to start with the question of living expenses. Most internships last for about three months. Many graduates can't afford to live away from home for such a long time without earning any money. Internships in London are completely out of reach for most of the UK's youngsters. There is a recent survey that reports a huge 78% of all 18- to 34-year-olds have said that they could not afford to live in the capital if they were offered an unpaid internship. That leaves companies in London with only 22% of all the country's graduates to choose from if they don't offer a salary. So by offering unpaid internships, these companies are limiting the choice of people they can take on. If the internship was paid, then the company could choose the most talented applicants, instead of only employing those candidates who have enough money to pay their own living expenses.

Presenter What other reasons do you have, Olga?

Olga Well, employing an unpaid intern for a long period of time is actually illegal. You see, the company is breaking the Minimum Wage Act of 1998. This law states that all workers must receive a wage. So far, all of the interns who have taken their employer to court for not paying them have won their case. And

the companies found guilty of breaking the law have all had to pay a heavy fine. So, you see, in the long run, it might actually be more expensive to employ an unpaid intern than to give them a salary.

Presenter But won't companies take on fewer interns if they have to pay for them?

Olga That certainly is a possibility, David, but I think that there is another alternative. In my opinion, we should go back to the traditional work experience placements of the past. These placements lasted only two weeks and they were much more suitable for graduates who couldn't afford to work free for a long period of time. If companies offered two-week placements instead of three-month unpaid internships, they wouldn't be in danger of breaking the law and they wouldn't miss out on the talent.

Presenter Thank you, Olga. Now, let's hear from Terence Littlewood. Terence, you don't agree with Olga, do you?

Terence Well, I take a number of Olga's points, but...

🔊 **5 A**

Speaker 1 I'm in my final year at school, so I spend most of my time studying. But some evenings I like to watch TV to relax. I'm not so keen on the programmes on national television, so I usually watch cable networks like Discovery Channel. My favourite programme is *How it's made*, which is like a kind of short documentary about how they make everyday objects in factories. Like most people my age, I often use the internet – usually to play games or to chat with my friends. I suppose I spend about 12 hours a week watching TV and 15 hours online.

Speaker 2 I guess I'm going off television, really. I just find that it isn't as interesting these days. There's so much more happening on the web with people talking about things that are going on. Social media is being updated every second, 24/7, so that you feel that you are actually part of the world around you. Whenever the TV is on, it only has a fraction of my attention, and my eyes are always looking over to my phone or my laptop, which are always within reach. I would estimate that I probably spend twice as much time online these days than I do watching TV.

Speaker 3 My wife and I only switch the television on when we know there's a programme that we want to watch. We both like some of the game shows, and we quite like a good film, but apart from that, our tastes are quite different. I like to watch the football when it's on, but my wife isn't at all interested. She prefers period dramas, which don't appeal to me. We only ever use the internet for emails or to talk to our daughter in Canada once a week. Although we don't watch that much TV, we spend even less time online.

Speaker 4 Yeah, I watch quite a lot of TV really. I never miss my favourite shows, and I've always got my smartphone on, so that I can comment on them with my friends as we watch. The *X-Factor* is the best – it's a kind of interactive talent show where different people come on stage to show what they can do. During the acts, my friends and I exchange our views on Twitter – it's almost as if we were in the same room together! I spend a lot of time online, too, but not as much as I do in front of the telly.

Speaker 5 I'm really into music, but not the kind of mainstream music you find on music channels on the TV. The only place you can listen to the bands that I like is on the internet. When I'm at home, you're much more likely to find me in my study in front of my computer than watching TV. There are some great videos online, not only music videos, but also news stories, too. I can't stand watching the news on TV because it's so boring and repetitive. You get a much wider view from reading different opinions on the internet.

🔊 **5 B**

Interviewer Susan, can you tell us something about where you live?

Susan Yes, it's a little village in north Germany called Molzen. It's about 90 km south of Hamburg, right in the middle of the countryside. There's a school, with about 80 pupils and there's a sports ground and a park. In the middle of the village, there's a big farm with lots of cows and there's a stream running through the farm. We used to have a village shop, but it closed down last year.

Interviewer Where did you live before?

Susan I used to live in Manchester – I went to university there.

Interviewer What do you do here in Molzen?

Susan I run an organic food company with my husband – he's German. We met while I was at university, and we came here because his family has an organic farm near here. Our company buys grain from organic farmers all over north Germany. We turn the grain into flour and then we make baking mixes from the flour. We sell the baking mixes to organic food shops in nearly every European country. I'm the sales and marketing manager, and I have to go to different cities to visit the customers. That's the part of my job I like most, really.

Interviewer What do you like about living where you do?

Susan I like going running along the country roads and through the woods right outside my back door. It's easier to drive in the country, too, because there are no traffic lights, and there isn't much traffic on the roads. I also like swimming in the heated outdoor pool in the rain when there is nobody else there except the village ducks. You can swim in the lake at sunset, too, as long as there aren't too many mosquitoes. In my free time, I play in the village band. We often go around the other villages playing at festivals, and there's always someone I know.

Interviewer Is there anything you don't like about living in the country?

Susan Yes, although I don't mind driving, I sometimes hate the fact that I have to drive everywhere because there are no buses or trams. The nearest train station is nearly 8 km away. It's also quite scary outside at night, because it is really dark and there are no street lamps.

Interviewer Do you think that you'll ever go back to the city?

Susan Yes, I hope so. I don't like being so far away from the city. If we lived nearer, I could go to concerts more often. I have to ride on a train for 45 minutes or drive for an hour if I want to go shopping in Hamburg. I'd like to live closer to an airport, too, so I could travel more often. I'd like to go back to living in a city when I retire. At the moment, it's nice to have a big house in the country, but I think when I'm older, a small house in the city will be better.

Answer key

1A

1 READING & VOCABULARY

a 1 to create a new image
  2 for fun
  3 to have more privacy

b 2 F
  3 T
  4 T
  5 F
  6 F
  7 T
  8 F
  9 T
  10 F

c 2 go about
  3 proof
  4 seek to
  5 stand out
  6 solicitor
  7 for fun
  8 birth certificate
  9 feel sorry
  10 maiden name

2 PRONUNCIATION

a 1 Alex, Sam
  2 James, Kate
  3 Emily
  4 Eve, Leo
  5 Bill, Chris
  6 Mike, Ryan
  7 Paula, Sean
  8 Joe, Sophie

3 GRAMMAR

a 3 I can't find them.
  4 ✓
  5 They haven't invited us.
  6 I can't find mine.
  7 ✓
  8 Their names are Sarah and Laura.
  9 Let's take yours.
  10 ✓

b 2 My parents gave us very unusual names.
  3 A friend is cooking dinner for me tonight.
  4 Our neighbour is going to lend us his apartment for the weekend.
  5 Becky's mum is making a party dress for her.
  6 I'm going to sell my old car to a neighbour.
  7 My dad writes a lot of letters to his old friends.
  8 We gave the hosts a box of chocolates.

---

c 2 sent them to her
  3 is reading it to them
  4 lent it to him
  5 found it for me
  6 brought them for us
  7 is going to buy it for her
  8 showed it to me

4 LISTENING

a 1 Gizmodo, design and technology blog
  2 Caterpillar, manufacturer of construction vehicles
  3 Twitter, social networking site

b 1 Twitter
  2 Gizmodo
  3 Caterpillar

c 1 two
  2 brainstorm
  3 week
  4 remember
  5 invent
  6 spelling
  7 animal / insect
  8 moved
  9 inspiration

1B

1 VOCABULARY

a 2 bossy
  3 possessive
  4 cheerful
  5 selfish
  6 reliable
  7 sociable
  8 glamorous
  9 powerful
  10 creative

b 2 noisy
  3 unprofitable
  4 unrecognizable
  5 spacious
  6 comfortable
  7 unhealthy
  8 impressive
  9 affordable

2 PRONUNCIATION

a Stress on first syllable: envious, sensible, stylish
Stress on second syllable: addictive, aggressive, desirable, rebellious
Stress on third syllable: inexpensive, irresponsible, unattractive, unsuccessful

---

3 GRAMMAR

a 3 more stylish than mine
  4 two different jackets
  5 as expensive as
  6 the most reliable
  7 darker than mine
  8 very colourful clothes
  9 ✓
  10 more popular than

b 2 ones
  3 –
  4 one
  5 –
  6 ones

c 2 more shocked
  3 stupidest / most stupid
  4 most thrilled
  5 cleverer
  6 more bored
  7 more stressed

d 2 a bit shorter
  3 much politer / more polite
  4 a bit better
  5 much more spacious

4 READING

a 2 C
  3 E
  4 B
  5 A

b 1 a
  2 c
  3 b
  4 b
  5 a

c 2 revealed
  3 synchronized
  4 consultation
  5 blue
  6 promotes
  7 the sick
  8 treatment
  9 cells
  10 Papyrus scrolls

5 LISTENING

a black and purple

b 2 blue
  3 cupboards
  4 neutral
  5 light blue
  6 lighting
  7 inviting

8 grey
9 pale blue
10 bright yellow
11 sea green
12 dark colours

Practical English A bad start

1 REPORTING LOST LUGGAGE
2 flight
3 just
4 medium size
5 belongings
6 contact

2 SOCIAL ENGLISH
1 your day
2 let me, Allow me
4 isn't it, miss you

3 READING
a 1 A national identity card or a passport.
  2 Yes, she can.
  3 Six months
  4 No, they can't.
  5 When they are studying an English language course.

2A

1 VOCABULARY
a 2 insect repellent
  3 adaptor
  4 memory card
  5 razor
  6 sunscreen
  7 swimsuit
  8 brush
  9 Flip-flops
  10 wash bag

b 2 hiking
  3 sailing
  4 on a cruise
  5 surfing
  6 camping
  7 on a tour
  8 sightseeing
  9 on a safari
  10 on package holidays

c 2 saw
  3 climbed
  4 had
  5 did
  6 watched
  7 sunbathed
  8 got

2 PRONUNCIATION
a 2 shorts
  3 cruise
  4 belts
  5 bottles

3 GRAMMAR
a 2 uses
  3 always packs
  4 aren't listening
  5 doesn't usually wear
  6 is never
  7 go
  8 is your girlfriend talking to
  9 speaks
  10 Do you go

b 2 am/'m going
  3 are, getting
  4 am/'m flying
  5 leaves
  6 does, arrive
  7 land
  8 is picking me up
  9 starts
  10 are/'re meeting
  11 don't want
  12 am/'m, looking forward

c 2 recognize
  3 is thinking
  4 Does it belong
  5 don't want
  6 're having
  7 don't agree
  8 don't see
  9 tastes
  10 doesn't matter

4 READING
a 1 Campbell Island, New Zealand
  2 No, he didn't

b 1 b
  2 a
  3 c
  4 a
  5 b
  6 c

5 LISTENING
a 1 B
  2 D
  3 E
  4 A
  5 C

b A speaker 3
  B speaker 1
  C speaker 4
  D speaker 2
  E speaker 5

2B

1 VOCABULARY
a 2 hypermarket
  3 florist's
  4 stationer's
  5 chemist's
  6 estate agent's
  7 butcher's
  8 baker's
  9 fishmonger's
  10 newsagent's
  11 jeweller's
  12 greengrocer's

b 2 dry cleaner's
  3 health food store
  4 travel agent's
  5 craft fair
  6 chain store
  7 off-licence
  8 DIY store

c 2 've looked round
  3 are opening up
  4 try on
  5 closed down
  6 was looking for

2 READING
a 2 B
  3 E
  4 A
  5 D

b 2 F
  3 T
  4 F
  5 F
  6 T
  7 T
  8 T
  9 T
  10 F

3 GRAMMAR
a 2 We saw James's new car yesterday.
  3 There's a barbecue at John's on Saturday.
  4 Karen is a very good friend of mine.
  5 That's a beautiful painting of a sunset.

b 3 The boys' bikes
  4 The door of the house
  5 our own shop
  6 a friend of yours
  7 my old shirt

c 3 my parents' wedding anniversary
  4 Linda and Dave's car
  5 his boss's office
  6 lid of my pen

4 PRONUNCIATION

a 3 ✓
   4 ✗
   5 ✗
   6 ✓
   7 ✓
   8 ✗
   9 ✓
  10 ✗

5 LISTENING

a C To make residents want to shop at their local high street.

b 1 5,000
  2 hardly ever
  3 Reinventing, High Street
  4 children's children
  5 experts, consumers
  6 click, collect
  7 celebrities
  8 High Street, Year
  9 residents

1 GRAMMAR

a 2 We took
  3 used to have
  4 We were sitting
  5 Where did you stay
  6 I didn't use to eat
  7 What were you doing
  8 you weren't listening
  9 Did you use to play
  10 stopped eating meat

b 2 woke up, didn't have
  3 was reading, was finishing
  4 didn't use to need, started
  5 didn't hear, was listening
  6 weren't driving, hit
  7 lived, was
  8 used to go shopping, built
  9 lost, were waiting
  10 used to spend, were

c 2 used to see
  3 was looking after
  4 were visiting
  5 was playing
  6 was cooking
  7 called
  8 was running
  9 caught
  10 hurt
  11 didn't think
  12 explained
  13 looked forward to/used to look forward to
  14 could
  15 was progressing

2 PRONUNCIATION

a 1 hoped, missed, washed, watched
  2 changed, lived, played, studied, travelled
  3 decided, ended, hated, started, wanted

3 VOCABULARY

a 2 Teenagers
  3 in his late thirties
  4 pre-teen
  5 in his mid-sixties
  6 Toddlers
  7 in her early twenties
  8 pensioner
  9 children

4 READING

a B Mums and teenage girls: a love-hate relationship

b 2 F   5 F   8 F
  3 F   6 T   9 F
  4 F   7 T   10 T

c 1 siblings
  2 rows
  3 eventually
  4 fall out
  5 answering back
  6 tantrum
  7 bad language
  8 brought up
  9 close
  10 despite
  11 priceless
  12 heart-to-hearts

5 LISTENING

a 2 neutral

b 2 twenties
  3 70
  4 new TV series
  5 shocked
  6 five hundred dollars
  7 junk food
  8 pop culture
  9 history
  10 Wednesday

1 READING

a 4 where she lives now

b 1 c
  2 a
  3 c
  4 b
  5 a

c 1 recalled
  2 claimed
  3 striking
  4 privacy
  5 arouse her curiosity
  6 assignment
  7 approach
  8 enquiries

2 VOCABULARY

a 2 in the bottom right-hand corner
  3 behind
  4 on top of
  5 In the centre
  6 in the distance
  7 in front of
  8 opposite
  8 opposite
  9 In the background
  10 in the top left-hand corner

b 2 lenses
  3 portrait setting
  4 enlarge
  5 zoom in
  6 flash
  7 out of focus

3 PRONUNCIATION

a Stress on first syllable: background, foreground, photocopy, photograph
Stress on second syllable: behind, photographer, photography, technology
Stress on third syllable: photogenic, photographic, situation

4 GRAMMAR

a 2 cycled over
  3 swam across
  4 sat next to
  5 ran along
  6 stood in front of
  7 walked past
  8 danced round
  9 fell down

b 3 proud of
  4 paid for
  5 told
  6 married to
  7 worried about
  8 asked for
  9 spend on
  10 arrived at

c 2 looking forward to going
  3 very good at drawing
  4 blamed me for breaking
  5 believe in having
  6 apologized for forgetting

5 LISTENING

a A – 2
   B – 3
   C – 1

b 1 March
  2 the third tallest
  3 enlarge it
  4 was taken
  5 the distance
  6 exotic
  7 begin in the foreground
  8 three men in the boat (with ducks)

Practical English All kinds of problems

1 RENTING A CAR

a 2 What kind
  3 Would you
  4 Will there
  5 Does that
  6 Can I

b b 5
  c 6
  d 4
  e 2
  f 3

2 SOCIAL ENGLISH

1 up
2 afraid
3 later
4 tone
5 Hang

3 READING

a 1 A first time driver in the UK should rent
    a car at their holiday destination.
  2 There's a speed camera 200 meters after
    a white sign with a camera on it.
  3 In towns you can drive at 30mph.
  4 You should only overtake a tractor if you
    have a long, clear view of the road ahead.

4A

1 VOCABULARY

a 2 bins
  3 waste
  4 packaging
  5 waste-paper basket
  6 throw away
  7 take out
  8 dustmen
  9 take away
  10 landfill site

---

b 2 packet
  3 jar
  4 tub
  5 bottle
  6 carton
  7 tin
  8 can

c 2 reused them
  3 reapply it
  4 recycle polystyrene trays
  5 replayed the last five minutes
  6 rethinking his future

2 PRONUNCIATION

a 2 rubbish
  3 garbage
  4 recycle
  5 away
  6 plastic

3 READING

a 1 D
  2 B
  3 E
  4 A
  5 C

b 1 a
  2 c
  3 a
  4 c
  5 b

c 1 binned
  2 special offers
  3 colossal
  4 edible
  5 go off
  6 starving
  7 shape
  8 budget
  9 undervalue

4 GRAMMAR

a 3 I'll call
  4 shall we do
  5 ✓
  6 I won't tell
  7 I'll make
  8 ✓
  9 It'll melt
  10 Shall I clear

b 2 shall we start
  3 I'll move
  4 I'll go
  5 Are you going to take
  6 I won't have
  7 I'm giving / I'm going to give
  8 He's coming round / He's going to come
    round
  9 Won't you have
  10 shall I do
  11 I'll help
  12 I won't drop

---

5 LISTENING

a The best is Sweden. The worst is South
  Africa.

b 1 600
  2 plastic bags
  3 480
  4 electrical goods
  5 0.5
  6 clothes
  7 0.7
  8 3.3

4B

1 VOCABULARY

a Across:
  5 faculty
  6 seminar
  7 tutor
  10 dissertation

  Down:
  1 webinar
  2 lecture
  4 postgraduate
  7 thesis
  8 professor
  9 campus

b 2 qualifications
  3 experience
  4 apply for
  5 skills
  6 referee
  7 covering letter
  8 attend
  9 got
  10 worked

2 PRONUNCIATION

a Stress on first syllable: residence,
  scholarship, seminar, vacancy
  Stress on second syllable: degree,
  postgraduate, professor, tutorial
  Stress on third syllable: dissertation,
  referee, undergraduate

3 READING

a 1 B
  2 C
  3 A

b 1 B
  2 C
  3 A
  4 C
  5 A
  6 B

c 1 domain name
  2 reviewer
  3 amassed
  4 coverage
  5 ventures
  6 articulate

4 GRAMMAR

a 3 we wouldn't complain
  4 ✓
  5 if we don't work late
  6 ✓
  7 unless they agree to his conditions
  8 He'll do a postgraduate course
  9 if I was / were a student
  10 ✓

b 2 she didn't have a boyfriend
  3 Becky won't go to an American university
  4 Matt would live in a hall of residence
  5 you have enough experience
  6 If you don't wear the right clothes
  7 you wouldn't miss your lectures
  8 the teacher will notice

5 LISTENING

a C The length of internships should be reduced.

b 1 fifth
  2 living
  3 78
  4 talented
  5 illegal
  6 fine
  7 fewer
  8 experience

1 READING

a 1 20th July 1969
  2 29th April 2011
  3 2nd June 1953
  4 4th November 2008
  5 27th July 2012
  6 14th October 2012

b 1 c
  2 a
  3 b
  4 c
  5 a

2 VOCABULARY

a 2 stand
  3 turned, on
  4 remote control
  5 was on
  6 turned up
  7 switched over
  8 speakers
  9 turned off
  10 turn down

b 2 cartoon
  3 live sport
  4 reality show
  5 cookery programme
  6 documentary
  7 period drama
  8 quiz show
  9 chat show

3 PRONUNCIATION

a 1 weather forecast, weekend
  2 voted, best band
  3 visited Vietnam
  4 watch, quiz, Wednesday
  5 volleyball, valuable victory
  6 very busy, business

4 GRAMMAR

a 3 has just finished
  4 for 20 years
  5 ✓
  6 Have you ever been
  7 ✓
  8 We've known each other
  9 I haven't ever liked / I've never liked
  10 ✓

b 2 has just resigned
  3 didn't turn off
  4 I haven't watched
  5 has been on
  6 I've already read
  7 all day
  8 for a month

c 2 has had his speakers for
  3 have/'ve just got
  4 has been an actor/actress since
  5 have/'ve moved house three times
  6 have/'ve never liked
  7 got married ten years ago
  8 have/'ve already had one

5 LISTENING

a 1 Speakers 3, 4
  2 Speakers 1, 2, 5

b 1 E
  2 A
  3 F
  4 D
  5 B

1 VOCABULARY

a 2 hill
  3 valley
  4 plant
  5 wheat
  6 ripe
  7 stream
  8 bush
  9 harvest
  10 gate
  11 cliff
  12 pond

b 2 hedges
  3 fences
  4 crops
  5 grass
  6 cows
  7 sheep
  8 lambs
  9 farmhouse
  10 barn
  11 hens
  12 cockerel

2 PRONUNCIATION

a 2 valley
  3 hedge
  4 grow
  5 stones

3 READING

a The farm opens at 9a.m. on Wednesdays. Visitors can buy ice cream, cold drinks, meringues, honey and sugar, as well as fruit and vegetables.

b 1 D
  2 F
  3 A
  4 E
  5 C
  6 B

4 GRAMMAR

a 2 have been going
  3 has been walking
  4 have been using
  5 have been drinking
  6 haven't been eating
  7 have been swimming
  8 has been playing
  9 has been making
  10 hasn't been adding

b 2 has been living in Paris for two years
  3 've been going out together for a year
  4 has been studying since she came home from school
  5 've been training for the new season for three weeks
  6 's been raining since about 8 o'clock

5 LISTENING

a   She'd like to live in the city.

b   1   Susan lives in north Germany.
     2   The village school has around 80 pupils.
     3   Their organic food company buys grain from other organic farms.
     4   The company sells its products in nearly every European country.
     5   Susan likes going running along the country roads and through the woods.
     6   She plays in the village band.
     7   She doesn't like going out at night because it's really dark.
     8   She would like to live closer to an airport.

Practical English Time to tell the police

1 MAKING A REPORT

  2   Did you notice anything unusual this evening?
  3   Is there anything else?
  4   Can you describe her?
  5   When did you last see her?
  6   Do you know what her plans were?

  b   4
  c   5
  d   6
  e   2
  f   3

2 SOCIAL ENGLISH

  2   listen carefully
  3   it mean
  4   all right
  5   message from

3 READING

  2   You contact the police.
  3   A police officer completes a computer report.
  4   The report is uploaded onto the Police National Computer.
  5   Police officers look for evidence at the missing person's house.
  6   The police encourage you to continue asking questions.